INTERRUPTED JOURNEYS

D1602374

Interrupted Journeys

YOUNG REFUGEES FROM HITLER'S REICH

ALAN GILL

SIMON & SCHUSTER
AUSTRALIA

First published in Australia in 2004 by
Simon & Schuster (Australia) Pty Limited
20 Barcoo Street, East Roseville NSW 2069

A Viacom Company
Sydney New York London Toronto Singapore

Visit our website at www.simonsaysaustralia.com.au

© Alan Gill 2004

All rights reserved. No part of this publication may be reproduced,
stored in a retrieval system, or transmitted, in any form, or by any
means electronic, mechanical, photocopying, recording or otherwise,
without the prior permission of the publisher in writing.

National Library of Australia
Cataloguing-in-Publication data

Gill, Alan
 Interrupted journeys : young refugees from Hitler's Reich.

    Bibliography.
    Includes index.
    ISBN 0 7318 1229 8.

    1. World War, 1939-1945 - Refugees. 2. World War,
    1939-1945 - Personal narratives. 3. Refugee children -
    Europe. 4. Refugee children - Australia. I. Title.

    940.530994

Cover design by Christa Edmonds, Christabella Designs
Cover photograph of Kindertransportees at Dovercourt Reception Centre,
reproduced with kind permission of Getty Images
Internal design and typesetting by Adam Hodson, Fly Design
Typeset in Celeste 11 pt on 15 pt
Printed in Australia by Griffin Press

Every effort has been made by the publishers on behalf of the author to locate the copyright
holders of material contained in this book. Where these efforts have not been successful,
the publishers invite the copyright holders to contact them directly.

10 9 8 7 6 5 4 3 2 1

This book is dedicated to Henry Lippmann
and the late Oswald Von Wolkenstein

CONTENTS

ACKNOWLEDGMENTS

Special thanks for their assistance to Rudolf and Li Brasch, Siobhán Cantrill, Barry Coldrey, Julia Collingwood, Konrad Kwiet, Leonie Peake, Suzanne Rutland, Jeanne Ryckmans, Henry Lippmann and the Dunera Boys, and not forgetting Daisy, my understanding wife. Also to Dominic Celio, Tim Ingham, Annette Larke, Jackie and Paul Pryce for unravelling the mysteries of the computer.

The author is grateful for permission to use extracts from the book and film, *Into the Arms of Strangers*, whose producer, Deborah Oppenheimer, is the daughter of a Kindertransportee. Likewise, for permission to use material from the late Cyril Pearl's *The Dunera Scandal* and Frank Heimans' *Class of '39*.

PREFACE

Whosoever rescues a single soul is credited as though they had saved the whole world.

Talmud

Like many other things in life, this book owes its origins to chance. In this case a conversation, about 10 years ago, with Henry Lippmann, organiser of the Sydney reunions of the Dunera Boys.

I told him I was writing a book about British child migrants.[1] He replied, matter-of-factly: 'We had them too.' By 'we' he meant the broadly based Australian Jewish community. He was right, of course, though it seems to have been a well-kept secret.

This book tells the story of (mostly) Jewish children and teenagers, and in a few cases young adults, who fled or survived Hitler's Reich and came to Australia from Europe as unaccompanied migrants or refugees before, after, and in rare cases during World War II.

Where the narrative demands – and because of the importance of the subject matter – the book includes the experiences of some who settled in third countries, notably Britain, for many the initial point of 'rescue'.

Two fringe groups – not quite migrants and not quite refugees – are also featured. They are the Dunera Boys, known to a wider circle mainly through the late Cyril Pearl's 1983 book, *The Dunera Scandal,* and the Vienna Mozart Boys' Choir,[2] whose astonishing story is told in print for the first time in the following pages.

Most Jewish arrivals in Australia during this period were refugees and most refugees were Jews. This book takes a broad sweep regarding the political machinations of the period. With the passage of time the once derisory word 'reffo' has become, like other sobriquets, almost a term of endearment.

For the sake of convenience, the people whose stories are told in this book have been divided into groupings, or categories, with a degree of overlap.

One of the most interesting groupings is also the smallest. It comprised teenagers who came to Australia from Germany and Poland, via European ports, in the lead-up to the war. The newcomers were sponsored by Australian Jewish agencies, and travelled on ocean liners with ordinary fare-paying passengers. There were less than 60, and would have been many times this number, had the Australian Government been more supportive.

The second category included children from Germany, Austria and Czechoslovakia, who left hurriedly by train and ship for Britain, where they had been promised sanctuary. Many arrived only hours before Neville Chamberlain's declaration of war. The plight of these children – some as young as three or four – aroused sympathy in Britain, with many ordinary men and women offering themselves as foster parents.

The rescue operation and the children themselves came to be known as *Kindertransports*. In this book the more grammatical *Kinder* is used. Good intentions were not always matched by reality, the children receiving treatment that was good, bad and indifferent. When the bombs fell, some were put on trains once again as evacuees. At least one child thought she was on her way to a death camp.

When peace returned, most of the *Kinder* – by now thoroughly anglicised – opted to stay in Britain. A few were reunited with parents. Many had their worst fears about their parents' fate confirmed. Even the 'lucky' ones had problems, some preferring the company of their English 'aunts' and 'uncles'. Several older *Kinder*, by now adults, migrated a second time as ordinary citizens to Australia, Canada, the US and elsewhere.

The third – and least fortunate – category featured in this book were Jewish children who had spent the war years in hiding, or incarcerated in concentration camps, where they bore the full brunt of Nazi horrors.

They re-emerged after the war as displaced persons (known to most simply as DPs) to await re-settlement in a new host country. Australia, by virtue of its remoteness, proved a popular choice. Shipping and other difficulties – including a notorious 'quota' restricting the percentage of Jews – meant that by the time of their arrival, up to five years had elapsed since the war's end. Many were therefore considerably older than their sponsors had intended.

With the possible exception of the *Kinder*, the existence of the above groups is not widely known, even within the Jewish community. This is possibly because the newcomers were, by and large, well cared for and, given the circumstances, reasonably content with their new situation. Happily, there have been none of the scandals and turbulence associated, for instance, with the child migration schemes for British 'orphans'.

Reference has been made to the existence of certain fringe groups, who, by accident rather than design, were to make Australia their home. The Dunera Boys – so-called after the ship on which they travelled – were low-level friendly 'enemy aliens', resident in Britain, who were interned and transported to Australia when Britain herself feared invasion. Alas, somebody forgot to tell Prime Minister Robert Menzies that these 'spies and Nazis' were not what they seemed. The unfortunates were incarcerated once again, then – when wiser counsel prevailed – released to form a special unit of the Australian Army.

Most of the 'Boys' were actually men. This book concentrates on the younger Dunera Boys, who were still in their teens (indeed, two were pupils at famed English public schools) when taken into custody.

As with the *Kinder* and other pre-war groups, those transported on the Dunera included a small number of non-Jews, Marxist Jews (two of whom became prominent in post-war East Germany), non-believing Jews, and Jews who had embraced other religions.

Though they are not Jewish, the story of the Vienna Mozart Boys' Choir, which was on tour in Australia when war broke out, is pertinent to other material in this book. One might say they were the world's youngest 'prisoners of war'. They, like the Dunera Boys, were blown this way by the fortunes of war.

In *The Dunera Scandal*, Pearl contrasted the treatment of the choristers, who were 'billeted with Catholic families' in Melbourne, with that of the Dunera Boys, who were interned.

The suggestion that the Dunera internees suffered disproportionately 'because they were Jews' has been made in other quarters and is hard to substantiate. To an unthinking Australian population anyone 'German', whether Jewish or Aryan, was 'the enemy'.

Additionally, there was a major age difference between the two groups. It would be hardly reasonable to place members of a children's choir amidst the rigours of Hay and Tatura. Understandably, the former choristers, most of whom now have Australian grandchildren, resent innuendoes that they were 'junior Nazis'.[3]

A former member of the Vienna Mozart Boys' Choir, Erich Troyna, helped provide the title for this book. In conversation with me, Erich referred to the break in his singing career as an 'interrupted song'. I remarked that all had 'interrupted journeys'. Bingo!

Alan Gill
June 2004

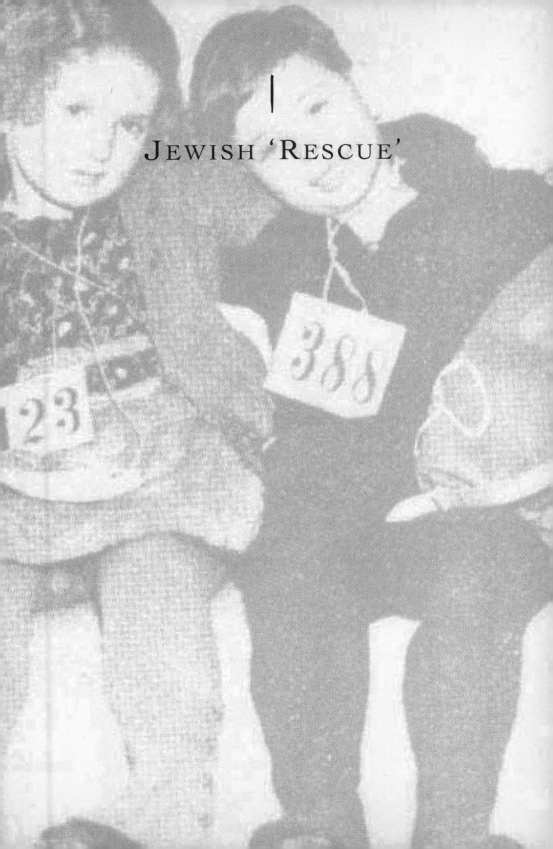

JEWISH 'RESCUE'

1
ESCAPE FROM HITLER

'At first nothing much happened.
The streets were full of people
in new uniforms.'

Lore Segal, Kindertransportee

UNEQUAL CONTEST

It has been estimated that one-and-a-half million Jewish children died in the Holocaust. In fact, less than 10 per cent of Jewish children in Nazi-occupied Europe survived.

Dr Paul Valent, a Melbourne psychiatrist[1] whose area of expertise is trauma, says the nature of the annihilation was unprecedented, and it was 'the most unequal contest ever'.

According to Dr Valent: 'Children were not spared any of the suffering and torture meted out to adults. On the contrary, because they could not obey orders and work, they were dealt with more harshly. For instance, in round-ups they were thrown out of windows and hauled by their hair into trucks. Children were not spared segregation, stigmatisation, overcrowding, hiding, round-ups, mass shootings, deportations, slave labour, torture, medical experimentation, humiliation or murder.'

In the period preceding World War II, with storm clouds already on the horizon, a small number of young German and Austrian Jews were brought into Australia, under Jewish community auspices, having fled their homeland – most leaving parents and relatives behind – to escape Nazi oppression.

These unaccompanied youngsters formed the first wave of *Kinder* (children) (though not part of the *Kindertransport* program operated from Britain) to find a new homeland in Australia.

Jewish youth migration actually dates back earlier than this – although the context was different. The Sydney-based *Hebrew Standard* reported in March and April 1913 the arrival of 13 Jewish lads who were to undertake training on the 'Dreadnought Farm' at Scheyville, near Windsor. Thirty other youths were said to be on their way. It is unclear if the youths were part of the Dreadnought Scheme[2], as some have suggested, or merely shared its facilities. The boys' fares (£10 each) were paid from money remitted to the London Jewish Board of Guardians by the Jewish Colonisation Association.

According to the *Hebrew Standard*, the lads 'created a particularly good impression on the officials and others with whom they came into contact.' On arrival in Sydney, they were met by Rabbi Lyon Cohen, who 'offered words of kindly counsel [and] assured the lads that their community would keep a friendly eye on their progress'.

Hitler's rise to power, in 1933, created an upsurge of interest in emigration. There were tensions among German Jews, as well as those in neighbouring countries, though of a lesser degree than might be imagined. Lore Segal[3] recalls: 'At first nothing much happened. The streets were full of people in new uniforms.'

The exodus from Germany began almost as a blip. Often it took the form of 'extended holidays' or, if they could afford it, the seeking of higher educational opportunities for teenage children in Britain and elsewhere.

Interestingly, among some British Jews there was a feeling that the wilder side of Nazism could be contained, even that it had some worthy elements.[4] Within the Australian Jewish community there were some who feared that the arrival of newcomers (albeit co-religionists) with different manners and customs could upset the applecart for themselves.

By 1938, the reality was evident. Hitler's regime was actively encouraging Jews to leave, provided another country would have them. They could not take money or valuables, and were regarded as having forfeited citizenship of the Reich.

CONFERENCE AT EVIAN

In July 1938 Australia participated in the so-called Evian Conference, named after the French city of that name. Its purpose was to facilitate the flow of refugees from Nazism, the vast majority of whom were Jews.

The timing was interesting – just four months before the notorious *Kristallnacht* on 9 November 1938 ('night of broken glass' – the launching of a major anti-Jewish pogrom, and when Jewish property was seized). It was also at a time when the Australian Government had already expressed a willingness to take unaccompanied teenage migrants from Holland, provided they were not Jews.

In preparing for the conference, the government of Prime Minister Joseph Lyons drew up a memorandum setting out reasons for preventing a 'flood' of refugees into Australia. The government argued that it would be extremely difficult to absorb large numbers of refugees without harming the position of Australian workers. An influx of uneducated Jews, who, the government claimed, almost invariably engaged in secondhand shop trading and cheap clothing manufacture, was especially undesirable.

According to the memorandum, most Jews were highly intelligent and successful, but failed to assimilate completely into their country of adoption because of their religious beliefs and rules regarding inter-marriage. The existence of a large, separate, ethnic minority with different religious traditions could also create racial tensions of a kind not previously experienced in Australia.[5]

Australia was represented at the conference by Thomas White, Minister for Trade and Customs, who said Australia was unable to increase its annual intake of refugees beyond the then current level of 5000 (with a three-year limit). He stated that Australia did not have a racial problem and was not desirous of importing one. According to Suzanne Rutland, Jewish historian and academic,[6] his speech indicated that the government had 'closed its ears to the pleas for help from thousands of Jewish refugees'.

As the situation in Europe worsened, so did the demand for a change in refugee policy. Stanley Bruce, a former Prime Minister, then Australian High Commissioner in London, suggested the intake should be doubled. His argument was that this would help Australia's image, particularly in the United States. However, it was not to be. On 1 December 1938, three weeks after *Kristallnacht*, the Minister of the Interior, John McEwen, told Parliament that Australia would keep to the original 15000 total, over a period of three years. The speech did not specifically mention Jews.

Some weeks later, after informal meetings with government officers and correspondence with the Council for German Jewry in London, the Australian Jewish Welfare Society (AJWS)[7] formally asked the Australian Government to admit 750 children and young people over a period of three years. On 15 March 1939, the government granted this request, but demanded a younger age group (between seven and 12) than was initially sought – also that the children be 'full orphans' with neither parent living. Finally, the point was made that the 750 children should come out of the 15000 total already announced for refugees.

Glen Palmer, a social historian who has closely studied the issue,[8] believes the restrictions imposed by the government were 'severe and unrealistic'. She claims – which others deny – that the Jewish community itself showed no great urgency in filling the quota.

According to Palmer, mishaps, bungles and disagreements of various kinds hampered implementation of the agreement, so that only 17 of that first year's intake of 250 actually arrived.[9]

The 17 German Jewish children, all under 13, arrived in Melbourne in July 1939. They travelled on the Orient Line vessel, *Orama*, and were met on arrival by officials of the AJWS. It was probably the first organised group of non-British child migrants ever to enter Australia.

Defining 'Orphan'

In the same month as the 17, a group of 20 Polish Jewish boys, aged 14 and 15, arrived on the *Oronsay*. Their precise status remains unclear. Meanwhile, the government of New Zealand also accepted 25 Polish Jewish children,[10] who were sent to an orphanage in Wellington.[11]

The Australian Jewish Welfare Society was not the only player in the immigration 'game'. Also in July, a party of 20 German and Austrian Jewish youths, aged between 14 and 17, arrived in Australia under a scheme administered by a newer organisation, the Jewish Welfare Guardian Society of Australia. On 9 July, a similarly sized group of teenage boys and girls arrived in Sydney under the umbrella of yet another group, known by its German title of Gross-Breesen.[12] A handful of other Jewish teenagers travelled independently.

The older youths among the newcomers went directly into the workforce. Younger migrants were cared for at the Larino Children's Home, in the Melbourne suburb of Balwyn, and the Isabella Lazarus Home in Hunters Hill, Sydney.

The Australian Jewish Welfare Society

The Australian Jewish Welfare Society, founded in 1936, has been described as the 'engine room' of Jewish refugee immigration. It existed to help adults as well as children. The Jewish Welfare Guardian Society of Australia (the 'Welfare Guardians'), whose aims and activities overlapped, was formed in 1939, specifically to help German and other Jewish youngsters come to Australia to undertake agricultural pursuits.

The AJWS also favoured the rural life for young migrants, and in 1938 opened the Chelsea Park Training Farm, in the Sydney suburb of Baulkham Hills, for this purpose. The property comprised a 12-hectare farm with a two-storey colonial homestead and various outbuildings. It was AJWS policy that young immigrants who were unable to find work in the city should train at Chelsea Park.

The farm operated with remarkable success, taking in Gross-Breesen boys and others, who found the training helpful. It produced some 200 'graduates' in its first year of operation and quickly became self-supporting. Sadly, the war interrupted its activities. When peace returned it offered temporary accommodation to newcomers and was a venue for Jewish youth camps. It was sold in 1952.

The advent of war effectively put a stop to all organised migration, both Jewish and non-Jewish, so the program announced by John McEwen went into limbo. Those Jewish youngsters who had already arrived were treated as bona-fide immigrants, with the right to remain permanently. Those who were old enough, including 17 of the original 20 Welfare Guardian intake, served in the Australian Armed Forces or in the associated Employment Companies.

WAR AND POST-WAR

With migration temporarily halted because of the war, and a paucity of reliable information about the situation of Jews in Europe, the AJWS found many of its aspirations frustrated. In 1941 and 1942 it received information from London that 'orphaned Jewish children' were 'wandering around France, most of them without any form of identification'. This was before implementation of Hitler's Final Solution.

Discussions were held with the Australian Government, which in January 1943 agreed that 150 children, aged seven to 14, could enter Australia on condition that the AJWS take responsibility for their reception and care. A 'Rescue the Children' appeal was launched, which raised £70000. Incredibly, some prominent Jews opposed it, on the grounds that it would clash with the Victory Loan Appeal in which all had been urged to participate.

At about this time contact was made with a similarly motivated organisation, OSE-ORT,[13] which had secured a pledge from the Swiss

Government via the Red Cross that children smuggled into Switzerland would be granted temporary asylum. This was subject to a proviso that some democratic country would issue long-term residential permits when safe transportation could be arranged.

Following this appeal, the Australian Government doubled the AJWS entry quota to 300. In addition, a further 100 permits had been granted to the Welfare Guardians, but 'safe transportation' proved insoluble – hence no youngsters arrived while fighting was in progress.

The advent of peace brought unexpected difficulties. According to Rutland: 'There were a large number of surviving Jewish orphans in Europe, but most now wished to settle in Palestine.'

Though the desired funds had been quickly raised, the AJWS 'Children's Committee', as it was called, found itself in a bind. A section of the community wanted the money to be transferred to *Youth Aliya*, a Hebrew word denoting emigration to the Promised Land, 'to help the children reach Palestine'. The committee could not concur, even if it wished, since tax exemption had been granted specifically for the one purpose. As often happens in Jewish community politics, rabbis were found supporting the arguments on both sides.

While the debate was in progress, most of the youngsters originally selected under the auspices of the AJWS opted instead for Palestine and the United States. There were other post-war problems. According to Anne Andgel, author of a history of the AJWS,[14] 'the issue of safety gave way to that of priority, and despite the great suffering that the orphans had endured, they were not given concessions or precedence in the allocation of berths on vessels travelling to Australia.'

At a meeting of the New South Wales Jewish Board of Deputies in September 1946, Saul Symonds, a founding member of the AJWS and its president from 1945 to 1952, said an approach for passages on behalf of the children had elicited a reply from the Immigration

Minister, Arthur Calwell, that priority would be given to 4000 Australians stranded in England. (While many Jews considered the Minister's approach discriminatory, the *Bulletin* magazine castigated him for being overly generous.)[15]

The Jewish Welfare Guardian Society, which had been temporarily inactive, was reconstituted when peace returned, with branches established in all states. A report published at the time said it was modelled on the Big Brother Movement (the largest of several organisations importing British youths for work on farms), with Jewish families undertaking to act as guardians for a boy or girl until they reached 21.

The Welfare Guardians and the AJWS Children's Committee were administered separately, but with a degree of overlap. John Wars, the Guardians' founding president, was for a time also president of the AJWS Children's Committee. Others who held dual roles included Walter Brand, secretary of the AJWS, who was an executive member of the Welfare Guardian Society, and Syd Einfeld (future state government minister and virtual 'father' of Jewish child and youth migration to Australia), who served on the Welfare Guardians' committee, as well as being long-term president of the AJWS.

In February 1948, a group of 26 Jewish 'war orphans'[16] arrived in Melbourne on the SS *Radnik*. Ten were sponsored by the AJWS Children's Committee, the remaining 16 by the Welfare Guardian Society. Several members of the group went on by train to Sydney, others to Brisbane, Adelaide, Hobart and Perth.

They were billed as the first post-war arrivals.[17] That it was three years after the war's end, and five years after the 'Rescue the Children' committee was formed, was an embarrassment for the organisers.

The papers of the newcomers gave their ages as between 12 and 17. This was in keeping with a new upper age limit agreed to by the government. In fact, some were much older. One '17-year-old' was actually 23. Like the British child migrants, their ages were 'adjusted' to meet requirements.

AGES 'DOCTORED'

The passage of time and the fact that most of those originally selected for Australia had opted to go elsewhere were not the only reasons for the 'doctoring' of ages. Generally speaking, only older children had survived the concentration camps. Those who were younger than about 11 or 12 on arrival at the camps would have been considered unfit for work, and condemned to die immediately, unless singled out by Josef Mengele or some other camp doctor for medical experiments.

According to teenage migrant, Braham Stern: 'The Australian government wanted children not older than 16. But they didn't exist.' To avoid drawing attention to the discrepancy, and the consequent loss of face, the AJWS (though not the Welfare Guardian Society) continued to refer to its charges, including those legally adult, as 'children'.

In Sydney, post-war arrivals supported by both the Children's Committee and the Welfare Guardian Society were accommodated for a 'settling-in' period at the Isabella Lazarus Home, now the nursing home section of the Moses Montefiore Home at Hunters Hill. Likewise, the two groups in Melbourne shared the facilities of the Larino Home,[18] later renamed the Frances Barkman Home.

By this time both sponsoring groups had dropped their agricultural emphasis, leaving the newcomers free to pursue a variety of occupations.

It was customary for Welfare Guardian boys to spend weekdays at their normal place of residence, and weekends with their guardians. This course was also followed by many of those sponsored by the AJWS Children's Committee, who had acquired unofficial guardians. The arrangement was flexible. It was felt that having been through the war they would be unused to families. Guardians had the responsibility of providing for their charge's material and spiritual well-being, including equipment and clothing.

Some youngsters required almost total support, others just needed help in establishing themselves in a job and finding accommodation. A few had problems of mental health, arising from their wartime experiences.

Neither of the two schemes generated the numbers originally anticipated. After the initial intake in 1948, a further 249 youngsters arrived in the following 18 months under the Children's scheme. This was less than had been anticipated, and in 1950 it was decided to disband the AJWS Children's Committee.

The Welfare Guardian scheme had similar problems, aggravated by the fact that suitable volunteer guardians were not easy to find. The scheme lapsed in 1951, by which time 67 teenagers had been brought to Australia under its auspices.

All in all, 316 non-British Jewish children and teenagers arrived under the AJWS and Welfare Guardian schemes in the early post-war years. It is thought that some Jewish orphans arrived independently. Syd Einfeld believed that the grand total, including pre-war arrivals and the Gross-Breeseners, was about 500. By comparison, Britain took 9 354 *Kindertransport* children, of whom 7 482 were Jewish, in pre-war arrivals alone.

Other comparisons show Australia in a more favourable light. It has been pointed out, for instance, that by about 1950 more than 20 000 adult survivors of the Holocaust had found refuge in Australia. It has been argued that on this basis Australia accepted more survivors in proportion to its population than any other country except the newly established state of Israel.

2

A PERCEPTION OF BIAS

'We had to insist that half the accommodation on these wretched vessels [to transport refugees] must be sold to non-Jewish people.'

Arthur Calwell, former Immigration Minister

It has been said of Australia's post-war immigration policies that the government was more welcoming to former enemies (Germans) than to friends (Jews).[1] While a number of unaccompanied Jewish youngsters were admitted, both before and after World War II, it was only as the result of intense lobbying by the Jewish community, which faced attitudes of indifference and hostility from Ministers and bureaucrats.

The Australian Government, whilst supporting the desires of British youths to have a 'new start in a new land', did not take kindly to providing a home for young, parentless refugees who were essentially 'foreigners'.

This raises the specific question: Was the Australian Government's response to the need to assist Jewish refugees – in particular children and teenagers who had lived through the horrors of Hitlerism – stingy, and was it influenced by prejudice?

Glen Palmer believes the answer is an emphatic 'yes'. She says: 'It was a paltry response. The need to provide refuge for non-British children and teenagers was immense by late 1938. But the Australian Government was unwilling to help in any significant way, or even to contemplate providing temporary refuge. It was blinkered by its pro-British migration policy. This response was a stark contrast to that provided for British [child] evacuees.'

Was there a degree of anti-semitism involved? According to Palmer: 'In terms of adults almost definitely. But not consciously in the case of children. I think they [the Government] just didn't want foreigners.'

Paul Bartrop, a Melbourne academic and historian, whose particular area of expertise is the Holocaust, points to the 1938 Evian conference and the 1 December speech by John McEwen,[2] as examples. He has claimed the Minister's announcement, while advertising itself to the world as a humanitarian gesture involving a growth in refugee numbers, was actually a cleverly worked-out means of 'containing' the number of Jews entering Australia.

According to Bartrop: 'In line with what it believed were the wishes of the electorate, the government held to the view that foreign European migrants should not come into the country in numbers greater than the nation could digest.' This policy was guided by a conscious desire 'not to allow any more Jews into Australia than could be avoided'.

Others consider the Minister's undertaking generous, pointing out that on a percentage of population basis, it compared favourably with that of many western countries.[3]

The resumption of peace, in 1945, created fresh concerns within the Australian Jewish community. At the time Rowland James was speech-making in support of young (Aryan) Germans,[4] Jewish community groups were pleading the case for child Holocaust survivors, whose parents had died in Nazi camps.

With the end of the war, old attitudes re-surfaced. Henry Gullett, MP for Henty (Vic),[5] had strong views about Jews. He said, in a speech to the Federal Parliament,[6] that Australia should 'not be the dumping ground for people whom Europe itself, in the course of 2000 years, has not been able to absorb'.

To a taunt that he was anti-semitic, he responded: 'Happily, in the past, men of the Jewish faith have played a very distinguished part in Australia's affairs. It is unfortunate, however, that many of the Jews who came to Australia in the years before the war and since the outbreak of the war have been notorious exploiters of labour. They set up sweat shops, have cornered houses, and evaded income tax.'

As previously noted, though the government did respond affirmatively to the requests by Jewish welfare groups, bureaucratic delays and a shortage of ships meant that the first organised group of post-war young Jewish 'war orphans' did not arrive until February 1948, some three years after the war in Europe ended.[7] By this time many had recovered from their initial trauma, and made the transition from childhood to being young adults.

A QUOTA

There is a common belief – to which many in the Jewish community subscribe – that the Department of Immigration, also its predecessor, the Immigration Branch within the Department of the Interior, controlled and restricted Jewish refugee immigration by means of a secret 'quota'.

The motive, it is said, was to restrict Jewish migration to a level that did not increase the overall ratio of Jews to non-Jews in Australia.

In his book, *Australia and the Holocaust 1933–45*, Paul Bartrop provides evidence for a quota system and reprints Cabinet papers warning that care should be exercised that 'no serious influx' of Jews come into the country, and that no 'special facilities' should be given to facilitate Jewish migration from Germany.

There is some disagreement about when the quota was introduced. Suzanne Rutland states it was introduced in 1946, before the 28 September federal election, and maintained until the end of 1948. Under the terms of the quota, no British ships could bring in Jewish refugees and non-British migrant ships were allowed to take no more than 25 per cent Jewish passengers.

Exceptions were made for the *Hwa Lien*, which brought Jewish refugees from Shanghai, and the *Johan De Witt*, with 700 Jews from Europe.

The question of bias is a tricky one. In his book *The Jews in Australia (Volume 2)*, Professor Bill Rubinstein, now of the University of Aberystwyth, Wales,[8] suggests that with or without restrictions, the Jewish population in the relevant period made astonishing gains.

He cites a survey attributed to Gerald de Vahl Davis, a former president of the Executive Council of Australian Jewry (ECAJ), that the Jewish population of Australia grew from 35 435 in 1947 to 45 500 in February 1950 and 53 750 in 1952 – an apparent growth rate of 52 per cent in five years. Official Census figures depict a similar pattern – that the Australian Jewish population grew from 32 019 in 1947 to 48 436 in 1954.

Statistics may be deceptive since the number of non-Jews also dramatically increased. Rutland says Jews were less than half a per cent of the Australian population in 1933, and remained less than half a per cent in the critical post-war years. Graham de Vahl Davis, the son of Gerald, concurs. He says there were some eight to 14 Jews on the First Fleet, giving them a ratio of about one-half to one per cent of the then white population. He believes that same percentage applies today.

In his autobiography, *Be Just And Fear Not*, written in 1972, Arthur Calwell himself admitted to imposing restrictions on post-war Jewish arrivals, but said he had little choice. A passage in the book refers to a conversation with Jewish leaders. The former Minister recalled: 'We had to insist that half the accommodation on these wretched vessels [to transport refugees] must be sold to non-Jewish people. It would have created a great wave of anti-semitism and would have been electorally disastrous for the Labor Party had we not made this decision.'

The Minister went on to state that when war broke out there were 'thousands of Australians who could not leave Britain for home' and 'a long waiting list' of United Kingdom citizens similarly stranded in Australia. For this reason, now that hostilities had ended, 'all British people within these categories had absolute preference in British shipping; [and] all foreigners without exception had to travel in ships flying other than the Union Jack.'

Calwell's explanation of a 50–50 split has upset some Jews who point out that it was actually – on the department's later admission – a 75–25 split.

The still-disputed 'quota' and attempts by would-be Jewish 'boat people' to circumvent it, received attention in Diane Armstrong's award-winning book, *The Voyage of Their Life*, about passengers on the *Derna*. Armstrong states, without sarcasm:

'Jews who had survived the war and wanted to migrate now faced discrimination in the form of quotas imposed by countries that had helped to vanquish Hitler. It was ironic that three years after the war had ended, Jews like my parents and me who had survived the Holocaust by keeping our Jewish identity secret, were obliged to conceal it once again in order to gain passage to our new land.'

Rust buckets like the *Derna*, and overcrowded, unsanitary conditions on ships like the *Ville d'Amiens* and *Monkay*, produced 'hellish' voyages, vividly described by Armstrong; while Suzanne Rutland, in a paper to the Australian Association for Jewish Studies,[9] drew a parallel to the *Tampa* incident, with its unwanted cargo of mainly Afghan refugees.

Problems arose when the quota was exceeded. In September 1947 Michael Blakeney, Secretary of the Australian Legation, Paris, sent a message to Canberra that the 25 per cent quota limitation would be exceeded on the *Tidewater* by 117 persons. Negotiations with the Hebrew Immigrant Aid Society (HIAS) reduced this number to 100 Jewish adults and 17 children under the age of 14. Blakeney insisted that the children be removed to maintain the quota, but the ship eventually sailed with the full complement.

In return HIAS had to agree that the next time they sent passengers they would reduce their quota numbers by 17 to make up for the excess. When similar problems arose with the *Partizanka* in

December 1947, Calwell insisted that the extra 150 Jews, who were to join the *Partizanka* at Haifa, not be permitted to embark.

The *Tampa* parallel would appear to be present in an incident[10] involving the *Struma*, an unseaworthy vessel which set sail from Romania in December 1941, carrying 769 Jewish refugees. Upon arrival in Istanbul on their way to Palestine, the Turks would not permit the passengers to land without a guarantee from the British that the refugees would be allowed to enter Syria.

The British refused and requested the Turks not to refuel the ship or supply it with provisions. The Turks sent the ship back to Europe, but on the way it sank in the Black Sea. There were only two survivors who, incidentally, were permitted to enter Palestine.

ARE YOU JEWISH?

That Jews could not travel on British ships and were subject to a quota system on the remainder was not the only problem. Passengers on some migrant ships were annoyed to be asked to respond to a question 'Are you Jewish?'[11] on Immigration Forms 40 and 47.

According to Rubinstein, the government claimed that it asked for this information in order to assist Jewish migrants rather than the reverse. In 1967 Joy Guyatt, researching an MA thesis at the University of Queensland, raised the matter with Calwell and through him with two senior officers of the Immigration Department.[12]

According to the two officers, the 'Are you Jewish?' question on Form 40 had been introduced before the war and was partly statistical and partly to ensure that the Jews were allocated a reasonable number of the 15000 berths set aside [but largely not taken up] in the agreement of December 1938.

After the war, the question was kept on the form to ensure the desired 25 per cent limit (on foreign-owned ships). It did not disappear until 1952. The officers claimed its retention was 'for the benefit of the Jews', and at the request of the Australian Jewish welfare authorities, which had responsibility for Jewish arrivals, and wished to avoid the need to place very large numbers at short notice.

Needless to say this explanation is regarded within the mainstream Jewish community as distinctly unconvincing. Suzanne Rutland, writing in the *Australian Journal of Jewish Studies*,[13] said the 'departmental subterfuge' employed was worthy of an episode in *Yes Minister.*

In a further twist to the tale, the officers said that from February 1949 the 25 per cent quota was replaced by a 'gentleman's agreement', brokered between the Chifley Labor Government and the Australian Jewish Welfare Society, voluntarily limiting Jewish refugee migration to 3000 individuals per year, with the quota on the ships being increased to 50 per cent at the same time.

According to the officers, the quota – in both its original and amended form – was beneficial rather than discriminatory [to Jews] 'since it enabled us to discriminate in favour of Jews who were of ex-enemy nationality'.

Rutland and others consider the 'beneficial to Jews' theory, and the alleged support given to the 'agreement' by Jewish community organisations, as untrue and misleading. In her article in the *Australian Journal of Jewish Studies*, Rutland cites a departmental memo[14] in which four different approaches were proposed to act as a brake on Jewish migration. These were, as interpreted by Rutland:

1. For the Minister to announce that the number of permits for Jews is out of all proportion to the number sought for other than Jews, having regard to the strength of the Jewish community in Australia, and for that reason applications will not be received in respect of Jews for a period of say, three to six months.

2. To impose a quota.

3. To restrict the eligible categories to certain classes of relatives.

4. To restrict migration to Australia from countries whose nationals comprise the majority of Jewish migrants.

The memo pointed out that the first three approaches would

'savour too much of anti-Semitism', but the fourth would be very effective since a breakdown of figures on European nationalities showed that most Jews tended to come from specific Iron Curtain countries.

Variations of all four proposals were, in fact, introduced.

Rutland also reveals the existence of a cable[15] from Noel Lamidey, then Chief Migration Officer in London, to Tasman Heyes, his superior, offering the following definition of 'Jew':

1. Any person of Hebrew race will be considered a Jew regardless of any later baptismal change.
2. Any person who is of the Hebrew faith will be considered of the Jewish nationality regardless of his nationality.
3. Any person whose passages are sponsored by the HIAS or any other Jewish organisation will be considered as of the Jewish race.

According to Rutland, an attempt to have British Jews defined as of 'the Hebrew race' (or Jewish race) was rejected by Calwell. They were treated 'as if they were British by race and Jewish by religion, unlike European Jews who were considered by the Australian Government to be Jewish in terms of both race and religion.'

JUVENILES

The restrictions on shipping applied also to unaccompanied juveniles. On 7 November 1947, Tasman Heyes, secretary of the Department of Immigration, wrote to Syd Einfeld as President of the Executive Council for Australian Jewry (ECAJ) stating bluntly that children under 14 had to be counted within the 25 per cent limit; that the 25 per cent limit had been exceeded on the migrant-carrying *Tidewater*, that the government would refuse to admit any vessels which exceeded this limit in future, and that in any case, where the rule had been infringed Jewish passengers in excess of the prescribed number would be declared prohibited immigrants and refused admission.

According to Professor Rubinstein, this restriction, which was punctiliously enforced, severely delayed the arrival of young

Holocaust survivors,[16] so that youngsters who were supposed to be 13 or 14 on arrival, were often 17, 18 or older.

On the other side of the coin, a case may be put that the Australian Government, in accepting some 600 young Jewish Holocaust survivors, was showing benevolence rather than the reverse, since Jews were almost the only 'foreign' unaccompanied minors allowed in.

I put this to Suzanne Rutland, who said: 'Yes, it was a sign of "benevolence", but I think the attitude was that 'these children can be assimilated and Australianised, therefore they're not much of a threat'.

'From the beginning,' Rutland said, 'the Jewish community had been pushing for Jewish orphans. The government's response was a sign of "benevolence", but it was also tokenism. And that was very much the government's attitude. "Yes, we'll let some Jewish refugees in, because we want to appear good and humanitarian, but Jews are only a tiny proportion of the population and we want to ensure that they remain as such".'

Both Suzanne Rutland and Glen Palmer agree that Australians were kind to the Jewish youngsters when they got here. Says Palmer: 'On the whole the young people were treated very well by Australians. I would say they did not experience anti-semitism.'

The youth migrants themselves are inclined to be supportive of the government and its actions. Tom Keleman,[17] who is active in several Jewish communal organisations, says the government's attitude to war orphans was generous.

"Australia was one of the very few Commonwealth countries that had a program for young people who survived the Holocaust. The US, which could have done it on a much wider scale, didn't have one and neither did Canada.'

He says the Immigration Minister, Arthur Calwell, 'was not anti-Jewish; he was a friend of the Jews, but apprehensive about Jewish migration. He didn't want large numbers of Jews living in Australia.'

The Churches

It is interesting to note the attitude of the Christian churches at this time. Bishop Charles Venn Pilcher, a Sydney Anglican, worked diligently to alleviate Jewish suffering. He was well liked, but considered eccentric (on this and other issues) by his colleagues. Pilcher believed the Christian world was, in part, guilty for the disaster that had befallen the Jews. There was also support from the Quakers, whose members later campaigned, with Pilcher, on behalf of civilian internees including the Dunera Boys.

The attitude of the Catholic Church in Australia was ambivalent. According to Rutland, its attitude was marked by a contradictory response which, on the one hand, deplored anti-semitism as 'unchristian and barbarous', but on the other, believed that too much publicity was being given to the plight of the Jews.

The latter approach was stressed by the *Freeman's Journal*, forerunner to the *Catholic Weekly*, which, in an editorial[18] as the Evian conference was taking place, accused the secular press of 'callousness and hypocrisy' because it ignored the plight of Spanish Catholics during the Civil War, whilst highlighting the 'lesser' difficulties of Austrian and German Jews.

The (Melbourne) *Advocate*, a week later, took a similar stance, claiming that 'the Jews' presence and influence are secretly disliked, even by those who hate their persecutors'. However, in the same month the Australian Catholic Truth Society published a pamphlet, *Why Are the Jews Persecuted?*, which set out to prove the injustice of racial persecution.

There was at that time no Council of Christians and Jews, whose influence might have been strongly beneficial. The omission was rectified by Archbishop (later Cardinal) Norman Gilroy and Rabbi Israel Porush, but not until 1943.[19] The Council fizzled out after about five years and was re-formed on a national basis in 1991.

A problem existed for Christian Jews,[20] by which is meant Germans of Jewish background whose families had become

Christians[21] perhaps two or more generations earlier. In their homeland they shunned Jewish community organisations which shunned them in return. The Nazis – who judged by race rather than religion – ignored such distinctions, banning their community organisation, placing them under the umbrella of the same organisations that dealt with Jews.

The Evian Conference of 1938 made allowance for the reception of a number of Jews turned Christian or Christians with part-Jewish ancestry, though the actual outcome is unclear. The German Lutheran churches in Adelaide received a list of some 75 German 'Jewish' Christians, in the hope that they would be sponsored as refugee migrants to Australia.

Those who did make it to Australia found themselves, at least initially, under the umbrella of the Australian Jewish Welfare Society. According to Professor Konrad Kwiet,[22] who has studied the topic, it was a difficult situation for both sides. 'They felt very German. They had no ties. They had first the experience of being classified and treated as Jews in Germany. Then when they came to Australia they were also regarded as Jews.'

3
LARINO MEMORIES

'The goodbye scenes, they'll always be there.
I don't think I was crying, but lots
of children were. I had no
understanding I might never see my
parents again.'

George Dreyfus, Larino Boy

'Yes, I was one of Hitler's children,' said Richard Dreyfus, responding to my telephone call, seeking information about pre-war Jewish child migrants to Australia.

Of course he was no admirer of Hitler. Making a jest of it all may have been a defence mechanism to blot out unhappier aspects of the past.

Richard and his brother, George, were among seven boys and 10 girls who arrived in Melbourne on 22 July 1939, on board the *Orama*, and were accommodated at the Larino Children's Home in Balwyn.

George Dreyfus has good reason to remember the date, which was his 11th birthday. He remembers, 'as if it were yesterday', the departure of the 17 children from Berlin's Zoo-Bahnhof station. 'The goodbye scenes, they'll always be there. I don't think I was crying, but lots of the other children were. I had no understanding I might never see my parents again. It didn't occur to any of us.'

The 17 children escaped the somewhat severe definition of 'orphan' demanded by the government. The London and German committees responsible for their selection interpreted 'orphan' as a child separated from his or her parents, as was the case for children entering England on the *Kindertransports*. When the Department of the Interior discovered that the 17 were not (according to its definition) orphans, it insisted – but later relented – that future children be *complete* orphans. The outbreak of hostilities rendered this argument of hypothetical interest only.

Richard, who was 12, was the oldest member of the 17 children, who were later joined by three others. The youngest in the group was a girl, Edna Lehmann, aged five. Unlike many of the others, the parents of Richard and George escaped the Holocaust. 'My brother and I were lucky enough to get our parents out; Matsdorf got them a visa.[1] They slipped out via a circuitous route two days after the war began.' The couple later joined their sons in Australia.

A former finance writer and stockbroker living in Killara on Sydney's North Shore, Richard was distressed at the lack of knowledge about the 'Larino Kids'.

'Nobody knows about us. When I retired from my last permanent job in the 1980s I wanted to write a book about our group, as quite a lot had been done about the Dunera Boys. 'I sent out a circular to the others and collected interviews on tape. I completely misjudged how sad and sorry it all was.'

While he was wondering how or whether to proceed, a producer from Film Australia entered the scene. 'She offered to make a film. I gave my material to her, but it fell through because of lack of production funding.'

Brother George disagreed. 'Lack of funds was not the main reason. People know about the Dunera Boys because of the "romance" in it. There were 2000 of them as against 17 of us, and there was the journey itself, the so-called "horror ship", and of course many of them did really well. Richard made money and I made music but none of us really became anything.[2]

The Larino Home, named after its first owner, was an attractive Federation-style home, described by some of the children as 'like a palace'. It had been saved from demolition, renovated and rented to the Australian Jewish Welfare Society by Samuel Meyers. It took up its new role in 1939 at the initiative of Frances Barkman, secretary of the Melbourne branch of the AJWS.

Barkman, who migrated with her parents from Russia, in 1891, was a tireless worker for Jewish and non-Jewish cultural causes, particularly in the fields of languages (her specialty was French literature, art and teaching) and dramatic arts. She helped found an AJWS women's auxiliary, and saw to it that representatives from the society met incoming ships with refugees on board.[3]

After a day to explore and settle into their new environment, the children were enrolled at Balwyn State School. Most have fond memories of the school and of the reception they were given by teachers and children. According to Glen Palmer, in an address to the 1995 Conference of the Australian Association for Jewish Studies: 'The headmaster, Mr Carter, was a particular favourite – a darling; they all adored him.'

Food was (by European standards) plentiful. The management committee had somewhat stuffy attitudes. Hedi Fixel, the matron, was admonished for indulging the children. According to surviving records, quoted by Palmer: 'On one occasion a child sucked an egg at the table and on others children resorted to the use of their fingers and neglected to use the cutlery provided.' They were also known to 'lapse into German', which was discouraged. The matron was additionally taxed with 'neglecting to enforce certain rules such as arranging for children to wash some of their own socks.'

According to Palmer, originally it was intended that the children would stay at Larino a few months, then be fostered by Australian Jewish families, with another group of children replacing them at the home. The difficulty of finding children who met the strict government criteria, together with the outbreak of war, changed those plans. 'It soon became clear that most of the children would be staying at Larino considerably longer. The parents of most of them would not survive the Holocaust.'

George and Richard Dreyfus were not in this category. They left the home when their parents arrived within a year. According to George: 'Just imagine it – a real mother and father visiting children at that place; think of the effect on the other kids.' The two boys went to live with their parents in modest accommodation in St Kilda. Says Richard: 'My father decided to volunteer for the Australian Army at age 40-something and joined the famous Labour Corps.[4] My mother went out nursing and we were very poor.'

Richard, influenced by the need to earn money, left school on his 14th birthday to work as a laboratory assistant, then became a trainee journalist and printer's help – an unusual combination – with the *Australian Jewish Herald*. 'I was a jack of all trades. It was a weekly paper published in English and in Yiddish; you could subscribe to the English version only, or take it with the Yiddish insert. I could actually hand-set type in both languages.'

From there he went to the *Launceston Examiner* as a sub-editor and music critic (the paper's first), and from there to Australian United Press, then to the Australian Associated Press, after which he decided to try his luck in Fleet Street. In London he briefly met Rupert Murdoch – which was to help in years to come. Back in Australia he worked on the Sydney *Daily Telegraph*, then joined the *Daily Mirror*, becoming features editor.

One day the deputy finance editor got the sack. 'I was called for and told, "We're sending you down to the stock exchange." At that time I didn't know the difference between a government bond and a mining share.' Not long afterwards, the finance editor, too, got the bullet and Richard found himself in the job.

Happily, he quickly developed the appropriate expertise, at which point Rupert Murdoch re-entered the scene as proprietor. 'I started to invest money for him and for the company; we got on very well.' It was a hectic period in his life. 'I was making children at the time and was working seven days a week – on the *Mirror*, the *Sunday Mirror*, and a paper called the *Financial Standard*. I lived in Mona Vale, didn't have a car, and I was hardly ever at home.

'I was also writing circulars for Rupert's broker and Rupert always commented on how much money brokers made. So, one day, I got a job with a broker who paid me as much for a 40-hour week as I had been earning for seven days a week.' The move was a success. Richard specialised in the financing of property companies. 'I guess I was the father of the property trust industry in Australia.' At 70, when interviewed by me, he was dismissive about notions of retirement, but agreed, under pressure from his family, to work 'in a more relaxed style'.

He said: 'I try to divide my time into three. A third with the family, children and grandchildren; a third with charitable and religious works, and the other third earning money.'

George Dreyfus, too, succeeded in his chosen field, and became one of Australia's leading modern composers. A writer in the *Sydney Morning Herald* said of him: '... the one Australian composer to fit all seasons and all reasons. His music maintains contact with every taste, every need, every level of sophistication.'

Compositions have included works for the cinema and the stage. He wrote the music for the Australian films *The Fringe Dwellers, Dimboola* and *Let the Balloon Go*, and also for the TV series *Power Without Glory* and *Rush*. He is as well known in his native Germany as in Australia, and his range is diverse – from 'pop' to grand opera. When I first interviewed George, he was putting the finishing touches to *Die Marx Sisters*, a German-language opera which looked at the founder of communism's behaviour towards the women in his mid-19th century household.[5]

The 'Larino experience' still features in the lives of those who passed through its portals. According to Richard: 'We had a 50th anniversary reunion in Melbourne, in 1989, like the Dunera people did a year later. Nearly everybody came – 15 out of the 17. A few of us still keep in touch with each other.' For the occasion George Dreyfus wrote a piece of music, *Larino Safe Haven*, which he played at concerts and recorded on CD.

As this chapter was being written, there were about 15 surviving 'Larino Kids'. Two live in Israel, one is in England, another in the US. The others live in Perth, rural Victoria, Melbourne and Sydney.[6]

Was their time at Larino a happy one? George Dreyfus said he had no grouse with Larino, but there were other problems. 'I have trouble with questions about happiness. At Larino I felt quite good in the company of the other children, whereas at Windsor State School I was the only "reffo". I knew there was a war on, but had no knowledge of what was going on where I had left from. I had no real concept of anything except that I was alive and I was probably safe.'

Brother Richard was more critical. 'Was I happy? Not really ... though I have to say that my brother and I were the fortunate ones.' It was the minor recollections that irked. 'When we were met at the wharf, the first thing that happened was that the kids were given new names. I remember a boy whose name was Rolf Schneider, he became Ralph Taylor.[7]

'We were anglicised, and the committee of the AJWS regarded us as second-class citizens. The clothing that we were given was very often clothing that their own children no longer wanted. We were also expected to become artisans and apprentices, and not to go to university like their children.'

The views expressed are echoed and amplified by other former Larino children. The management committee went to unusual lengths to assimilate the children, to the extent (according to Glen Palmer)[8] of denying an Orthodox boy the opportunity to participate in the full expression of his religion. 'Assimilation' did not include much socialising with the wider community, Jewish or otherwise.

According to a Larino girl, Marion Paul, quoted by Palmer: 'We were an island. We went to school and we went home. We were taken places occasionally, but only as a group. Occasionally we would be invited to a Jewish family for lunch and I enjoyed that. Sometimes we would go to the pictures afterwards with the other children, as they would have children of their own ...

'They were kind to us, but we felt a bit out of it ... We would notice that they [the children] had new clothes. They were brought up differently from us. We had hand-me-downs. People used to send suitcases of their old clothes for us.'

Richard Dreyfus agreed. 'It was a very traumatic period, and a number of the Larino kids have had severe psychological problems. Of course, one must make allowances. What is known today about how to treat human beings wasn't known 50 years ago.'

George Dreyfus said he considered many of the above statements petty. 'I say "stuff the change of names". I think we owe nothing but gratitude to the Jewish Welfare Society. It was a life-or-death situation and they saved our lives. The change of names meant nothing; you could change it back if you wanted to.'

GROSS-BREESENERS

'I was among the younger ones, and I was terrified.
The boys were locked in a horse stable.
The girls in another barn. An SS man stood guard outside.
We didn't know what was going on,
but in fact all the older ones had been put in
a lorry and sent to Buchenwald concentration camp.'

Bert Cohn, Gross-Breesener

'We're a big happy family, and we're spread all over the world. We've never made a fuss about ourselves. Once we all die it's finished.'

Herbert (Bert) Cohn, a retired businessman from Bondi Junction, is contact person for one of the world's more unusual Old Boys' associations. The title, *Gross-Breesen*, doesn't reveal much. It refers to an estate in Silesia, owned by a Jewish family, who, after Hitler came to power in 1933, were obliged to return to Poland.

From 1936 to 1939, when heightened persecution of Jews forced it to drastically scale down its activities, the estate, near Breslau was home to a kind of boarding school, known in German as an

Auswanderer Lehrgut (migration training centre). It took young people of both sexes, aged 15 and over (about one in four students were girls), and offered academic and practical training with an agricultural bias.

The school opened in the fourth year of Hitler's rule. Students and staff regarded it as a kind of oasis. The Jewish historian and academic, Werner Angress,[9] describes it as 'a charmed and protected island in a sea of hatred, persecution and fear'.

Emphasis was placed on behavioural and leadership skills, and a philosophy of living known as *Lebenskunde* (life skills). This reflected the tenets of the school's director and guiding force, Professor Curt Bondy. This remarkable man demonstrated perseverance and strength of character in his own life, and succeeded in passing these traits to others.

The school was one of a handful of similar centres established by the Jewish agency commonly known as *Zentralverein* (Central Agency).[10] The aim was that graduates should form the nucleus of a Jewish settlement in a part of the world free from anti-semitism, and where Jews would be both safe and welcome. Several potential host countries were investigated, including Argentina (where the Rothschilds had already established a colony) and Bolivia.[11] The concept was not uncommon among Jewry at that time.

A group known as the Freeland League (or 'Territorialists') hoped to establish a similar colony in the Kimberley region of Western Australia. The Kimberleys proposal met with a mixed reception from Australian Jews. Though supported by the Western Australian Government, it failed to win backing from the Commonwealth Government in Canberra. Its chief emissary, Isaac Steinberg, was trapped in Australia by the outbreak of war, and was unable to leave until 1943.[12]

Kristallnacht upset all plans for an orderly migration program. '*Kristallnacht* changed everything,' says Bert Cohn. 'I know because I was there.' Even a semi-rural community like Gross-Breesen did not escape the ravages of that terrible day. 'All of a sudden all these trucks arrived with SS personnel, whips in their belts and pistols in their holsters. They shouted: "Line up, boys and girls!" They soon had us sorted; under 18 on one side; older ones on the other.

'I was among the younger ones, and I was terrified,' Cohn recalls. 'The boys were locked in a horse stable, the girls in another barn. An SS man stood guard outside. We didn't know what was going on, but in fact all the older ones had been put in a lorry and sent to Buchenwald concentration camp.'

Before *Kristallnacht* the school had about 100 boys and 30 girls. When the SS departed there were less than half this total. 'We came out of the stable and made our way back to what we called the *Schloß* [meaning 'castle', but in this case, more a manor house]. We were shocked by what we saw. They had smashed windows, wrecked our piano, and even made holes in the dining-room tables. They had been through the entire place with their hammers and axes.'

It was November, and it was getting cold. The adults and older students had gone; now the younger ones were in charge. They had been taught to be jack of all trades, and their training showed. Bert Cohn had spent six weeks in the carpentry shop and also knew the rudiments of glazing. The few unbroken panes of glass were removed and put into other window areas to make key rooms habitable.

There was a more pressing danger. Some of the non-Jewish labourers, who worked on the estate, had become friendly with the SS thugs and had broken into the cellar, where wine was stored. The intruders got drunk and were carousing throughout the night. Bert and his friends, housed in the same building, were fearful for the girls in their dormitory below. 'We got some axes and other weapons to protect them. Thank goodness nothing happened.'

The director had been away from the school when the SS paid their visit. He was picked up elsewhere and imprisoned in Buchenwald with the older students, but eventually released. Bert

Cohn remembers the look of horror on his face when he returned. Bondy, a man of culture and refinement, was 'particularly upset about the piano'.

At that time (November 1938) Hitler's Final Solution had not yet been implemented and it was still possible for Jews to leave Germany – including those Gross-Breeseners already interned – provided another country was willing to accept them. Bondy himself obtained a visa for Holland, becoming involved in refugee work there, and later in Britain and the US. Bert Cohn still marvels at the 'miracle' of how he came to find himself en route for Australia.

'It's an incredible thing. I don't know how long after *Kristallnacht* it was, but one day the female secretary, a non-Jew who had not been harmed by the Nazis, came up to us and said, "I've just got a telegram from a man in Australia; he says he is making arrangements for 30 visas."'

The man was Wolf Matsdorf, a German-born resident of Australia, who had been a friend of Bondy and was at the time a migration officer with the Australian Jewish Welfare Society in Sydney. He worked tirelessly to obtain guarantors in Australia for young German Jews, without which the Immigration Department would not issue entry visas.

Matsdorf, a hero to many Jews, was physically small, with an outsize social conscience. His work for the AJWS was interrupted when he was briefly interned as an 'enemy alien'. He was released to join the Australian Army. In the late 1950s Matsdorf quit the AJWS to join the NSW Corrective Services Department as a parole officer, in which he served until his retirement in 1972. Gross-Breeseners and others interviewed for this book owe their lives and those of their families to his intervention.[13]

Sadly, not all the Gross-Breeseners were able to emigrate. Bert's younger brother, Alfred, also a Gross-Breesener, was removed from the list of those bound for Australia. Bert recalls the school secretary, who, in the absence of senior staff had assumed greater responsibility, coming to him one day and saying: 'I'm very sorry; I've had to take him off to give preference to older people.'

The decision, though painful to both boys, seemed reasonable at the time. Older boys, some of whom had already seen the inside of concentration camps, were clearly at greater risk. This assumption was correct. They were not to know that within a few months the Nazi horrors were to apply equally to young children.

The story has a tragic sequel. After his brother left for Australia, Alfred continued at the school, then went to another farm as virtual slave labour. While there he married a Gross-Breesener girl (both were about 17) in the belief that married couples were less likely to be persecuted.

It was a vain hope. Alfred, his young wife and presumably their small child died in Auschwitz in 1943. The surviving brother heard about it after the war from a camp survivor (also a Gross-Breesener). Bert speaks about it matter-of-factly: 'That was his destiny.' By a cruel irony, not all the 30 places for Australia were taken up. This was because some of those with passes for Australia instead went to the US.[14]

Twenty-one Gross-Breeseners (19 youths and two girls)[15] sailed on the *Slamat* from Rotterdam, changing to the *Strathallan* in Port Said. Five of the party left the ship in Adelaide. Two girls had already arrived in Sydney, travelling independently. Another five or six arrived later.

Those who arrived in Sydney were met by Matsdorf, taken to the Maccabean Hall and then to Chelsea Park Farm in Baulkham Hills, owned by the AJWS. From here jobs were arranged on rural properties in all parts of NSW. Bert Cohn found himself on a dairy farm in Forster. 'I couldn't speak a word of English, but I must have picked it up fairly quickly because I've got letters I wrote in English after three months. The spelling was pretty bad but they were understandable.'

He got on well with his employer: 'They were very nice people and quite cultured.' He was delighted when other farmers began to ask:

'Are there any more where you came from?'. Within a few months (thanks to Bert) there were six Gross-Breeseners working within 15 km of Forster.

Companionship was important for the new arrivals, who communicated with each other by chain letter. Some of this correspondence survives. Inge Rosenbaum (now Inge Kaye) described life on a sheep farm, 700 km from Sydney: 'We work from 7 am to darkness; about 5.30 there is a one-hour meal break. After dinner we still peel potatoes. We always change for dinner, but this is not possible for lunch.'

Bert himself wrote: 'People here are very nice to me ... I work here for one pound weekly and keep. This is nice money but not too much if one intends to buy a farm.' Gerhard Wachsman (Harry Winston) was lonely: 'Sometimes I feel really sorry that I cannot play any instrument. Good music is so poor on the wireless, and I cannot even play my father's records as I have no gramophone.'

Hanni Flaschner (Hanni Jonas) said her employer allowed her to talk with another Breesener girl by telephone. 'Ten days ago I came here as domestic help. Now there is hardly a distinction between the family and the "maid". I am treated almost as their daughter.'

Many Gross-Breesener boys volunteered for the army, but their 'alien' status caused difficulty. Bert Cohn wrote in a chain letter: 'Unfortunately, they did not let us join their fighting forces, so am now in a Labour Company.[16] I think now that it doesn't matter in which unit you are as long as you have a chance to do your share in this fight for freedom.'

Though they were personally happy, the lack of news about families and loved ones left behind was devastating. In addition to his brother, Bert Cohn lost his mother, aunts and uncles, and some 30 other relatives in the Holocaust. Influenced by their shared upbringing, Gross-Breesener boys and girls in Australia 'stuck together' and sometimes married each other. All except one of these unions was successful.

Thirty-four Gross-Breeseners ultimately made their homes in Australia. This figure includes some who went initially to British Commonwealth countries in Africa, then migrated a second time to Australia.

At the time of writing, 12 of the Australian 'Breeseners' are thought to be still alive. Like the Dunera Boys they are getting on. The youngest, Herbert Born, who lives in the Sydney suburb of Oatley, is 80.

The largest number of Gross-Breeseners live in the US, but Greater Sydney – with 11 at the last count – has the highest concentration of any one metropolitan area.

Former students and others associated with the Gross-Breesen project have achieved fame and fortune, the best known being Professor Ernst Cramer, until recently deputy chairman of the Axel Springer publishing empire.

Curt Bondy returned to Germany in 1950. He settled in Hamburg, where he became director of the Psychological Institute of Hamburg University. For many years he acted as a kind of one-man Old Boys' Association. Gross-Breeseners throughout the world would write to him. He would print extracts from their letters and lists of names and addresses in irregular bulletins, some of them of 50 pages, known as *Rundbriefe* (newsletters). Upon Bondy's death, in January 1972, the task was taken over by Ernst Cramer.

About five years ago Cramer wrote that the *Rundbrief* then being distributed would probably be the last. Bert Cohn dashed off a letter in response: 'Please don't ever say it will be the last. If it must be the last, okay, but don't let's say it will be the last.' In fact, it wasn't the last. Contact is now maintained on a regional basis. Says Cohn: 'I've kept everybody together here, and a chap called George Landecker has done the same thing in the US.'[17]

A 50th anniversary reunion, organised by Alexander Neumeyer, who had become secretary and treasurer of Shavey Zion Kibbutz in Northern Israel, was held in the guest house of the kibbutz in 1986.

It was a great success. According to Bert Cohn: 'I have one regret. You know how in Israel they plant trees in memory of so and so? I was very keen on having a tree planted with a plaque specially for Bondy. He was such a great guy, like a father to us. I might still get around to doing it.'

The question is often asked: 'Whatever happened to Gross-Breesen?'. A diary by a former student, Gunther Marcuse, provides details of the final years. When war broke out, the school somehow stayed open despite the fact that all of its students were Jews. A letter from Gunther to his parents in Gibraltar, sent via the Red Cross and subject to censorship, states: 'Am healthy and sound. The work goes on ...'

In mid-1940 the Germans appointed a new director, Walter Bernstein, to take charge of the school. For a while, in view of the importance of agriculture to the Third Reich, things continued much as before, with the emphasis on manual work rather than teaching. The Jews called it 'farming for survival'. In August 1941, the Gestapo announced the liquidation of the training centre and the conversion of Gross-Breesen into an *Arbeitseinsatz* (labour camp).

For a while the Jewish 'students' (now slave labourers and numbering about 40) were allowed to remain. They were subjected to numerous indignities such as having to eat off the sideboard in their own dining room, denied all meat and even permission to eat the bread they had been baking.

In 1942 there were rumours that the estate would be used to house Russian prisoners. About 40 duly arrived. Within months, however, this role was abandoned. The estate became a convalescent home for wounded soldiers. Gunther noted in his diary: 'Probably not much can be expected in the way of co-operation, since they are all amputees.'

This use continued until February 1943, when the site was taken over, for an unspecified purpose, by the Land Settlements Bureau. There is little more in Gunther Marcuse's diary. His last entry, dated

26 February 1943, reads: 'For us, the prospects ... are diminishing. [We are] filled with apprehension [and] await coming events.' It is known that some of the remaining 'students' were transferred to a labour camp at Grussau, to await 'transfer to the East' – a euphemism for the concentration camp at Theresienstadt.[18] Others, including Bert Cohn's brother, as well as Gunther himself, went to Auschwitz.

Gunther Marcuse died in Auschwitz on 23 March 1944. Somehow, his diary found its way to his sister in Israel, who submitted it to the Yad Vashem Centre for Holocaust Studies, where it has been translated into English.[19]

II

CHILDREN OF THE HOLOCAUST

4

THE BOY WHO MET EICHMANN

'As he came out of the list he turned
round and I saw him face to face.
Our eyes locked ... Perhaps he wondered
what an Aryan-looking Jewish boy
was doing there.'

Tom Keleman, on meeting Eichmann

They arrived in the early post-war years, Jewish 'war orphans' with a very special bond. Travel documents, now faded, show young faces with a slightly haunted look. All had experienced at first hand the horrors of Hitler's tyranny. Australia considered them refugees, but a more appropriate term would be 'survivors'.

Tom Keleman, an accountant now living in the Sydney suburb of Northbridge, was the first post-war Jewish youth migrant to Australia. A polite, unassuming man, he agreed to tell his story because of the 'importance' of the issues raised. However, he is anxious to stress: 'I am not a publicity-seeking person.'

He states matter-of-factly that he lost 35 (out of 50) members of his immediate and extended family, plus a similar number of school friends and neighbours. His story is not uncommon.

Tom Keleman arrived in Australia on 19 July 1947. He was a 'Welfare Guardian' boy (ie. sponsored by the Australian Jewish Welfare Guardian Society), but travelled solo, beating by seven months the first group arrival under the same auspices.

Transport and other problems had delayed the migration of the youngsters, as a result of which the newcomers were older (in some cases considerably) than was anticipated.[1] Tom Keleman was 17 but looked 14, which was to his advantage. He had sandy hair and a fair complexion, which had proved a help (though on one occasion a handicap) during his time on the run.

He was born in a suburb of Budapest. His father, Bela Keleman, was a journalist, who, when barred from his profession, found employment with the Jewish Community Council.

On 19 March 1944, the Germans formally occupied Hungary. Tom was then in the fifth form of a Jewish community high school which closed down the day after the Germans marched in. On the tram home from visiting friends he saw leather-jacketed Gestapo men and SS soldiers escorting people to waiting trucks. Though he was not to know it, the family he had been visiting was among those arrested that day.

After his school was closed down by the authorities, Tom and others from his class volunteered to be couriers for the *Judenrat*, the Jewish council sanctioned as a liaison body between the new masters and the (now subjugated) Jewish community. He received a pass, which enabled him to move around the city during curfew hours.

While on duty as a runner, Tom saw Adolf Eichmann.[2] 'I was outside the office of the couriers, on the same floor as the Judenrat meeting room. We were supposed to sit and wait. Eichmann had come to meet the Judenrat. As he came out of the lift he turned round and I saw him face on. Our eyes locked, then he turned around and went into the council chamber. Perhaps he wondered what an Aryan-looking Jewish boy was doing there.

'I shall never forget that experience. He was in uniform and wearing that hat with the death's head on the peak. He had very hard eyes. I was shocked. He did not look Aryan: I thought he had distinctly semitic features.'[3]

Eichmann paid further visits, though usually the task was undertaken by his lieutenants. 'His attitude in the beginning was calm but threatening. I think he wanted to prove himself a good Nazi.[4] His lieutenants also took this line. Their attitude basically was "Do what we tell you and nothing will happen to you. But if you step out of line the German Reich will use its weight to crush you".'

In addition to his messenger duties, the Germans got the lad to deliver equipment used for making air-raid shelters to buildings taken over by the SS. It was known that hostages were kept in the cellars. Tom began a dangerous double role, reporting what he saw to the Jewish 'rescue committee' and, where possible, passing messages to Jews in safe houses or on the run.

In October 1944, Tom's father was taken by the Nazis for labour service. Soon afterwards he was handed over to the SS, who deported him with thousands of others to Germany. A few weeks later Tom was tipped off by a Red Cross contact that the district where they lived was about to be raided a second time. His mother refused to leave her elderly parents. For this she died in Ravensbruck early in 1945.

By this time Tom and others knew of the existence of Hitler's Final Solution, and had no illusion about what it meant. For a bright 14-year-old, on his rounds as an 'errand boy', the sight of trains in marshalling yards and gendarmes[5] supervising the loading of the wagons with human cargo bound for the death camps 'remains one of the most painful memories of my life'.

One day he looked out of the window of the 'Jewish house' where he was living, and was surprised to see and hear 'Russians' singing in the marshalling yards below. He was uncertain if they were liberators or prisoners. In fact, they were Ukrainians, in black uniforms, brought in by Eichmann to help with the deportations.[6]

The Vatican and several neutral States intervened to try to prevent or limit the slaughter. Many Jews were saved thanks to letters of protection issued by the Swedish[7] and Swiss Consulates. Tom obtained Swiss papers, which helped him for a few weeks, until the Nazis decided such papers were not acceptable.

Tom moved from one 'safe house' to another. Tipped off that the Germans were about to raid a Swiss-protected house, Tom was given the names of two other shelters – a convent and a Spanish-protected house. He went first to the convent. 'The nuns wouldn't take me because they thought I didn't look Jewish and might have been an agent of the Arrow Cross.'[8] Happily the Spaniards were more accommodating. He spent the final weeks of the war in an auxiliary hospital of the Red Cross.

DESTINATION AUSTRALIA

For the Jewish war orphans, the choice of new homeland was somewhat of a lottery. Tom Keleman found refuge in an Austrian DP camp, run by the United Nations Relief and Rehabilitation Administration (UNRRA). From here he lodged applications through the American Joint Distribution Committee,[9] to migrate to Palestine, Canada, the US, New Zealand and Australia.

'For some reason the Australian papers came through first. I knew very little about Australia, except that it was a very large country, similar in wealth and standard of living to New Zealand where my father had a friend. It seemed to me like Utopia, far away from Europe, which was good.'

Tom sailed on the *Ville d'Amiens*, owned by Messageries Maritimes, which had a regular service from Marseilles to Australia via the Panama Canal. The voyage took 11 weeks; the French-owned vessel stopped at interesting and unusual ports, including Martinique and Guadeloupe, Panama, Tahiti, the New Hebrides (now Vanuatu), New Caledonia and, finally, Australia. According to Tom: 'It was wonderful, an adventure. More so because I was young and on my own.'[10] There were advantages in travelling unsupervised. He acquired a girlfriend on board, a French-speaking teenager from New Caledonia who was coming to Sydney to study.

The ship's arrival at Circular Quay is permanently ingrained in his mind. 'It was a beautifully clear, sunny winter day. Everything was shining; there were boats in the harbour, it was something unbelievable, like paradise.'

Perhaps because they had suffered so much, Tom, like other youngsters who would follow him, gave little attention to what would happen to them on arrival. 'I thought there might be a representative of an organisation who would say, "Here is some money for the first couple of nights. Come and see us in the office." I certainly didn't realise anyone would take such an interest in me.'

Some were met on the quayside, others on the ship. When the *Ville d'Amiens* berthed in Sydney a 'distinguished-looking' man came on board and spoke, by coincidence, to Tom's *amie de voyage*. 'Do you know someone called Tom Keleman?'. 'Oh yes, he's my friend.'

She took the newcomer across to where Tom was standing. The man said: 'I'm Julian Rose, I'm going to be your guardian. Welcome to Australia.' Tears fill Tom Keleman's eyes as he recalls the words and the man who spoke them.

Julian Rose, who was of Russian parentage, was a former actor who had trod the boards with Roy Rene (Mo McCackie) and others. He was a talented commercial artist and, after giving up the stage, formed his own advertising agency.

'Uncle Julian was my appointed guardian – he got me by a ballot. I didn't know anything about the scheme. All I knew was that my permit said something about the Jewish Welfare Guardian Society, but I didn't even know who they were.'

They disembarked and Tom was introduced to 'Aunty Vi' (Mrs Rose) who was waiting on the quay. 'They both embraced me.' Again Tom's eyes fill with tears. 'They're dead now.' The couple then took him to meet Julian's mother, who was in hospital. 'She was like my grandmother. They were the loveliest family.'

The Roses found a room for him in a flat owned by an old lady, Mrs Lipson, at Vaucluse, a 10-minute tram ride from the Rose Bay unit where Julian and his wife lived. 'I used to see them always on a Friday and at least one other day during the week.' The old lady was a 'darling' but feared intruders. In the evening she would bolt her door, then take a sleeping pill and go to bed. After being forced to spend several nights on the street, Tom moved in with the Roses and later found board at Rose Bay and Maroubra.

A week after his arrival in Australia, Tom started work as an accountant and migrant liaison officer with the Australian Jewish Welfare Society. In this capacity he got to know John Wars,[11] who later invited Tom to work for him in his import-export business.

'In those days welfare and social workers received very little money. Mr Wars said to me, "If you want to get on you'll have to move into the commercial world. You've had training in accountancy; you can be the accountant of my business."'

Tom strongly rejects the criticism of Wars by some Jewish war orphans. 'He was energetic, forceful, a visionary. I personally found him a very capable person, fair but not always easy to work with. I was with him for three years. The experience effectively determined my career.'

Julian Rose, died in 1962. 'I started looking after the affairs of Aunty Vi after that. We had a very close relationship. She died in 1990.'

THE SEARCH

While some of the Holocaust children saw their parents die, others lack certainty about what became of them. Like the British child migrants, the quest for information is important to them.

Tom Keleman last saw his father on 20 October 1944, when he was taken away for service in a labour unit. Tom was then 14, and the memory haunts him still. 'I shall never forget our last farewell and the expression on his face as he looked up at our balcony for the last time.'

Tom has certain knowledge of the death of his mother, in Ravensbruck, early in 1945, but for years lacked information about his father, creating a special void in the young man's life. The first clue came when Tom was in a DP camp in Europe. He learned from a survivor that his father had been handed over to the SS by the Arrow Cross and sent to Buchenwald.

For 41 years Tom made exhaustive inquiries through many sources, visiting the Yad Vashem Holocaust Centre in Jerusalem, whose records were initially unhelpful. Just as he had given up, a breakthrough came in 1986, when the centre received information from East Germany, via the International Red Cross, which included not only his father's name, but his number as a prisoner and even distinguishing marks.

Tom learned that in January 1945 his father had been moved from Buchenwald to Bergen-Belsen. Three months later, he was among 8000 prisoners who were moved from the camp, between 7 and 10 April, and put on three trains bound for the Theresienstadt camp in Czechoslovakia.[12] Possibly they were to be a bargaining tool with the Allies, who were by then almost at the gates of Bergen-Belsen.

His father's group left on 10 April, and numbered 2600 prisoners. One of the trains made it to Theresienstadt, another was liberated by the Americans at Magdeburg (later part of East Germany). The third – which included Tom's father – was condemned to making a meandering and fruitless journey along the narrow corridor which was all that was left of the German rail system. It could not get anywhere because the bridges were blown up. The Americans were approaching from one side and the Russians on the other.

Allied bombing meant frequent stops, during which the dead were buried by the side of the track. There was no food. SS guards were replaced by middle-aged men who allowed the captives to get out of the wagons and gather whatever they could find in the fields – raw potatoes, turnips and grass, which they boiled. They drank water from polluted streams.

The prisoners continued to perish from a combination of cholera, typhoid and malnutrition. Among them was Tom Keleman's father. Train leaders kept a record of the victims, including where they were buried. His son states without bitterness: 'My father died on 20 April 1945, and was buried two days later. He died five days after British troops entered Bergen-Belsen and three days before that train was liberated by the Russians.'

Having gained this information, Tom now desired to pay respect to his father at the gravesite. He elicited the help of a local historian, Erika Arlt, and the local *Bürgermeister* (Mayor), Martin Riedel, and visited the region for this purpose. Unfortunately, the search for the grave proved fruitless. The German railway system had marker stones, beside the tracks, supposedly indicating the distance in kilometres from Berlin. He had been told his father was buried near marker 101.6, whereas it should have been 106.7. Hence the search was conducted in the wrong place.

Upon returning to Australia, Tom made contact with the Dutch Red Cross through the Consul in Sydney. He was acting on a hunch that because of the presence of several Dutch prisoners on the train, he might be able to obtain further information. He was right. The correct marker stone was now indicated, together with details of 16 other prisoners buried at the same site.

Erika Arlt, contacted by Tom, got together a group of volunteers, including the Mayor, a botanist and others with 'war graves expertise'. They visited the site – a siding near the small village of Langennaunddorf – and found the grave almost immediately.

On 20 April 1995, the 50th anniversary of his father's death, Tom and his wife, Eva, visited the communal grave in the company of the local historian, Erika Arlt, and said *Kaddish*, the Jewish memorial prayer, for Bela Keleman and the other victims. A train hurried past, its whistle sounding, as they were thus engaged.

Tom told me: 'The question of where my father lies buried had been with me for 50 years. The fact that I found it, and was able to say *Kaddish* there, has given me peace.'

Later, a commemoration at the site was attended by, among others, *Bürgermeister* Riedel, the parliamentary representative for Brandenburg, Herbert Knoblich, a local Protestant minister, Pastor Zimmerman, and the rabbi and members of the Jewish community of Potsdam, approximately 110 km away.

During his visit, Tom happened to mention his intention to visit Ravensbruck, where his mother died in the gas chamber. Martin Riedel, who was born after the war, insisted on driving him there. Tom believes gestures such as this offer hope for a better future. 'Through all these people I came to terms with the Germans. At one time I could not stand anything or anyone German. Then came these kind acts. I realised they're also people and have feelings.'

Today, a memorial paid for by the local community stands beside the railway line at Langennaundorf. An inscription reads: '*In ehrendem Gedenken den Judischen Opfern des Faschismus*'. ('In eternal memory of the Jewish victims of fascism.')

There is another memorial in the nearby Jewish cemetery at Trobitz, where the nightmare train was finally halted by the Americans. It contains the names of *all* the victims, including some 300 who died after liberation.

MISTAKEN IDENTITY

Tom Keleman, formerly vice-chairman of the B'nai Brith Anti-Defamation Commission, and president of the Alfred Dreyfus Anti-Defamation Unit, was for some years a volunteer assistant with the now disbanded Australian War Crimes Unit. In that capacity he accompanied witnesses from Australia to the war crimes trials in Toronto, Canada.

While assisting the War Crimes Unit, Tom had an unusual experience involving a namesake. It came about when he wished to have a minor building job done in his home and advertised in the local paper for a bricklayer. One of those who replied was Hungarian. 'He said to me on the phone before he came, "You must be related to Charles Keleman." I said, "No, never heard of him."

'The bricklayer came and looked at the job, then told me about this other fellow whom he mentioned casually had been a sergeant in the Hungarian Gendarmes. My ears pricked up because the gendarmes were the worst possible types, like the German SS.'

Tom believes his visitor was a right-wing sympathiser, who didn't realise the man he was talking to was Jewish. 'What he said was as revealing about himself as it was about the other Keleman. "Interesting old fellow, bumped off a few Yids." That sort of thing.'

The next day Tom rang the War Crimes Unit. 'I asked if they had a Charles Keleman[13] on their list. "Oh yes, we've got a whole file on him."'

'I discovered that the other Keleman lived in the next suburb to mine. In 1941 and 1942 his specialty had been to kill people on the ice floes on the Danube. He had some devilish ways of doing it. He drove people on to the floes, then cut the ice round them, so they were floating down the river. He then machine-gunned them from the banks. He killed this way because he enjoyed it.'

Tom Keleman never got to meet his namesake, who died before he could be prosecuted.

A Man Called Syd

'The photographs of some of the Jewish teenagers
he helped were in the loungeroom...
His wife, Billie, laughed at the suggestion
that she and her husband were a Jewish Mr and Mrs Chips.
"That would be right, I suppose. We knew them all, of course."'

It could be said of Syd Einfeld that he had a boxer's face but a heart of gold. As their train pulled into Central Railway or their ship arrived at the wharf, many new Jewish arrivals would have observed a tall, craggy-faced man pacing up and down like a father awaiting his returning sons.

If there was a father figure to the NSW Jewish community it was Syd Einfeld, who was president of the Australian Jewish Welfare Society for 27 years,[14] also chairman of the Children's Committee and of the reception committee for all (adult and juvenile) Jewish migrants. In the latter capacity he met every ship and train coming in.

Tom Keleman recalls: 'I have the greatest respect for Syd, who moved mountains to help us, and knew how to put pressure on the relevant minister or public servant. On several occasions he went to Canberra to see the Secretary of the Department of Immigration, Tasman Heyes. Heyes was an anti-Semite but at the same time fair. Syd knew just how to handle him.'

Sydney David Einfeld was born in Kings Cross in June 1909, three weeks after his parents arrived from London. His father had come to Australia to take up the post of Cantor at the Great Synagogue. They named their son after the city which he was to make his home.

Syd himself was a religious man, a very unstuffy, unorthodox (in the sense of unconventional) Orthodox Jew. His first conversation with me, in the early 1970s, was about sermons. He thought most were too long and too boring, and that the general standard – by both Jews and Christians – was declining.

Syd – somehow the use of the first name seemed entirely natural – was fond of saying that he was a 'parliamentarian' rather than a 'politician'. Those with whom he had disagreements were disarmed by that impish smile and his knack of being able to 'come on strong' without causing offence.

His formal entry into politics came in 1961, when he won the federal seat of Phillip. He lost it again in the 1963 swing against Labor. He turned to State politics and in 1965 won the seat of Bondi by 76 votes. In 1968, he was elected deputy ALP leader to Pat Hills.

He promoted inter-faith dialogue and reconciliation, albeit in a low-key, practical way. In 1960 he was appointed Australian representative to World Refugee Year in Geneva. In 1965, he was made first chairman of the Australian Council for Overseas Aid (ACFOA), earning the friendship and respect of the Christian aid agencies which were a majority on that body.

During the 1970 papal visit he was commended on his work by Pope Paul VI, who gave him a medal. Syd told me he had thought of having it engraved 'From Paul to Syd'.

In 1976 he was made Minister for Consumer Affairs and Co-operative Societies in the NSW Wran Labor Government. From 1978 to 1981 he was additionally Minister for Housing.

I recall interviewing Syd Einfeld during this period.[15] There was a dispute at the time involving supermarkets. The way he tackled it was unforgettable. In one room were the bosses of a grocery chain. Syd spoke to them rather like a headmaster chiding the sixth form. A consumers' group delegation was in another room. Syd addressed them like a family doctor counselling his patient.

If there were Liberal voters present, probably they would have changed their vote. Syd championed both Jewish and non-Jewish child and youth migration. Claims that the traffic in British children was morally questionable and allegations of paedophile activity in the orphanages did not lead him to change his mind. 'I supported the concept then and have no regrets about that. I think it [child migration] was valuable for Australia, and valuable for the children too.'

The photographs of some of the Jewish teenagers he helped were in the lounge room, when I visited him for the first of several interviews. His wife, Billie, chipped in: 'He knows the histories of every one of them.' She laughed at the suggestion that she and her husband were a Jewish Mr and Mrs Chips. 'That would be right, I suppose. We knew them all, of course.'

In the 1980s the former Jewish youth migrants organised a 'thank you' dinner for the Einfelds at the Maccabean Hall, Darlinghurst. According to Billie: 'It was a celebration, a huge party, and when we walked in, I wondered what had struck us. They had come from all parts of Australia. They practically knelt before Syd and kissed his toes. I just was moved to tears. I couldn't hold back.'

Syd Einfeld died on 16 June 1995, the eve of his 86th birthday. About 800 people attended his funeral at the Great Synagogue. Many of those present felt as if they had lost a blood relative.

Rabbi Raymond Apple stated in his funeral oration: 'Syd was driven by dreams and visions. He responded to the human condition with emotional feeling and passion.'

Referring to Syd's extended family, he said: 'Unbelievable numbers of Jewish families think of Syd as their brother, their father figure, their friend, their champion, their mainstay, their prince ... I don't think any of the countless people Syd helped ever disappointed him or let Australia down.

'Shakespeare said: "One man in his time plays many parts". That too was Syd, but he played them all together ...'

5
ECHOES OF THE CAMPS

'Some people had brought money with them. Of course, when the Germans
gave the order to undress it was left blowing in the wind. Being a poor
chap from a very poor family, I just couldn't believe the amount of money
and valuables that were lying around in Auschwitz.'

Albert Halm, post-war youth migrant

In February 1948 Syd Einfeld and many of his colleagues from the
Australian Jewish Welfare Society, Welfare Guardian Society and
other Jewish bodies were at Central Railway to meet the Sydney
arrivals from the *Radnik*, which had docked in Melbourne.

Some of the new arrivals were 'raring to go, others shy and
apprehensive'. One lad, Albert Halm, caught his attention. According
to Syd: 'He seemed to follow me as I walked up and down the station.
So I rang up my wife and said, "I'm bringing this young fellow
home."' Albert Halm became virtually an addition to the family of
Syd and Billie Einfeld.

Some 55 years on, Albert, now in his seventies, is modest about the
incident. 'I don't think I followed him around; I was very reserved.'
However, he doesn't dispute that a bond developed. 'Syd became
grandfather to our children,[1] and our greatest friend,' his wife, Ruth,
chips in.

Albert Halm was born in Yasina, Czechoslovakia, an area now part
of the Ukraine. 'We were very poor. My father died when I was very
small and I lived with my grandparents and my mother.'

The onset of war brought a confused situation with Hungarians
and Ukrainians (both allies of the Germans) fighting for control of
the territory. For Jews this was bad enough. 'Then the Germans came

and immediately took us away. That was that. They cleared the area completely. *Judenrein* (Jew-free) was the motto. We were sent to Auschwitz in Poland.'

The shock of being in this charnel house was very great. So much so that he has blocked a large part of it from his mind. 'I remember very little about Auschwitz. I don't remember the block I was in, I don't remember the *Appels*. I don't remember how long I remained there.'

Though he could be forgiven for wishing that it did, his loss of memory does not apply to the arrival scene. 'It was unbelievable. People of both sexes being ordered to strip, Alsatian dogs biting and barking, the Germans screaming, the children screaming, mothers screaming, elderly people crying.

'Some people had brought money with them. Of course, when the Germans gave the order to undress it was left blowing in the wind. Being a poor chap from a very poor family I just couldn't believe the amount of money and valuables that were lying around in Auschwitz.'

He has another recollection. As he was going towards the initial *Selection* a man called out to him in Yiddish 'Look tall, look tall.' 'I didn't know what he was talking about. Another man threw an oversized jacket over my shoulders and said, also in Yiddish, "Put it on." I was a scrawny kid; these two gestures probably saved my life.'

Albert's mother had been transported to Auschwitz with him. They were separated in the melee. He assumed, incorrectly, that she was dead. Though he cannot remember the time span, it seems likely that he spent only a few weeks in Auschwitz. Like his former near neighbour, Braham Stern (see page 59), he was transferred to Mauthausen, in Austria.

Later, he was moved again to Ebensee. 'It was the third camp in my travels. At Ebensee I developed chickenpox. I was with my cousin working, building roads. I didn't feel well and went to the first aid station. They panicked and said I'd got an infectious disease.

'People who had infectious diseases were very quickly got rid of. There was no gas chamber at Ebensee, but people were shot and their bodies sent to the crematorium. I was certain it was the end for me. They kept me in the Jewish infectious block. After two days I was still alive. My cousin was working in the street near the hospital and I had to let him know that I was alive. There was a crack in the boards – we had no windows – and I was able to call his name and speak to him.

'I got a little better, so they put me to work cleaning the block. I did that for a while and it was then discovered that I had reasonably nice handwriting, so the man in charge of the block asked me to work in the office.

'Again, my life was saved. The *Blockaltester* (block supervisor) was a German, a non-Jew, a prisoner like ourselves. He was a particularly nice person. I was so impressed with his humanity; I never saw him hit anybody or scream at anybody, which was most unusual in that dreadful place.

'He was a political prisoner. They stood out from the others – the gangsters, the robbers and murderers, who were usually the ones appointed *Blockaltester* or in similar roles.'

After the war, in fact after arriving in Australia, Albert tried to resume contact. 'I wrote letters to Germany, I wanted to do at least as much for him as he did for me. I regret I was unsuccessful.'

On 6 May 1945, the camp was liberated by the Americans. Albert returned to Czechoslovakia, and became a trainee radio mechanic at a firm called Tesla in Prague. He lived in a hostel with other young people, most of them returning refugees.

Conversation among the returnees was largely about emigration - to the United States, Palestine, South Africa and to Australia. Albert was excited about the latter. 'It was not because I feared democracy would disappear in Czechoslovakia, nor for any strictly "political" motive. Quite frankly, I just wanted to get away as far from Europe as possible, and to get away from the Holocaust.'

Contact was made through a Jewish migration agency and its European representative, Mrs Anita Glass.[2] He was accepted by the AJWS Children's Committee, but was subject to the delays experienced by other Holocaust survivors.

While the application was pending, an extraordinary thing happened. 'One day, when I got back from work, somebody downstairs told me, "There is a lady waiting in the dormitory for you." I went upstairs and opened the door. The room had about 30 beds. She was sitting on one of the beds, and it happened to be mine. I found my mother sitting on my bed.'

Though wonderful news for Albert, it was potentially embarrassing because Jewish war orphans migrating to Australia were supposed to be just that – *orphans*. Happily, the fact that he had a mother was glossed over, as was the matter of his age. By the time he reached Australia he was 23. His travel papers said he was 17. His mother also sought to migrate, opting to go to Palestine.

Upon arrival in Australia, Syd Einfeld found Albert a five-year apprenticeship with Leo Edel, part-owner of the Radio Centre, Kings Cross, and a fellow board member of the AJWS. Albert completed his apprenticeship and worked as a tradesman for a while. Increasingly, he found that the market was being inundated with German products, which distressed him. He began to seek another profession, unrelated to trade with Germany, choosing a two-year evening course in diagnostic radiography.

This led to a career which bore interesting fruit. In 1990, Albert Halm retired from the position of manager of the Department of Diagnostic Radiology and Chief Radiographer at the Prince of Wales Hospital, Randwick, having held the latter post for an astonishing 35 years.

As previously noted, there existed a special bond between the Halm family, including their children and grandchildren, and the Einfelds. On a visit to Israel, in 1954, Syd Einfeld decided, on his own initiative, to seek out Albert's mother. His task was hampered because she had re-married, and now had a different name. With assistance from several quarters Syd found her in Beersheba, where she was running a kiosk selling soft drinks and stationery near a school.

According to Billie Einfeld: 'Syd sent a message home that he would ring me at a certain time, and that it was important that Albert should be here. There we were, all slobbering at this end waiting for the call to come. Our own children were here as well. Then Syd came on the line and made his great announcement.

'Later she came to Australia for an extended holiday. There were language problems because she couldn't speak English. But Albert spoke to her in a mixture of Czech, German and Yiddish.'

Like many Holocaust survivors, Albert Halm was initially very reticent to talk about his experiences. Billie Einfeld recalls: 'He wouldn't tell us anything. I think it was about five years before he opened up.' According to Albert: 'I still don't like to talk a great deal about my experiences. My children have reproached me from time to time as has my dear wife, but the tragedy was not theirs. Why burden them or other people with my background?'

In what may appear a contradiction to the above, Albert formed, a year or so after his arrival, an organisation for young Holocaust survivors called 'The Revival of Jewish Youth'. He explains: 'We didn't really fit in to the mould of young people. We were odd; most of us had no parents, no brothers and sisters, we were so different. I thought it's an opportunity to harvest whatever talent there was and tell our story as a group rather than as individuals.'

The 'group' aspect was important. 'There was a need to be surrounded by others who had had the same experience, and at the same time be able to ...', he searches for the right phrase. 'People were reluctant to talk about these things, but as an organisation we were able to get them to open up and talk a bit more freely. "Cathartic", I think the word is.'

In 1983, mindful of the role played by the now defunct 'Revival of Jewish Youth' some 30 years earlier, Albert founded another organisation, the Australian Association of Jewish Holocaust Survivors. Many of its members had belonged to the former body – 'by now they had children and grandchildren of their own and were more relaxed about it.'

In 1985 the new association sponsored the International Gathering of Holocaust Survivors, held over several days at the University of NSW. It was well publicised and well attended; the first of its kind in the southern hemisphere.

Albert is proud of the success it achieved. 'It's another era now. It's something that we experienced. People here were not responsible for the tragedy that befell us. There are happier issues to talk about. On the other hand I feel we are dying out very quickly, and there is a need to tell our story just so that people know what happened and it doesn't die with us.

'It's not for the sake of generating tears and sorrow because of the six million dead. We want people here and now to have an inkling of how the thing started, so that if those in the next generation and the generations after that see the signs they can do something about it.'

In pursuit of this aim, aware of the passage of time and inter-generational needs, the Australian Association of Jewish Holocaust Survivors, with a membership of about 600, is now known as the Australian Association of Jewish Holocaust Survivors and Descendants.

BRAHAM STERN, PRISONER 67957

I met Braham Stern and his wife, Barbara, in one of the better addresses in Australia. As we spoke, wild birds fluttered around the swimming pool of their Sydney home, behind which was a panoramic view over Rose Bay.

The tranquility of the scene contrasted with much of what was being recorded on tape. It seemed as if fate and the fruits of hard work had sought to make amends for what was, in Braham's case, a singularly cruel childhood.

He was born in Svalava, a small town close to the city of Mukacevo, near the Carpathian mountains. Previously part of the Austro-Hungarian Empire, it became part of Czechoslovakia after World War I, and was later absorbed into the USSR. It is now in the Ukraine.

He was one of five children. Two older sisters are still alive, having survived Auschwitz, as did Braham himself. A younger sister and a younger brother 'went straight into the gas chamber', as did his parents.

Braham's father and an uncle had gone to the US before World War I. The uncle died fighting in France and the father, rather unwisely, returned.

Braham has bittersweet memories of his early childhood. Anti-semitism in his own region was 'very strong', and Jews were 'second-class citizens'. Braham recalls: 'As children we were ostracised by other kids. Come Easter, there were crucifixes in the schools, villages and churchyards, and they were very graphic – Christ on the cross; his head looking down at you as you walked past, large nails sticking out of his hands and feet.

'One year I was playing in the yard, I suppose I was about nine. Some kids came over and beat me up. They said it was because the Jews killed Christ. It hurt me mentally more than it did physically.'

In 1939, there was much worse to worry about. Enemy forces arrived in the form of the Germans' Hungarian fascist allies. His father at that time still had a US passport, but did not flee on the grounds that 'Europe has always had anti-semitism and this [present phase] will pass.' It did not pass. As Braham puts it: 'Nobody guessed about the Holocaust; it wasn't on the list.'

The Hungarian occupiers instituted a pogrom and Jews were put in ghettos. At the beginning of 1943, after many privations, Braham and his family were moved into a disused brick factory, where guards devised barbarous punishments as 'sport'.

'The factory had water-filled pits where the workers must have dug for clay. A guard would come up to you, put a brick on each hand and order you to swim. You'd be bashed if you couldn't do it. Another officer had a stick like a conductor; he'd hit you over the ear until it was half-severed.

'Things like that get into your brain and are never forgotten, particularly if done on a regular basis.' At this time the family remained together, which was a comfort. 'We slept on the ground and used little bits of straw to line our beds. It was like a nesting colony.'

Like other industrial sites the brick factory had a branch railway line. Trains left daily for larger sidings where prisoners were transferred to cattle trucks. After about six weeks in the factory, Braham and his family found themselves part of this cargo. Braham was just 13 years old.

Although he did not know it, the destination was Auschwitz. The journey took three days. There was standing room only; one bucket of water for 100 people, and no toilet facilities.

ENTRANCE TO HELL

The great gates, with their slogan *Arbeit macht Frei* (Freedom through work), were like the entrance to Hell. The process of *Selection* began immediately upon arrival. 'It was like a sorting yard, where the lambs go one way and the sheep another.' Braham was among the 'lucky' ones, being directed through the gate with those considered capable of, and suitable for, work.

He was taller than most lads his age, but thin. 'We knew we would not be allowed to bring suitcases, so my mother had made me put on three shirts, a jacket and overcoat and cap'. This 'padding' made Braham look bigger and stronger, which possibly saved his life.

His older sisters were spared with him, but, sadly, not his parents, nor his other sister and younger brother. During the sorting process he briefly caught sight of them. They were being ushered through the opposite gate, condemned to die. 'My father didn't bother even to wave, he kept on going. My mother turned round; she called out to me something like "Look after yourself and wear your extra clothes to keep warm".' Telling the story is not easy, even after 52 years, and Braham is temporarily overcome.

The prisoners had their heads shaved, were given numbers – Braham's was 67957 – and issued with the familiar white and blue striped prison uniforms.

Concentration camp survivors disagree as to whether the tattooed numbers should be removed. Some wear it as a badge of pride; others see it as a cause of shame. One of Braham's sisters has retained her tattoo, the other has not. 'People notice it and talk about it. They say things like "It's sad" or "What a shame", and their partners feel uncomfortable. It's a bit like an ex-serviceman with one arm missing. Some are proud of it; others are not.'

A matter of tremendous importance for all prisoners was footwear. 'I was fortunate that everything was too big for me, including my shoes. It was a big advantage; there were those who had a size 12 foot and got a size 9 shoe. Imagine their predicament.

'We wore wooden clogs with linen or cotton material at the top. If these were too large you could find an old cement bag and wind it around, which would keep your feet warm. Alternatively, you could find paper. The more paper you had the more comfortable you were, but if it rained, it was worse. Sometimes when standing at *Appel* (roll call), you'd pull the paper off and skin would come off with it.'

Apart from the cruelty of the guards, there was the horror of overcrowding. Prisoners had three-tier bunks; five people per bunk, two on one side and three on the other. 'We were like sardines. No movement was possible. I was fortunate that when I arrived it was Spring time.'

In order to stay alive, prisoners had to appear healthy, particularly when fronting up for the twice daily *Appel*. It was here that SS officers decided who would live and who would die. Hygiene was a nightmare. The Germans had a rule '*Eine Laus ein Tod*' (one louse one death). 'The latrines were so packed, if you had *Scheißerei* (diarrhoea) you'd never make it.'

After several weeks Braham and several others were transferred to Mauthausen, in Austria. Though less well known than Auschwitz, the regime was just as cruel. He was sent to work in a stone quarry. 'My job was to pick up rocks which had already been hammered out and load them on to railway carriages.'

The task would have been hard for a grown man, let alone a skinny child just entering his teens. 'SS thugs swung their rifles to make you move faster, and whoever was in the way just copped it.' One day it was Braham's turn. He put up his right arm to protect himself, and felt a crushing blow. His arm was broken. 'I had to go to work the next day with a broken arm because we had no medical facilities whatever. If you failed to appear they simply crossed out your number and your ration was stopped. Even if you were still alive you were thrown on a heap of bodies.

'After two or three weeks the pain was gone and I was able to conceal it [my injury] behind my jacket. I was like a lame dog or fox whose leg has been trapped, but eventually releases itself.' He also suffered lasting injuries through being bitten by the guards' Alsatian dogs. 'I put some rags on the wounds, but they got infected.'

Eventually the camp was liberated by the Americans. Braham returned to his home town. The house was there but had been ransacked. A neighbour came and said: 'Mr so-and-so has your lounge suite. He collaborated with the Nazis.' A few days later the man accused of taking the lounge suite called by and said: 'Your dining room suite is in the home of Mr so-and-so', mentioning the name of the first accuser.

'They'd all been at it and had guilty consciences. I felt uncomfortable and decided to leave.' Braham discovered that his two older sisters were alive. The fiancé of one of them was a pastry cook and had decided to set up in business, taking advantage of a rule which allowed camp survivors to take over premises in the former German-occupied Sudetenland.

The bakery was in the small country town of Friedland, near Liberec (Liberetz), now in the Czech Republic. Though the venture was successful, his sisters thought that a youth who still suffered the effects of a broken arm (he had earlier changed from being right-handed to left-handed) should not be pounding dough. Braham left the business to be apprenticed to a watchmaker – an event which was to shape his life.

In mid-1946, Braham and his younger sister heard about a scheme to bring Jewish war orphans to Australia. It was in fact the scheme organised by the Children's Committee of the Australian Jewish Welfare Society (AJWS).

Both were accepted, travelling by train to France in a party totalling 20 boys and two girls, before departing from Marseilles in a Greek-owned ship, the *Tati*. Braham has good reason to remember the voyage. 'I was very sick; I had some spaghetti with cheese, and got a stomach upset. I vomited all the way to Haifa.' From Haifa they transferred to the *Radnik*, arriving in Australia in February, 1948.

The ship ended its journey in Melbourne. Braham and several others travelled by train to Sydney, where they were taken straight to the Maccabean Hall for morning tea and goodies. 'A man came and sat next to me, and started talking to me. I said, "I'm sorry, I don't speak English." He said, "Do you like Australia?" and I said "Yes". So he said, "You do speak English." That was Syd Einfeld. He was actually the first person who talked to me in Sydney.'

From the Maccabean Hall – now the Sydney Jewish Museum – Braham and his companions were taken to the Isabella Lazarus Home, where they were to stay. On the Friday morning, Walter Brand, secretary of the Australian Jewish Welfare Society, collected them and took them to Palmers menswear shop in the City, where each was kitted out with two shirts, a pair of trousers, and appropriate underwear.

The youngsters were told that arrangements had been made for each of them to have a *Shabbat* (Sabbath) meal with a Jewish family. In Braham's case this meant taking a bus and tram to Bellevue Hill, or as he understood it 'Bellevua'. He made the journey without mishap, arriving earlier than expected.

'I got there at about 3, holding under my arm the cardboard box with the items Mr Brand had bought for me. 'Mrs Lewinnek, that's the lady on the wall,[3] came to the door and welcomed me, but we were virtually unable to communicate and I was flustered. She had her mother with her, and said her husband [John Lewinnek] would not be home until about six.

'She opened the bathroom door and turned on the bath for me. I'd already had a bath before coming, so didn't know what to do. I let the bath run for a considerable time, but did not get undressed. I switched off the taps and sat on a little stool for about 20 minutes. I then emptied the bath and came downstairs. When I came down she started having a conversation with me, but it was useless. She gave me a cup of tea and went into the kitchen with her mother. I was left sitting on her veranda.

'I knew her husband could speak German, so I wasn't really worried. Of course the whole atmosphere changed when he arrived. He started talking; he took me to the Great Synagogue on the Saturday; we've been members ever since. I stayed the Friday and Saturday night with them, then on Sunday took the bus and the tram to Circular Quay, and the ferry back to Hunters Hill. I did that on a regular basis every week.'

Life in the hostel, certainly in the early weeks, seemed idyllic.[4] 'There were about 20 kids living there. The dormitories – about eight to a dorm – were 'clean, bright and comfortable'. Girl migrants (there were two in Braham's intake) were accommodated in private homes.

GENEROUS COOK

'We had a good cook, who was very generous.[5] When we got down to breakfast there was cereal followed by fried or scrambled eggs and coffee. We felt quite guilty. We had been starving in Europe and here we were with two eggs for breakfast and a third one if we wanted it. It's like children with cookies. You look over your shoulder to see if someone is watching you for being greedy.'

The 'generosity' was not confined to breakfast. 'You could come home at any hour and go into the kitchen. There would always be a shoulder of lamb, a piece of cold turkey or chook.'

These living arrangements – weekdays at the hostel, *Shabbat* and weekends with the Lewinneks – continued smoothly for several months. Braham was now 17, and decided to resume the career that had been chosen for him as a result of his broken arm. He became an apprentice at Saunders, a well-known watchmaker and jeweller in Railway Square.

'The journey into town was an awkward one, and our stay in the hostel was supposed to be temporary. I obtained a room in Old South Head Road. The rent was three guineas, and I was paid three pounds. So the mathematics didn't work out. I went to my guardian, who said he would give me one pound a week. It meant that I had a total of four pounds; I had enough left over for fares and a little pocket money.'

Braham thrived in the job and found there was plenty to do. There were so many orders that his boss was having to turn away jobs, mainly repairs to larger clocks. Braham got permission to take on some of this work in his own time. 'After leaving the shop I would run down George Street, and pick up a chiming clock or Big Ben clock and take it home. At that time a retail repair job would cost seven shillings and six pence. I would do it for half that amount.

'I bought an ordinary desk at an auction, and stood it on fruit boxes to raise it to shoulder height. I put it in the room where I was boarding. After five or six weeks I was earning more repairing those clocks than I was earning as an apprentice. I thought, even if I lose my job I'll still be able to keep myself. I felt like a millionaire at that time.

'At Chanuka[6] Mr Lewinnek gave a party for migrants. After the party he asked me to say a few words. I took him aside and gave him a cheque for 52 pounds – refunding the money he had given me during the past year. He was proud of me and was very touched. I think that our friendship developed from then on.'

Braham responded modestly when I praised him for this gesture. 'I don't think anyone likes to queue in soup kitchens. Certainly, there is no way that I would have asked for money if I could have supported myself. All the other boys were in the same situation; nobody wanted handouts.'

Life was not totally dedicated to work. While still at the hostel Braham had joined the Great Synagogue Youth (GSY). 'If you were to meet a Jewish girl, take her out three or four times and then perhaps drop her, you'd be very unpopular. So some of us used to go to the Trocadero[7] and look for company of the opposite sex there.

'It was our hunting ground; we didn't know them, they didn't know us. We kept away from the Jewish girls, I guess we didn't want to be involved at that time. For that matter we foreign boys were not that acceptable to the Australian Jewish girls.'

There was also a psychological factor. According to Braham: 'You'd be introduced to their parents and they'd ask, "What do you do for a living?" If you weren't a university student they might not approve of you. It's a catch-22 situation. It might not be true, but that's what we imagined.

'I met a nurse, took her out a few times and introduced her to my guardian; he was polite but not very pleased.' The attitude of his guardian changed when, at the age of 21, Braham started dating Barbara Basser, who was already known to the Lewinneks. Though excited at this development, the Lewinneks were disappointed when Braham declined to become formally engaged until he had reached his self-defined goal.

This came about in 1954, when Braham decided that he was ready to trade entirely on his own. He could not afford to buy an existing watchmaker–jewellery business, so bought a cake shop in Hurstville, put a bench in the window and converted it. When it looked like succeeding he proposed to Barbara, who accepted. The Lewinneks were chief guests at their wedding in the Great Synagogue.

Having married, Braham then invested in a car, later a second business in Burwood. This too prospered. He found he now had substantial savings – a new and welcome experience. 'I had never had so much money in the bank and it bothered me.' With a fairly hefty mortgage he bought the first of the four homes they have occupied since their marriage.

Though retired from business the family tradition is continued by his son, Timothy, who has a shop in the local Westfield Shopping Centre, trading under the name 'Sterns of Hurstville'.

Sixty years on, a slightly disfigured right arm and marks from the dog bites are reminders of an unhappy past. Plastic surgery has all but obliterated the leg wounds, though mental scars, including the loss of his parents, brother and a sister, remain.

When he was released from captivity a US Army doctor 'looked at the arm, but found they had more urgent jobs to do'. In Australia the AJWS asked if it hurt and arranged x-rays. 'They said it could be fixed, but no one did anything about it and I wasn't in a position to demand that it be done.'

The years passed. 'It continued to bother me psychologically. I had a crooked arm and thought I must have it fixed. I have a stubborn streak, and when I was financially capable of doing so, I saw a specialist who assured me he could do something about it. Unfortunately he didn't succeed.'

His wife, Barbara, has an interesting hobby, collecting miniature shoes, of which she has several hundred, acquired in shops, bazaars and from individuals all over the world. The collection includes wooden clogs. Was it influenced by her husband's experience in the camps? 'No, it is pure coincidence.'

6
CRUELTY AND KINDNESS

'A mouse or a bird, I always wished I was a bird, the way they flew in and out of the camp. I wished I could do that. If only I could be a bird and fly in and out.'

Jack (Zoltan) Schwartz, post-war youth migrant

Zoltan Schwartz was born in the village of Nyircsaholy, in the 'motherland' region of Hungary. 'My father was a simple man, a carrier, or porter. He carried things in a horse and cart. My father was proud of his medals, gained as a soldier in World War I. Some of those with whom he served subsequently helped send him to the death camps.'

Zoltan, who is now known as Jack, was caught in Budapest on 4 December 1944. He was then 15. His parents and two sisters, who remained in the village, had been seized eight months earlier, and taken to a ghetto, which was subsequently demolished. What became of them is a mystery. He assumes they perished in a concentration camp, but lacks confirmation. 'I've never been told anything, up till today.' It is possible, though Jack has no certain knowledge, that at the time of his own arrest they were already dead.

Jack himself was taken into custody by the ruling Arrow Cross Fascists, acting for their German masters. His only offence was 'being Jewish'.

Jack Schwartz remembers his capture well. 'Arrow Cross men entered the cellar where we were living, and rounded us up. An old lady, who was dear to us, was in the middle of cooking a pot of potatoes spiced with paprika. To this day I have the taste of it on my tongue, though I never touched it.'

Outside, it was a cold winter day, already dark at about four in the afternoon. 'I was a quick-witted person at that time, and very slippery. I could wriggle my way out of most situations. I had been taken into custody many times before, but had got clear. This time I was unlucky, and had no chance of escape.'

The war by this time was going very badly for the Germans. 'You could hear the Russian canons around Budapest.'[1] This was not much comfort for Jack and his companions, who were marched to a railway station and bundled into cattle trucks for an unknown destination. This turned out to be the infamous concentration camp of Bergen-Belsen, between Hamburg and Hanover in northern Germany.

The new captives reached their destination on 15 December. The horror train journey took seven days to cover 200 km. Jack recalls: 'They put 90 people in one wagon which was supposed to hold eight horses and 20 people. We sat back-to-back and holding on to each other. As you fell asleep, your limbs went anywhere and you found yourself in all sorts of odd positions; someone could be sitting or lying on you.

'We had 12 deaf mute people in our wagon. They couldn't communicate when it was dark. By three o'clock it was dark, and of course somebody might have been sitting on their hands. They were screeching in a funny voice, and they couldn't explain why. Then they lit matches to see each others' signs. This angered the guards who shouted that they were giving signals to the enemy.

'We had a boy whose arm was shot through. The doctor found a piece of wood and they strapped his arm to it. But there was no space for his outstretched arm, so we tied him to the wall of the wagon and he was standing there 12 days. He was literally tied to it so he couldn't let go.'

Bergen-Belsen had a crematorium but no gas chamber. Unlike Auschwitz, it did not purport to be a work camp. 'We had no work, there was no factory set up. What it offered was a slow death, because there was no food. It was made to house 15000 to 20000 prisoners, but by the time I got there it held close to 100000.

'In such a situation nothing could function; the bakery, the kitchen, the toilets, nothing. So it was chaos, just chaos. And they kept bringing in more people. As I have said, they were doing this almost until the end.'

The cruelty of the Germans remained undiminished, even when it must have become clear to the dimmest of them that their days were numbered. One of the cruellest was known as the 'bed board man'.

According to Jack, the 'bed board man' was a sadistic thug. 'He could not, in truth, be referred to as a "person", nor will I insult the animal kingdom by placing him among them. As soon as the call was sounded for the muster he would rush into the nearest barracks, grab a plank from a handy bunk and attack anyone he could reach with it, on any part of the body, as they were trying to leave their huts.

'This thing, this enormous hitting machine, was, to me, one of the symbols of the Third Reich. When he struck, it was not only with the strength of his arms but he swung with his whole body behind it. He never uttered a sound. People would crowd the doorway and in their attempt to get away from him would push each other over. He would then block the doorway and force others to step on the fallen. He just continued to swing as if he were chopping wood.'

In contrast to the 'bed board man', there was a *good* German. 'He was an old man, thin, with no teeth, who looked for all the world like Popeye. He wore clothes twice his size. He never spoke to anyone, and we knew nothing about him, other than that he was German. I was going by one day, and I saw an astonishing sight. He pulled a piece of bread from his pocket and gave it to a little boy.'

Recalling the incident brings tears to Jack's eyes. He pauses to regain his composure. 'Who was this man? Who could have imagined an act of kindness in a place like that?'

Women who served the Nazi cause could be as cruel as men. 'I saw a woman kill another woman. Every morning a big cart came by, but it was being pulled by female prisoners, women and girls, instead of horses. Their task was to collect the corpses. If somebody died in one of the huts, the body would be put outside, where it would be picked up, loaded on the cart and taken to the crematorium.

'There was this beautiful, blonde, very elegant German girl in uniform. She was nicely coiffeured, and wore a light blouse with her green uniform; she really looked most attractive. One day she passed right in front of our gate; the sun came out, but the road wasn't very smooth and the surface was slushy. As the cart went by, one of the wheels sloshed some water on her uniform.'

Jack cries again, as the memory returns. 'She turned round; she had a large leather whip. She took it off her shoulder and beat one of the women pulling the cart until she died. When she was finished she put the strap back on her shoulder, fixed her uniform and just carried on. There had been seven or eight prisoners pulling that cart; now there was one less, and one more body to carry.

'I kept asking, I still keep asking myself, "How can a beautiful girl like that be so horrible?". Then there was that old fellow who was kind, but he was the exception. With most of them ... that air of superiority, the way they looked at you, the way they belittled you, the way they walked.

'I don't think any of the Allies could understand what those Germans were. They were just ... I don't know where they picked it up, where did they get that understanding of things? Even a fly I wouldn't kill.

'A mouse or a bird, I always wished I was a bird, the way they flew in and out of the camp. I wished I could do that. If only I could be a bird and fly in and out.' Jack cries again at the recollection.

Starvation and lice affected prisoners' morale as much as actual cruelty. Many a night he lay awake mentally tasting the potatoes spiced with paprika, the serving of which had been interrupted by the arrival of the Arrow Cross.

For Jack the mental anguish was worse than the physical. 'It was the absence of names, the impersonality which got to me. I was never asked my name. Nobody said "Who are you?", "Why are you here?". We were not told anything, no one was interested. It was like when you buy cattle, they don't each have a name; we were numbers.'

(Actually, Jack did not have a number. Such was the overcrowding and emergency conditions that by the time of his arrival in Bergen-Belsen the Germans had abandoned the practice.)

Inmates and guards shared a common attitude. 'Nobody knew my name was Schwartz and nobody knew my name was Zoli (Zoltan). There were no friendships because your friends were here today and gone tomorrow; those who shared your bunk could die the next day.'

In the absence of real names there were nicknames. Jack came to be known as 'the Army-cap boy' because of a cap he wore constantly, which had belonged to a soldier. A companion was known as 'the fat man'. 'He had a big tummy when he was caught and it went down to nothing. He kept showing us all that empty area of his trousers.'

In the hut with Jack was a prisoner who would talk about the importance of religion and religious observance. 'He used to say that we could not afford to relax our observance because of "times and conditions", and that had we done so in the past there would have been no observance left.

'This man's eyes lit up when he explained to anybody within earshot that God "sees and knows what is happening" and the reason why it is happening.

'He could never explain it in a way that I could accept. I believed that God had completely forgotten us, and had abandoned us. I felt that since there is only one God, the one the Germans believed in had to be the very same one and he had given them food; he had given them guns and the means to lock us up, starve us, beat us and kill us.

'It seemed to me that the more religious a person was the harder it was to believe in a God who would permit all this. I thought about it often and long, but I wasn't sure. Nevertheless, it was beautiful, it was a comfort to see a certainty, a conviction in so many others who possessed faith and to whom it provided concrete help.'

Although Jack Schwartz didn't know it, his ordeal was about to end. Jack and several other prisoners left Bergen-Belsen on 7 April, 1945,[2] by which time the Russians were already on the outskirts of Berlin. Rare in Nazi Germany, the prisoners were given a choice. 'They just said they wanted a given number of people to assemble the following morning at the gate. You could say, "I don't want to go, I'd rather stay here." That was okay. But I said, "I want to go, I can't stand this place." So they counted 1500 people and we were off.

'We were put on trains; I believe they were planning to use us as hostages. That's what we were told on the latrine news. For six days we kept going. There was a little window which was boarded up, but you could see through it. You could see the war was virtually over because planes were flying practically non-stop, and all the stations and railway lines were bombed out.

'We came to a halt in a place called Hillersleben, about 30 km from Magdeburg where the Americans and Russians later met. The wagon doors were opened and the Germans just disappeared. We saw that the locomotive had been detached from the wagons, and was about 500 metres along the track. Suddenly it was blown up.

'It was about 11 in the morning. Soon after this there were voices in the front of the wagons. We went to investigate. There were two American soldiers; they had found us.'

Jack's voice breaks with the emotion. 'We nearly tore those soldiers apart in our joy; everyone wanted to touch them. They had helmets on and rifles in their hands. They brought and gave us every bit of food they had; chocolates and tins of food. Had God descended from heaven we could not have been happier.'

One of the Americans drove off to the village in his jeep, shot five geese and brought them to the newly-liberated captives. 'We tried to clean them, to cook them, but how? We had no paper, no matches, no dishes, no knives, we had nothing. We were bloody all over, feathers were flying everywhere. We just gave up. Then they came back with some cooked rice in milk. They tried to give everybody some of that rice. We were crowding them, and they couldn't serve it ... Finally, the dish spilled over and we were ...' His voice breaks again.

It was Friday, 13 April – unlucky for some, lucky for Jack and those freed with him. The liberated prisoners were taken to a commandeered military barracks at Hillersleben. It was clean – at least, it started that way – and there was a garden. There was a hospital and other amenities. To Jack and others it seemed 'just beautiful.' Jack was put into a ground floor billet for single soldiers. It was a very long room with a toilet at both ends.

Upon leaving Belsen the prisoners had helped themselves to clumps of beetroot which had upset their already weakened stomachs. That and the food given to them by the Americans was to create havoc. Jack recalls: 'We couldn't control our bowels; we all had diarrhoea, I couldn't make it to either of the toilets. I used a helmet; the whole place stank.'

Unfortunately people kept dying. 'I was fortunate. By this time it was 20 April. I found a patch of onions, very young spring onions, I got to like that; I kept eating bread and butter and spring onions and I think it helped.'

Jack discovered that he had left Bergen-Belsen a week before the camp was liberated by British troops. Months later, in a Paris cinema, he saw the famous newsreel showing Joseph Kramer, the 'Beast of Belsen', camp commandant, being led away in chains, and former guards, now prisoners, digging graves and burying the dead. All this in front of local townspeople, who were forced to watch.

After his own liberation Jack had plenty of opportunity to study his former captors in defeat. 'Those men who used to come in dressed to the nines in their uniforms, with buttons and boots gleaming, and that fixed contemptuous look; once their faces got dirty, that haughtiness gone, and the shine came off their buttons and their boots, they were like ordinary people. 'Of course, we ourselves were in a horrible state; we had completely lost our dignity as human beings ...'

Jack Schwartz decided not to return to Hungary, which faced many uncertainties, but to live in France, where settlement rules were flexible or could be circumvented. On the long train journey to Paris he and other former concentration camp victims were involved in an incident which highlights questions of 'dignity' and revenge.

'We were several hours into our journey. The train was still in Germany. The tracks were not good and you had to stop here or there for hours. Even when moving we were going extremely slowly. We stopped at a spot where there were beautiful cherry trees; they were harvesting the cherries. Somebody noticed and called to the others. Everybody got off and went for those beautiful crunchy cherries. There were 500 of us; we ate until we couldn't eat any more.

'When we had finished eating, we pulled the rest of the cherries out and squashed them with our feet. The Germans looked at us with much hatred, and we looked at them with the same hatred.

'They were ordinary people picking cherries, their own cherries from the field. We had just pulled out the beautiful juicy cherries and trod on them, and they couldn't sell any of them or eat them. It was a horrible sight, and, I suppose, a horrible thing to do. I still think about it and what makes people act in certain ways.'

When they arrived in Paris, members of the group were treated like VIPs. General de Gaulle himself was in the welcoming party. Jack, still only 16, spent four years there, finding enchantment not only in the city but in the company of several charming Parisiennes. 'I became a fur cutter; I settled down there and I was very happy. I learned the language quite well.'

In 1948, his brother, the only other member of his family to survive the Holocaust, invited him to visit him in Hungary. He was away for three weeks. On returning to Paris, he found that he had lost his job and there were other complications. 'And that's when Australia came into the picture.'

Jack originally applied to migrate to Canada: 'I thought it was cold there and fur would be more useful. I got a letter to say that I had been turned down for Canada, I've no idea why, but I had been accepted to go to Australia. Up to that day I had never heard of Australia. I said, "Where is Australia? What is Australia?". And the lady, Anita Glass, said, "It's on the other side, on the bottom of the world, and it takes six weeks to go there by ship." I said, "Then I will go. It's a long way from everything."'

His emigration was arranged by the Swiss-based *Oeuvres de Secours aux Enfants* (Works for helping children), better known by its initials OSE, which helped many Jewish war orphans. 'I was told Australia had a hot climate and I thought what would a furrier do there? I queried this and was told, "You will do what all the others do and if there isn't any fur business you will find something else".'

Jack arrived in Sydney on the *Napoli* in October 1948. There were several other young Jews, most of whom, like himself, had been temporarily living in France.

The newcomers were taken to the Isabella Lazarus Home in Hunters Hill. 'It was paradise, absolute paradise. We were about two dozen boys; I stayed there about four months, and I loved it there. I left when I was kicked out like Adam and Eve from the Garden of Eden.

'I remember we had a wonderful cook,[3] a big garden; we played cards, we played football, we played ping pong. Unfortunately, they kept trying to push us out in order to make room for the next lot.'

SENT BY GOD

Like the cook, whose name is forgotten, Hugo Schneider, manager of the Isabella Lazarus Home in the early post-war period, is remembered with respect and affection. He was of Hungarian origin and had come to Australia briefly in 1928, as an exporter of agricultural machinery. He returned as a migrant in 1939.

Schneider spoke several languages, which impressed the newcomers. Jack Schwartz recalls: 'On our first afternoon he greeted us solemnly and said, "Children, you have to be careful. You must not go out at night barefoot, because there are poisonous snakes and spiders about." We were stunned. We said to each other, "What on earth is this bloody place we have come to after beautiful, shiny Paris?".'

In dealing with his charges, Schneider took into account their deprived backgrounds. When he saw a boy taking food from another's plate, he gently chided him, saying: 'You do not have to do that here. If you want more food, tell me and I will give you some.'

Despite some early misgivings, Jack took a liking to his surroundings and to Mr Schneider. 'He was a man sent by God, who understood us, where we came from, what we had been through, and how we should behave. He told us how people live in Australia, that you are free, you don't have to have identity papers, that you are innocent until proven guilty.

'He taught us English. He had a strong accent, but was excellent and poured the language into us like a funnel. While teaching us he explained, not just the language, but everything that goes with it. Everything that he knew we had to know. I had a lot of respect for that man; we considered him old; he was about 60, very tall, slightly bent. He was a fantastic person.'

Australia at the time was 'backward in many ways'. According to Jack: 'You could buy a good old Sargents pie and that was about it.' Nevertheless, he took a strong liking to Australia, and was determined to succeed.

Within a few weeks of his arrival, and with very limited command of English, he set out to find a job. 'I was surprised to find there were furriers here and I came to the conclusion that women like to look good and wear expensive clothes regardless.'

He returned to his former trade as a fur cutter, but lost his job during a brief slump about two years later. He decided to change tack. 'I gave away the fur coats. There was too much competition, and you needed too much capital.

'I had on many occasions seen soft toys in shop windows and thought that this was something I could do, something I could get into.' With assistance from John Lewinnek[4] he started his own business. 'I made fur toys, I'm still partially in it. We call ourselves Lina Products.'

It was a solo occupation, which meant that he could choose his working hours. 'Every suitable afternoon would find me on the beach, after which, to make up for the lost hours, I would work till midnight.' He led an active social life, dining, dancing and going to parties, in the course of which he met a 20-year-old girl, 'attractive, elegant, with a mass of curly blonde hair brushed to one side', who was to become his wife.

Some 60 years on, when he looks back on his life and experiences, Jack finds, like other Jewish war orphans, that the good memories compete for space with the bad. His brain is unable to resolve the many contradictions. 'There was the horror, the things we saw in Budapest and in Germany, the cruelty and inhumanity. Then you go over to the other side of life and you see the kindness, generosity and understanding and all the good things people can do.

'The contrast between one person and one set of circumstances and another ... it can make you very mixed up ...' He shakes his head. 'I shall never understand it, personally.'[5]

JOHN LEWINNEK: OPEN HOUSE FOR NEWCOMERS

*'To me he was more than an employer. More, even, than a friend. I have had
no closer relationship with anyone. So much so that when I married, he and
his wife took the place of my parents.'*

Henry Lippmann, Dunera Boy, speaking of John Lewinnek

Jewish tradition holds that in every generation there are 36
hidden righteous people, known in Hebrew as *Lamed-
Vav-Tzaddikim*, who profoundly influence, though they
themselves may not be fully aware of it, people or events of
their time.

Isidor (John) Lewinnek may be deemed by history to be one of
these. Grown men cry when they recall the man who befriended
them when they were young and vulnerable. Photographs of him and
his wife, Peggy, are in many homes.

To the post-war Jewish youth migrants, depending on how well
they knew him, he is 'Mr Lewinnek', spoken deferentially, or
'Uncle John'.

Tom Keleman remembers a man who was 'very humane, very
friendly and helped a hell of a lot of people'. To Albert Halm he
was 'a lovely man, a wonderful, wonderful man, who was
involved in every humanitarian activity in the Jewish and
non-Jewish community'.

According to Albert: 'Saturday afternoon was open house at the
Lewinneks. The boys and girls used to come and browse through his
library and through the whole house. Afternoon tea was laid on. We
had a truly lovely time.'

Jack Schwartz echoes this view. 'They [John and Peggy Lewinnek]
replaced our parents. You could just go in there and you were at
home. You could tell them your problems; they would help you
financially. I started business and he lent me some money.

'He was such a generous person; he would arrange an evening, which was supposed to be paid for by some organisation. He would never bother about that; he just paid for the whole thing himself.'

Boys who were not strictly speaking his wards nevertheless refer to him as their 'guardian'. I asked Braham Stern why he did so. 'He was not my guardian, directly. I was a Welfare Society boy.[6] But he became the best guardian any of us could have wished for. He was a very kind man.'

Braham pauses to regain his composure. His wife breaks the silence: 'He [John Lewinnek] actually wanted to adopt Braham. Braham said he didn't want it because he remembered his own father who died in Auschwitz, and he didn't want to change his name.'

John Lewinnek was a pre-war refugee from Germany, who achieved success as a wholesaler in ladies' fashions, in particular coats, representing leading overseas brands. He was financially secure and had obvious business acumen. He enjoyed his work, and regarded financial success as the means of improving the lot of the less fortunate.

According to Braham Stern: 'He loved "stray dogs". Anybody he found in the synagogue who was a stranger in town he would bring home for Friday night or Saturday dinner, usually unannounced. Quite often he would bring a whole family. Aunty Peggy would say "What am I going to feed them on? I wish you wouldn't do that to me." But she always managed to cope.'

Mrs Peggy Lewinnek was what nowadays would be called an 'identity'. She came from an established Australian family, had been married (and widowed) before, and was considerably younger than her husband. The couple had no sons or daughters of their own.

It was their custom to take regular holidays in the Blue Mountains, staying at The Chalet in Medlow Bath. Braham would accompany them. 'Aunty Peggy would love walking and I would go with her. I jumped from one rock to another and I slipped and broke my leg, ending up in the Katoomba Hospital.

'When I woke up from the anaesthetic I found her crying next to my bed. Our relationship became much stronger then. Before that time I had thought that she was kind to me because her husband insisted on it.

'We remained close, even though, by this time, I was going out steadily with Barbara. Aunty Peggy loved dancing and Mr Lewinnek didn't dance. He would start talking to everyone, wandering around. So I used to dance with her. Sometimes I had arranged to go out with Barbara to the movies and Aunty Peggy would say "What are you doing next Sunday?". So I had my preferences changed.

'Of course it wasn't like the way it sounds. I was going out with the Lewinneks. I never took dancing lessons; to me it came naturally. I wouldn't win a prize but I could go from A to B without tripping.'

Jack Schwartz was another young migrant who became part of the Lewinneks' extended family. 'I remember the first time I met them. She said "Hello" to me and I said, "Sorry, no speak English". She spoke a school French, so we started in that. They invited me to their home that weekend.

'On one of these visits there was an amusing incident. We were sitting in the front garden and she asked me to go in and put the kettle on. I had no idea what the bloody kettle was, so I went in and just looked around. Then I saw the cat sleeping. So I picked up the poor cat and put it out into the back garden.

'A few minutes later she said, "Let's make the tea." She came back with a puzzled look and said, "I thought I told you to put the kettle on and you said you had done it." I told her about the cat. She just smiled.'

Girls as well as boys had good reason to be grateful to John Lewinnek. According to Greta Silvers: 'Every season he would say, "Girls, you come up and choose something." He had these really beautiful garments. We were never asked to pay.'

Henry Lippmann had a special association with John Lewinnek, having worked for him as a salesman. He says of his former employer: 'I learned many things from him but one thing above all others, that is that you are happiest in life when you are helping someone else.'

Their association began casually when Henry and a friend, both in the uniform of the 8th Australian Employment Company, struck up a conversation with a stranger in a restaurant.

As Lippmann tells it: 'We were stationed in Albury at the time, and I was on six days' leave. This man said to me, "Where do you come from?". I said "Albury". He said, "Where do you really come from?". I said "Berlin".

'We talked for a while. He said, "I have to sit at the other table with my friends." After a while he came back to our table, and said, "Look, boys, I have to go now. I have a meeting. I wish you both all the best." Later, when we got up and went to pay, the owner said, "Mr Lewinnek has paid for you already." It was embarrassing because we received six shillings and sixpence Army pay, and did not consider ourselves poor.'

The young soldier and the older man kept in irregular contact. When the war ended, Henry Lippmann, newly demobilised, came to Sydney. 'I bought myself a suit, a shirt and a tie and I felt like a millionaire. I met him by chance in Market Street, corner of Castlereagh Street. He said, "Hello, Mr Lippmann" – people were formal in those days – "How are you doing?" I said, "Very well." I had a bit of deferred pay in my pocket and looked prosperous. He said, "Why don't you come and see me? Come tomorrow."

'I went to see him. There was an office with a carpet, and the smell of cigar. There were some garments hanging up. He said, "Ah, Mr Lippmann, there you are." He opened a box and put an order book in it and said to me, "You go out and sell." I didn't want to act stupid and didn't even ask questions. I went out on the road and sold. I never looked back. I worked for him for 15 years.

'Because of my association with his business I was an eyewitness to all the voluntary work he undertook. His dedication was embedded in philosophical beliefs. This was evident when he once confided to me the simple motto, "Life must have a purpose". At a function I heard Syd Einfeld describe him as the "model of an immigrant". His whole life was the opposite of the common attitude of "take, take, take".'

Each year John Lewinnek organised a Channukah party[7] at Sydney's Maccabean Hall for the young migrants and other new arrivals. Bernie Weiss, a war orphan, met his wife, Sarah, at one of them. 'Bernie and I went up and lit the Channukah candles. That's going back over 45 years. We met again at their home.'

She added, when her husband had left the room: 'You have to understand that these boys came from Europe and they had no one. They had no language, no profession, no one to turn to; and suddenly they had this wonderful couple to act like substitute parents. It was like an anchor for these boys.'

In 1954, the tables were turned on John and Peggy Lewinnek when over 1000 people attended a Channukah party to pay tribute to their role in assisting the 'Children of the Holocaust'.

John Lewinnek died on 21 December 1961. His widow re-married, twice. She died, aged 71, in 1978. They are buried together in the Jewish section of Rookwood Necropolis.

On the grave is a tablet: 'A Tribute of Love from Braham, Bernard, Jack, Henry and Morris.'[8] The headstone carries the inscription, 'His righteousness walketh before him' (Psalm 85:13).

7
A SHORTAGE OF RELATIVES

'In my family not one single person survived. I have no cousins, no nothing. I feel very deprived; so whenever I see people with lots of aunts and uncles I say, "I haven't got any. How about giving me a couple?".'

Greta Silvers, post-war youth migrant

Greta Silvers (also known as Greta Alsberg) is smiling as she speaks, but her pain in recalling her early years is real enough. 'It's difficult to come to terms ... Sometimes, even now, it really hurts.' Her friend, Agnes Adler, seems almost lucky by comparison. 'I have two cousins,' she says proudly. 'One can remember me as a child; the other is younger than me.'

Between them the two women have had three husbands (Greta has been married and divorced twice), and four children (Greta has two sons and Agnes has two daughters). Agnes has two grandchildren and Greta would like to achieve the same. Both believe it is important to have a family *upwards* (parents, grandparents, uncles) as well as *downwards* (children, grandchildren).

According to Greta: 'You can be compensated to a point by marriage, children and whatever. In my own case it was long ago, the very big pain. If I meet people who have lost a family member, a father, or grandfather, I say to them, "I sympathise with you, but I can't *feel* for you because I have done it long ago. My grieving was long ago."'

Agnes nods in agreement. 'I tell people who have lost someone dear to them, "You had another 40 years with your sister, mother or whoever, which we didn't have".'

About two-thirds of Jewish youth migrants to Australia, as well as to other countries, were boys. Why the imbalance? Various theories are offered. Greta believes it was because 'fewer girls survived'.[1]

The two war orphans have been friends for over 50 years. When they came to Australia, Agnes was 17 and Greta 15. Their birthdays are five weeks apart. Agnes Fenster, as she was then, came from the Hungarian capital, Budapest, and Greta Tabakova from Kosice, a country town which has been at various times claimed by both Hungary and Czechoslovakia (now Slovakia).

They met in April 1949, at the Redleaf Pool in Double Bay. It was the day Agnes arrived in Sydney. The purpose of the outing was to 'meet boys and have fun'. The boys were mostly fellow war orphans, who had come two months earlier with the first post-war group of Jewish youngsters. Someone took an informal snap of the pool gathering. The girls' costumes are not – by today's standards – flattering and some of the boys look awkward. But all are clearly enjoying themselves.

It had been a long day for Agnes, which began when she arrived at Central Railway from Melbourne, having disembarked in that city from the Greek vessel, *Cyrenia*. Greta had arrived with the earlier group on the *Radnik*.[2] Along with several others in that party, her papers were 'doctored' – two years were deducted from her age – to meet immigration requirements.

Agnes recalls: 'I did a lot of things that first day, and then quietened down. In the evening I went to the movies in Double Bay and saw *The Great Waltz*.

'What I remember about arriving are the colours and the smells. It smelt so different from anywhere else; I can't put it into words. It was April and it was still beautiful and warm. I'd always lived in a big city; here it seemed a little town. You couldn't even get sliced bread, never mind salamis. When we ate a capsicum, they thought we were eating grass.'

She spent her first few nights in Sydney at the home of Gerald de

Vahl Davis, later president of the NSW Jewish Board of Deputies. A former school friend in Budapest, who had been among the welcoming party at Central Station, met her again at lunchtime. She and Greta, who shared a room in the home of the Rev. Marcus and Doris Einfeld,[3] invited her to the swimming party.

Greta's first night in Sydney was at the Isabella Lazarus Home. This was unusual, to say the least, because the hostel was officially for boys.[4] She then went to stay with Julian and Violet Rose. The arrangement lasted until she had learned a modicum of English, at which point she boarded with an Australian family in Rose Bay.

She continued to stay with the Roses at weekends, alternating with weekends with John Wars[5] and his wife. 'I never had an official guardian, though in fact I had two. I just floated between one and the other every weekend. Both treated me like their daughter.'

Shared ages, interests and compatible temperaments led to a natural affinity between the two girls. They found they had less pleasant things in common. The fathers of both died in forced labour battalions assisting the Germans' Hungarian allies.

Greta was taken prisoner with her mother and other family members in a round-up of Jews in Kosice in May 1944. They were sent to Auschwitz. 'We were separated – one side for the living and one side for those who would die. Before going through, a fellow called to my mother, "Don't hold on to her, or she'll go with you." My mother pushed me away but my little brother was holding on to her.' Greta lost sight of them; she assumes they went straight to the gas chamber.

Greta says she survived in Auschwitz because 'I stayed out of trouble. I hid under the bed ... I wanted to live so badly. All I wanted to do was survive and go home. That kept me alive; it kept my hopes up.

'After about three months we were transferred to a labour camp at Weisswasser. It was a factory that made light bulbs. From there I went to Bergen-Belsen. I was there just under a week when we were liberated. There were rumours that we were going to be given poisoned bread to kill us. Instead, the British came and freed us.

'I was very sick. People continued to die – many because they were given rich food and couldn't take it. In hospital I cottoned on to some people and they said they would take me back home to Kosice. We walked and sometimes soldiers gave us a lift. We were so weak physically, I don't know how we made it.

'When I got home I went to a kind of welfare society and they had all these names written out – names of people who had come home and people looking for people. I found some people I knew and they took me in.'

Agnes, unlike Greta, managed to avoid imprisonment and incarceration in a concentration camp. This was partly because of the more chaotic conditions in Budapest and because their apartment building was designated as a ghetto. This did not save her mother. The Arrow Cross men who took her away said that being a war widow – her husband had died in 1942 with other military 'slaves' on the Russian front – she would almost certainly be sent home after her papers were checked.

This did not happen and Agnes, who never saw her mother again, sat out the rest of the war in the ghetto. She believes her relative youth (she was 14) shielded her from mental anguish as she did not fully realise what was happening. 'I had only a few months of the ghetto. I walked past dead bodies because there was no way of getting them to the cemetery. Luckily it was winter and it was snowing. I was not even frightened; it was more like an adventure.'

She remembers vividly the day Budapest was liberated. 'The Russians came in at six in the morning. There was still fighting in the street; I was going the other way breaking into shops trying to get food. The little boy who was with me had no shoes. I went into a big department store to steal some. Everyone was doing it. When I got back my grandmother said, "How can you do these things?". She wouldn't have dared go anywhere.'

Meanwhile, having returned to Kosice, Greta's life took an unexpected new turn. She had been back in her home town about a year when a man contacted her, saying that he had served in the labour battalion with her father and that the two men had made a pact that if either of them survived, the survivor would look after the other's children. 'He took me to his town of Liberec (Liberetz) and I went to live with him and his sick wife.'

It was not a happy arrangement, and with hindsight she feels his story may have been untrue. She was still only 14. The man, who she regarded as her guardian, reneged on a promise to send her to school, restricted her movements, and regarded her 'as a maid'.

She came to Australia almost by accident. 'Somebody put my name down [for emigration] because they were feeling sorry for me. I really was like a prisoner there. The husband of a person I knew in Kosice came to Liberec, and knocked on the door to say "Hello". It was a Sunday, I remember, and my guardian gave permission for us to go out for a walk. My friend's husband said to me, "I have two tickets. We're going back home tonight." I had only the clothes I stood up in, but I agreed.'

Once in Kosice a tug-of-war developed. Her 'guardian' made threats, tried to get her back, but the police would not intervene. In the midst of this, Greta fled to Prague, where she met Anita Glass, who took her to Paris on the first leg of her far longer journey to Australia.

Agnes, like Greta, has an odd story of how she came to be in Australia. 'According to my papers I was supposed to go to Canada. I heard nothing for ages, then received a postcard telling me to go to Paris immediately. When I got there they said that I was too old and couldn't go. The committee[6] that was running the show then sent me to Australia.'

The experiences of many years ago now seem dream-like. Both women are glad that a scheme for Jewish child migration existed. Says Greta: 'Wonderful, wonderful. Where I come from it was only a small place. Had I stayed I would have been married, miserable, and very poor.'

Though their temperaments are similar, there are also differences between the pair. Greta is artistic and a little 'dizzy'. Agnes is cautious, more reflective, staid. Within a week of her arrival she moved to more permanent lodgings with a Hungarian couple in Bronte. 'They were very nice people who were renting out a room with full board. It was a happy arrangement. I stayed with them until I got married. I'm not a "moving person". I've only moved five times since I've been here.'

Her first job was in a trouser factory. 'They put me to work on an electric machine which I hadn't a clue how to use. My grandfather had been a tailor, so when I arrived I said I had experience in "sewing". I really knew nothing.

'On my first day in the job the boss, who was quite nice, asked me if I had brought any lunch with me. I said "No", and he produced a meat pie. I bit into it and I didn't know what to do because I never had anything like that and thought I would die. It was pretty revolting. Now I love meat pies, I really do.'

Agnes stayed in the job a few months. 'Then a man at a Maccabean Hall dance said he'd get me a better job and he did. It was in Newtown and paid six pounds a week. The job was supposed to be for an experienced tailoress. After two hours he realised I knew nothing. But he was nice about it and actually taught me a lot. I stayed there several months, then moved to another job, also as a tailoress. That was the last paid work I had. It was where I met my husband who was also a tailor, but left to go into another business.'

Greta's entry to the Australian workforce was more glamorous. She was employed as a junior in a high class *salon* – an upper-class dress shop – patronised by the rich and famous. The work involved 'sitting and sewing, cleaning up and making tea and coffee. I stayed there two years and then moved to a similar establishment where I had a better job with 10 shillings more.

'I was never good as a dressmaker, I hated it. I was too lazy to go to college to learn because I didn't think I had what it takes. But I was good with the ladies; I could suggest things that they should have and was good at fittings. I stayed there for a number of years. She [the proprietor] looked after me and made my wedding dress.' Did she choose her husband? 'No, perhaps it might have been better ...' She smiles and leaves the sentence unfinished.

In the past 30 years Greta has found moderate fame as an artist. In the 1970s she studied sculpture under Tom Bass, and opened a gallery in Woollahra with her then husband, Peter Alsberg. She attended Woollahra Art School, and later Frankston TAFE College, in Melbourne, concentrating on etching on foil. She has many works in private collections, and in 1983 was invited to the Melbourne Women's Registry as a permanent exhibitor. In 1985 she returned to live and work in Sydney.

Both Greta and Agnes have used the Red Cross and other tracing agencies in an attempt to find missing relatives. In Greta's case it was futile, but Agnes's story is different.

As she tells it: 'I tried for many years to find my two cousins, whom I had last seen [in 1944] as small boys of five and seven. I was told they had been taken by some underground means to Palestine, but had no means of verifying this.

'I did everything I could. I advertised, tried various ways, for so many years, but never had any response. Then about six years ago I went to the Red Cross again. A wonderful person, a beautiful lady helped me. Incredibly, after three or four months she found one of my cousins.

'He did not know that he had anybody in the whole world. He was just so thrilled. Mind you, we cannot communicate easily because he can't speak Hungarian or English and I can't speak Hebrew. So I talk to him through his children; he has five children, the older two girls speak English. One of them lives in New York. He went to the US to see her and I went there too. It was wonderful.'

Both women still dream about the parents they have not seen for nearly 60 years. According to Agnes: 'I close my eyes and dream that I have found them somewhere. Also my brother because he was young and maybe he would have survived. I went to a clairvoyant, a famous Dutchman. He said, "Your brother is alive and he is in Paris." So, of course, I went again to the Red Cross and to Paris. There was nothing.'

Greta chips in: 'We'll all meet, we will meet up there.' The conversation pauses. The silence is broken when Greta rises to prepare morning tea.

ANITA GLASS: SPECIAL AGENT

Some see her as a Jewish Florence Nightingale. Others as a female Scarlet Pimpernel, or perhaps a queen. Mention this to Anita Glass and she laughs loudly. 'A queen bee, perhaps?,' she says, in heavily accented English.

It's an appropriate term for a grand old lady, who, in the immediate post-war years, was a familiar sight in hospitals, displaced persons' camps, and other centres of population in former German-occupied Europe.

Her task was to seek out Jewish war orphans – boys and girls who had lost their parents in the Nazi Holocaust – and arrange their migration to Australia.

She is herself of Czech/Jewish origin, and was interned for three-and-a-half years in Theresienstadt concentration camp, along with her husband and son. After the war her husband was convicted by a Czech court of having collaborated with the enemy. It's a topic she doesn't care to talk about, and there is argument to this day about his guilt or innocence.[7]

Anita Freiberg, as she was then, returned to live, alone, in Prague. The Chief Rabbi of Great Britain arranged for her son to be educated in that country.

In 1946 she was offered a position with the Jewish rescue organisation *Oeuvres de Secours aux Enfants* (OSE) in Switzerland. The job involved organising a TB sanatorium and providing disadvantaged children with 'catch-up' educational opportunities.

At about this time Anita remarried, becoming Mrs Glass. Her new husband was a Swiss widower, who had lived for 30 years in Australia and had dual citizenship.

While engaged in this work she had an offer she couldn't refuse. 'A letter came from the Paris office that children who survived the Holocaust[8] would be allowed to go to Australia. The numbers were limited – I forget how many – and I was asked to help in the selection.

'The Australians wanted them to be about 14 years old and absolutely healthy. I started looking, but it was a pretty heavy job ...' The request from Paris was, on the face of it, relatively simple. In fact, there were problems.

A child of 14 in 1947/48 would have been 11 or 12 when the war ended and six or seven when the terror against Jews began. Children of this age in the camps were considered to have no work potential and – unless 'saved' for medical experiments – were likely to be assigned for liquidation. Not only were there relatively few survivors in this age group, but those who did usually did not have perfect health.

Anita solved the 'age' problem by doctoring travel documents so that youngsters of 17 or 18 were registered as 14. Where necessary, she obtained false passports and identity papers.

This was not to 'fool' the Australians, who couldn't have cared less about a person's name and nationality, but to fool newly created Communist regimes who might not wish a citizen of their country to leave.

A potential difficulty arose when young people bound for Australia passed through various checkpoints in Europe. Where necessary, her charges had to be taught words and phrases from the language of their supposed country of origin.

'I told them, "You must speak only Polish or Russian or whatever." Of course, some of them had no idea of these languages, but when we crossed the border they had to speak the language of their passport.'

The health problem was more difficult. A number of the child concentration camp survivors who wished to go to Australia, and whose need was greatest, had suffered mild forms of tuberculosis. Some had spent time at the clinic which was under her care. TB was the great 'no, no' as far as Australia was concerned.

Anita Glass feared that chest X-ray plates might show signs of the disease. She adopted an unusual solution to this problem – substituting X-ray plates of herself for those of 'suspect' teenagers.

After about three years in this work the Communist government in Czechoslovkia passed a law that anyone helping a person of or approaching military age to leave the country would be shot as a spy. Arrangements were quickly made for Anita herself to leave the country.

Anita Glass returned with her husband to Melbourne, where for the next 18 years – having 'retired' from her unusual and sometimes dangerous occupation – she kept 'open house' for her former charges and (in the words of one of them) 'any odd bod who needed a helping hand or friendly shoulder to lean on'.

In the early 1970s Anita and her second husband were divorced. She decided to move to Israel. A great sadness developed in her life when her daughter, who was also in Israel, and a figure of some importance, took poison and committed suicide.

Another 18 years or so went by, at which time – by now a somewhat lonely figure – she was persuaded by a Jewish youth migrant to return to Australia. That was in 1988. A place was found for her at the Moses Montefiore Home in Hunters Hill.

Advancing years[9] and frailty have taken their toll. Sadnesses in her personal life have scarred her, but she is bright and chirpy when talking about 'my children' – she believes there were 61 – whose migration to Australia she personally arranged nearly 50 years ago. She laughs at my suggestion that she has 'the largest family in Australia'.

Some of these 'children' are themselves of pensionable age. A few are unable to claim government benefits because official records show them to be younger (in one case seven years) than they really are. 'I have had phone calls about this. They ask me, "What do I do?". I tell them "This is the price you have to pay. You must keep to the years that are on the passport."'

Anita has a handful of regular visitors and for some years enjoyed the companionship of an elderly male resident[10] of the home. By and large, the 'children' whom she once helped no longer call. She makes light of this. 'They have families and their families have families, so they are all very busy. They know where I live and contact me from time to time.'

She reminisces about the early days and, in particular, her arrival in Melbourne, when she came to Australia the first time. 'They gave me a huge party, which was wonderful. They wanted me to reply in English and I couldn't.'

DAVID GELBERMAN: TWICE
In December 1947 a boy called David Gelberman was scheduled to sail to Australia with other young people sponsored by the Jewish Welfare Guardian Society.

A few weeks before the departure from Europe Gelberman told Anita Glass,[11] who was in charge of the arrangements, that he had changed his mind. The reason was that he had fallen in love with a girl who had an uncle in the United States, where both hoped to live.

The organiser of the group rectified the problem in an unusual way. She cornered a 17-year-old Dutch youth, Aaron Mantel, and asked if he would like to take his place. She then gave Gelberman's papers and travel documents to the newcomer, and the switch in identities was complete.

Aaron Mantel, alias David Gelberman, like most of the young people with whom Anita had to deal, had a grim background. He was born in Amsterdam of Polish Jewish parents, who had gone there to seek a better future. Alas, fate caught up with them when the Nazis invaded their new country.

The entire family – apart from an older brother who escaped to Switzerland – were put into a holding camp and from there transferred to Bergen-Belsen.

After four-and-a-half years the boy received an upturn in his fortunes as part of an extraordinary 'deal' negotiated by his brother and others in Switzerland. It involved the issue of false passports to selected inmates declaring they were citizens of Paraguay. They would then travel to the Latin American state where they would be exchanged for about 400 German nationals who wished to return 'home' to fight for the Fatherland.[12]

Aaron Mantel knew nothing of this until, one winter's day, wearing just shorts and a shirt, he was marched through the snow to the station. 'There were about 40 of us. We really had no idea what was happening. The train had Red Cross emblems on the roof, which I thought was odd. There was much activity, people coming and going. The train started moving. I thought it might be a trick and we'd all be shot.' Instead, they were taken to a camp at Biberach an der Riß, in Baden-Württemberg.

The camp, near the major city of Stuttgart, housed mainly civilian prisoners, including Italian political prisoners (taken captive after that country changed sides) and British subjects from the Channel Islands.

The camp was run by the *Wehrmacht* (Army), not the SS, and was 'heaven in comparison. I made porridge for the other prisoners in the morning. Life was almost enjoyable.' Aaron learnt that his stay was temporary and that he and the others from Bergen-Belsen were supposed to be leaving for Paraguay. However, the declining war situation ruled this out and, early in 1945, the camp at Biberach was liberated by French troops.

After the war the youth made his way to Czechoslovakia, 'where I had quite a good time until the Russians came and the country was under Communist rule'.

As he tells the story: 'I had no papers, nothing at all to prove who I was or what I was doing there. That's where Mrs Glass came on the scene. She asked me if I would like to go to Australia. I said, "Yes, please, I certainly don't want to end up in Siberia". So that was it. I became David Gelberman and that's how I came to Australia.'

Once in Australia, the newcomer quickly settled down. As David Gelberman he took out Australian citizenship and later changed his name by deed poll to David Gilbert.

The 'anglicising' of his name was intended to help in business and other contacts but – coupled with the unusual circumstances of his arrival – has proved a handicap. When he inquired about receiving a grant from the German Government under its reparations program for Holocaust survivors, they wouldn't believe his story and demanded proof, including evidence relating to his life in Holland, which was difficult to obtain.

Some 55 years on, David Gilbert (Gelberman) hardly remembers that he was once Aaron Mantel. 'To me we are strangers.' By coincidence, Mendel Gelberman, brother of the real David Gelberman, also came to Sydney as a war orphan.

The real David Gelberman, having changed his mind about migrating to Australia, got his wish and (in 1949) married his girlfriend and emigrated with her to the US. Having given his name to someone else, it was thought better that he be given a new name.

In the US he entered the retail trade and currently owns and manages a furniture store in a major city on the east coast. About 25 years ago he visited Australia for his nephew's bar mitzvah.

Perhaps curiously, he and the lad who took his name have never met or had contact of any kind. As David Gilbert explained: 'I hope this doesn't sound selfish. I came here to carry on living, to become an Australian ... to forget the past.'[13]

8
A CONTRAST IN CARE

'With the English kids it may have been different. With us it was simple.
We came here knowing there was no other place to go. This has got to be
home, and is going to be home for the rest of our lives.'

Bernie Weiss, post-war youth migrant

There is an interesting parallel between the children of the Holocaust
and British child migrants to Australia. The Jewish children knew
who their parents were but in most cases lost them, while the *Leaving
of Liverpool* kids, most of them, grew up without knowing who their
parents were – or if they had brothers and sisters – and spent a
lifetime trying to find them. Both groups have suffered an acute
sense of loss. They have grown up lacking aunts, uncles and the
family support others take for granted.

Jews have a tradition of looking after their own; the Jewish
community was at that time closely knit, and the Holocaust children
were regarded (correctly) as valuable remnants of an endangered
people. British orphan children, on the other hand, particularly if
they suffered the additional burden of illegitimacy, were socially
disadvantaged – at the very bottom of the heap, which is largely why
the mother country 'exported' them.

In their first months in Australia the Jewish war orphans had little
contact with non-Jews, other than at work. Jack Schwartz recalls: 'A
lot of people resented newcomers in a general way. But there was no
real hostility. Australians had their own way of life and as long as you
were prepared to go along with this, go to the pub with your mates
after work, and so on, you'd be the best of friends.'

The hospitality extended to newcomers from within the Jewish community has occasionally created jealousy. According to Jack: 'I had a friend who migrated to Brazil. Even today they always make sure that whoever needs help gets it. When the ship arrived someone from the local Jewish organisation came on board and collected the Jewish migrants. Others had to wait God knows how long before anything was done for them. People were swearing, "You Jewish bastards, you always get the privileges." Really, it's in the Jewish tradition that you must help your fellow man, particularly another Jew.'

By and large the Jewish teenage migrants now living in Australia give the impression of being stable and well adjusted.

Some challenge the veracity of this statement. 'They've done well, they look all right ... But they're different,' was a comment by one prominent member of the Jewish community to me.

Clearly, several of the Jewish war orphans did have problems in the years immediately following their arrival.[1] According to Tom Keleman: 'We were all traumatised by the Holocaust. I believe I adjusted easily, but some of the others found it very difficult. They found it difficult to live in a family; some were almost like wild animals, others just couldn't cope.'

One young Holocaust survivor committed suicide. Another spent much of his later years in mental institutions.

Certainly, the situation for those who remained in Europe was far worse. According to the Australian writer, Tom Keneally[2]: 'During the research for my book *Schindler's Ark*,[3] I met and interviewed a number of survivors of the Holocaust who had been children at the time of their ordeal. It only took a short time to see that they were the most damaged of any group of survivors; the group to whom the very word *survivors* was most appropriate.'

In 1948, Albert Halm, himself a newcomer to these shores, wrote a letter to the Sydney *Jewish News* commenting on some of the difficulties experienced by the new arrivals in Australia. He stated:

'In some cases misunderstandings may have occurred between guardians and boys. This [is] probably due to the lack of understanding and patience towards those who were not used to normal family life ...

'[It] is especially difficult for a foreign orphan, who lost his parents before he realised what parents mean; who was a slave of the higher German race while he should have been studying, and who neither enjoyed childhood nor parents' love.'

A report by a welfare officer described one Jewish teenager, who had been an inmate of Auschwitz, as 'distrustful of all human beings'. A report by another welfare officer said new arrivals at the Isabella Lazarus hostel needed 'much warmth and understanding'. Evidence suggests this is precisely what they received. Within a few weeks most were requiring merely routine assistance.

All in all, as previously suggested, the Jewish youth migrants have adapted remarkably well. This may be because Australia picked the 'best specimens'. More likely, it is due to the bonding which they experienced with the people appointed, officially or unoffically, as their 'guardians'.

Men like John Lewinnek, Syd Einfeld and Julian Rose are remembered with singular gratitude for this role. Grandchildren are named after them;[4] in preference to relatives who died in the Holocaust. So strong is this bonding that some of the child migrants become more emotional when speaking of the people who were kind to them – an experience not shared by the British child migrants – than when recalling the horrors of the Holocaust.

COMING OUT

Remember the days of yore,
Learn the lessons of the generation that came before you.

(Deuteronomy 32:7)

'Coming out' as a holocaust survivor is now gaining momentum. Holocaust survivors, as with many English child migrants, have an ambivalent attitude towards self-disclosure. A natural reticence and desire to sweep 'the past' into the subconscious is matched by a feeling that people 'must be told' for the sake of future generations, and to ensure that 'it doesn't happen again'.

Added impetus is given by the existence of a growing Holocaust denial industry. There is a belief that 'letting the world know' will scotch the claims of David Irving and other Holocaust revisionists that the death camps didn't exist, or fulfilled a lesser purpose, and that the number of victims is exaggerated.

Braham Stern, who arrived in Australia as a war orphan in 1948, says the revisionists must be challenged. 'I feel it's time [to speak out]. So many people are claiming it didn't happen. Others just don't know about it.'

Nearly 50 years ago his attitude was very different. Like most Jewish child migrants, he had no desire to talk about his experiences. 'I just wanted to assimilate as soon as possible. I wanted to become an Australian. I loved this place. It was a home to me; the home that I had never experienced. I didn't have to wear the Star of David on my jacket.'

There were other reasons. 'In 1948 or 49, can you imagine my telling the people at work what I had been through? Would they have understood? They knew I had been in a camp, and that was it.'

He said some of his workmates faced a similar problem. 'Take an ex-servicemen who had fought in New Guinea. People might know that he had been in the tropics, and that it had been hard. But would they have really understood the humidity, the stench and the disease?

'Anyway, who would want to know? If I had got hold of an average Aussie and talked of all the cruelty and the suffering, he would have listened for two or three minutes and then said "Oh well, I've got to go." He'd probably be thinking I should see a psychiatrist.'

Nearly 60 years on, attitudes have changed. There is another reason why Holocaust survivors are now willing to talk about their experiences. It is that age is taking its toll, and their numbers are getting thinner.

Braham Stern would like his grandchildren to know about his own grandparents. 'Out of 73 immediate relatives, three survived. I myself nearly died. I've got two fine sons and three grandchildren. I get overwhelmed when my grandchildren come to see me. It's like a tree that was devastated and is living again. I'm talking about the family tree. It has been replanted in new soil and it is thriving.'

ANTI-SEMITISM: A LEGACY

'A couple of years ago I was driving to the city. I found a parking spot and got in there just as another chap came along. Whether I was wrong or he was wrong, I really don't know. But he called out "You bloody Jew!".

'I would not have minded if he had said "You bloody bastard!", or "You bloody reffo!", but when he said "You bloody Jew!", it hurt me. I am touchy on this point.'

Jack Schwartz, Jewish war orphan

Survivors of the Holocaust have noted how Hitler's Reich, even in the final months of the war, was prepared to divert men and materials from the front into organising transports to labour and death camps.

Many claim the attitude of some of Germany's foes was not much better. The Polish underground resistance movement, with some exceptions, would not allow Jews to join.

It has been said that in Poland, from which many would-be migrants originated, a new-born baby took in anti-Semitism with its mother's milk. In the late 1930s Polish Jews were denied entry into higher education and most professions, and had to pay higher taxes merely for being Jews. Germany itself – prior to the advent of Nazism – was a relatively tolerant society in which Jews were fully assimilated.

At Easter, when European churches taught how Christ died on the cross and held the Jews of Biblical times to blame, simple peasants, deprived and hungry, were looking for a scapegoat. Their hatred, fanned by ignorance, was strong enough to result in pogroms against the Jewish people living in their midst.

For many young Holocaust survivors, the advent of peace did not mean an end to their problems. Braham Stern, who returned to his home in the Czech Republic, recalls: 'We were freed from the camps, but we were locked in mentally. Our surroundings were not happy. Everybody knew us and what we had been through, and they all said they were innocent.

'But it was like the Italians blaming Mussolini, and the Germans saying they were only carrying out orders. The Ukrainians, the Croats and everybody else; they never did anything, but they collaborated indirectly.

'Hatred against Jews went with the masses and was very entrenched. Very few people had the courage or brains to deviate from that path, which is why we wanted to get out.'

Braham believes this pattern of oppression explains the success stories of many Jewish migrants in Australia. 'Having got out you were determined to succeed. People who were denied good jobs, or lived in places where only two per cent were allowed a higher education were so determined to succeed that they probably didn't have any failures. I am sure this is why people like Sir Peter Abeles [TNT], Frank Lowy and John Saunders [Westfield Shopping Centres], did so well.'

The Jewish war orphans have mixed feelings towards the nation primarily responsible for their trauma. Greta Silvers says she 'bears no animosity' towards the Germans, and certainly not to the present generation. 'When I used to say that to my friends they got very angry. But I cannot help what I feel. Certainly, I cannot be angry at the kids for their fathers' sins.'

I put to Greta the question: 'If you saw a coach load of middle-aged German tourists in a city restaurant, would you feel uncomfortable?'. She replied: 'Not at all. It doesn't help anyone by hating them.'

Her friend Agnes Adler disagrees: 'I do [dislike Germans] very much, and feel uncomfortable with them. I will give you an instance.

My husband was working in a factory where they needed a designer. They brought somebody out from Germany.

'My husband said we should invite this gentleman with his wife and two little children for afternoon tea. And we did. He said, "You're Hungarian, how interesting. I was there in 1944." What he meant was he was there in 1944 as a German soldier. How do I know what he did? How could I be at ease with a man like that, wondering what he had done in my country at that time?'

ATTITUDES

'In our home we had a tailoress, a Christian lady, who came once a fortnight to our place. We were friendly; I called her Aunty. Her sister's husband had two boys, we were friendly and sometimes played together. The father was a Social Democrat and had a job in the post office.

'When I was here after the war and settled in Sydney I had a letter from one of these boys. "Dear Henry. You may remember me and my brother, we used to play together and my Auntie Mucky used to come to your place. I knew that you had gone to Australia and I found your address. We were both in the German Army; my brother fell at Stalingrad. I survived. I would like to come to Australia. What is it like? Please write to me."

'Well, you know, I got that letter. At that time I didn't want to see another German, to be quite honest, and I just didn't answer it. There were meetings here in Sydney at that time not to allow any Germans into Sydney, and I was actually active in it. I have changed my opinion a little bit since. We know, however, a lot of suspicious characters slipped in.

'Anyhow, after a while I got another letter. "Dear Henry. You may not have received my letter, but in the meantime I have got engaged and we're both thinking of coming to Australia. Please write to me. You're the only person that I know there. It would be good to keep in touch."

'I still said no. I didn't answer that letter. I didn't want to have any contact. Then arrived a third letter, this time from Port Augusta. "Dear Henry, I'm now here ... etc." I still didn't answer that third letter. I don't know why. I never met that boy. He probably thinks, "These bloody Jews". Well, that cannot be helped. You cannot get out of these things.'

Extract from a taped conversation with Henry Lippmann

III

OPERATION KINDERTRANSPORT

9

SEPARATION: AN AGONISING CHOICE

'I took my teddy bear. I wore a cross, star and a little angel, so that the Almighty could choose what religion I should belong to.'

Eva Hayman, Kindertransportee

On 14 June 1999, a plaque was unveiled by the then Speaker of the House of Commons, Betty Boothroyd, in the Palace of Westminster. It states simply: 'In deep gratitude to the people and Parliament of the United Kingdom for saving the lives of 10 000 Jewish and other children who fled to this country from Nazi persecution on the Kindertransport 1938–1939.[1]

Rail and sea journeys are often evocative, but none more so than the journeys and subsequent experiences of this large influx of mostly German and Austrian Jewish children, plus a smaller number from Czechoslovakia and Poland, who participated in a unique and little-documented rescue operation in the months, weeks – and in some cases even days – before World War II.

In what is generally considered to have been a magnanimous gesture, the British Government recognised the immediacy of the hour and the perils likely to be faced by Jewish and other minority[2] children in Hitler's Reich.

Special trains took children from Berlin and other major centres of population to the Hook of Holland. From there ships took them to Harwich, and occasionally other English ports. Some children from Hamburg and other coastal cities sailed direct.

Some 'rescued' children went to other European countries – notably France – only to fall victims to Hitler once again. A few used Britain as a transit point to the United States, Canada and Australia. Others migrated to these countries – as naturalised Britons, rather than refugees – when peace returned.

The children travelled with, and sometimes without, the required documentation. Many hid their true intentions, wearing several layers of clothing and pretending crammed cases were light, to give the impression they were going on holiday visits to relatives. Actually, this deception may not have been necessary. The Germans were at that time only too pleased to be rid of the despised *Juden*,[3] provided another country was willing to take them.

Henry Mendelson, journalist and marketing consultant, currently chairperson of the Australian Council of Christians and Jews,[4] says the Kindertransport concept was a compromise reached between the Jewish communities of Germany and the Nazi regime.

According to Mendelson, himself a Kindertransportee: 'The Jewish community sought to persuade the Nazis that allowing Jewish children to leave the country was simply an alternative means to achieve its notorious *Judenrein* [5] objective. Children were permitted to leave Germany, consigned to unknown destinations as far as the German authorities were concerned, but in fact pre-arranged by the Jewish communities, at not inconsiderable monetary cost and untold psychological strain.'

For the *Kinder*, depending on age, the process may have been frightening, an adventure or a blend of both. Younger ones generally fared better. Henry Mendelson recalls being taken with his sister, Marion, to Hamburg's main railway station with admonitions and instructions about future behaviour, 'comforted by our parents' stoic assurances that they would soon follow'.

'To me, a wide-eyed barely eight year old it was just like a family outing, with little or no foreboding as to its implications. For my sister, a little over two years older, it was different. She had been told to look after me, and understood all too well that this was more than a short separation from *Mutti und Vati*.'

For the parents, faced with the likelihood of long-term separation, it offered the most agonising choice. Forced smiles cloaked the reality that the majority would never see their offspring again.

Inge Sadan (née Inge Engelhard), who has edited a book[6] of the experiences of *Kinder* now living in Israel, has dedicated it, appropriately: 'To our parents, who gave us life – twice'.

The imagery is strong. The very word *Kindertransport*, meaning 'transport of children', conveys a sense of the exodus.

The concept of a rescue operation for European Jews had its origins in initiatives by a group of prominent English Jews in the mid-1930s. The organisation behind it, the Central British Fund for German Jewry, was established only four months after Hitler came to power in 1933.

The British Government was not in the early stages sympathetic. Neville Chamberlain, later to become Prime Minister, is said to have made a remark about not wanting any more 'wailing Jews'. Some English Jews, likewise, were not particularly supportive, fearing, no doubt, that their own comfortable situation in the pecking order might be threatened.

(A female *Kind*, now a clinical psychologist, told me: 'I don't think the British Jewish communities had a lot of money at that time. And they were very anti-German. The German Jews who came over were looked down on. The established Jewish community didn't want newcomers to rock the boat.')

Many Jews in Germany at that time took a wait-and-see attitude towards Nazism. Older Jews had lived through pogroms elsewhere, and thought they could 'ride out' the excesses of the new regime. Lorraine Allard (née Lore Sulzbacher) recalls her father saying, 'I'm too old to start again. This madman [Hitler] can't possibly last.' Of course, no one realised the true extent of the horrors which were to follow.

Gradually, even to a child, the signs of change were evident. Ursula Rosenfeld recalls her parents organising a birthday party at which her non-Jewish friends declined to come. 'You become aware that there's something different about you.' Jewish youngsters gradually found themselves barred from schools, parks, theatres and swimming pools.

Kristallnacht – the night of 9 and 10 November 1938 – was to end any illusions of 'riding out' State-sponsored anti-semitism. To English-speaking ears the name sounds almost pleasant, perhaps suggesting tinkling glass. The reality was different. During the 'night of broken glass', Nazi Stormtroopers and their allies attacked Jewish shops and homes, smashing or looting everything in sight, beating and humiliating those whom they found.

Ruth Rack, who later made her home in Australia,[7] remembers seeing a venerable old man in a dark suit and coat being dragged by the beard and beaten by Nazis in black boots. Being a child was no protection. Jack Hellman was thrown through a plate-glass window by assailants who called out 'Jew bastard'. Hedy Epstein (née Hedy Wachenheimer) was told by her father to 'hide in the wardrobe if you hear strange noises'. She saw men trampling on the Torah. A man who complained about the removal of shoelaces and braces from old people was beaten to death.

There were violent crowds growing thicker and there was the smell of smoke. Synagogues were burning, with fire brigades deliberately standing idle. Within a few days 20000 Jews were rounded up and sent to concentration camps.

The excuse for the attack was an incident on 7 November, involving Herschel Grynszpan, a teenager then living in Paris, who had received a letter from his parents complaining of being caught up in a tug of war between German and Polish frontier police. It arose when Polish border police refused to implement a German decree deporting Jews of Polish origin from Germany to Poland. The impasse forced victims to live in a kind of no-man's land without basic facilities.[8]

Grynszpan, born in Hanover, had himself fled to France in 1936. He decided on a dramatic attention-seeking measure. He went to the German Embassy in Paris with the intention of shooting the German Ambassador. He did not know what the ambassador looked like and let him pass in the corridor. Instead he shot the third secretary, who later died of his wounds.[9]

The incident was the perfect pretext for stern retaliation. Those who had thought, 'Things will calm down, sort themselves out', realised this was not the case and that they were wrong. Even the dumbest realised that Jews no longer had any rights as citizens in that country. There was a rush to escape – and if adults could not, at least there was an opportunity for their children.

Parents besieged the various refugee organisations. A report to the Council for German Jewry[10] from the Jewish community in Frankfurt showed that parents were indifferent to the type of care provided for their children. 'There is a fervent desire among Jewish parents at least to see their children moved quickly, it is immaterial whether they are offered individual hospitality or accommodation in camps, so long as they are removed from Germany.'

Kristallnacht, horrible though it was, helped create a change of climate towards refugees in British official circles.

Men and women of vision set about persuading the government to allow persecuted Jews, with particular emphasis on children, into the country. On 21 November 1938 – just 11 days after Kristallnacht – representatives of the Central British Fund (now World Jewish Relief) had a meeting with the Home Secretary, Sir Samuel Hoare, seeking to impress on him the seriousness of the situation.

It appears they succeeded. That evening in the House of Commons, Labour MP Noel Baker made an impassioned speech about the plight of Jews in German-occupied lands. Hoare then made an announcement that unaccompanied Jewish and other threatened children would be allowed into Britain without special visas.[11]

On 2 December 1938, the passenger ship *De Praag* arrived at Harwich with a party of 320 German Jewish children, about one quarter of whom were to go on to other countries.

Most came from a Berlin orphanage which was subsequently burnt down by stormtroopers. Ten days later a transport arrived from Vienna with another 200 children.[12] Thereafter there were at least two *Kindertransports* a week, with transports arriving daily and all but overwhelming the organisers.

As stated earlier, not all those seeking refuge were from Germany. Vera Gissing (née Diamant), and her sister, Eva (now Eva Hayman), hailed from the small town of Celakovice, in Czechoslovakia, where, until the Nazi invasion,[13] a relatively tolerant attitude prevailed.

According to Vera: 'In my little town it didn't matter that I was Jewish, that my best friend was Catholic. The only thing which mattered was that you were Czech, and proud to be so because Czechoslovakia had only been founded in 1918. We were the children of the first generation of the Republic.'

DEPARTURE

There was little time to prepare for departure. Vera recalls: 'We had about three weeks.[14] Our mother bought loads of material and had the local dressmaker working hard so she would send us both to England with a decent wardrobe. All the clothes were made to fit. There was no allowance for growth. It was my parents' way of coping with the forlorn hope that our departure was only a temporary one.'

To excite their children about the future, parents gave a rosy view of life in the British Isles. According to Hedy Epstein: 'My parents painted such a wonderful picture, I accused them of trying to get rid of me.'

Despite such attempts, there were heart-rending scenes as parents, who were unable (or in some cases unwilling) to join them, said goodbye to their children at German main-line railway stations. Lore Segal (née Lore Groszmann) recalls: 'Mother kept up conversation as if it [separation] was an ordinary occurrence. But her face inside her fur collar was red and hot.' Lore also recalls: 'Each child was given a number. Mine was 152. There was the same number on my suitcase.'

As the trains were about to leave, fathers forced themselves to smile, though suffering inner turmoil. Their last glimpse would have been of young faces pressed against the thick glass windows giving a final wave.

The parents of Lory Cahn (née Lory Grünberger)[15] from Breslau, found it all too painful. On impulse her distraught father pulled her from the train window – cutting her in the process – as the train pulled out. It was not a wise move. In 1941, she and her parents were deported to Theresienstadt, where she was confined for a year-and-a-half before being separated from her parents and sent to Auschwitz.

In the years which followed, Lory was transferred to a further five camps.[16] Near the war's end she was liberated by the British Army from Bergen-Belsen, weighing 58lb (26kg).[17] Her mother perished. Her father, though considered frail, miraculously survived. He died in Germany, in 1972.

For the *Kinder* on the trains, their ordeal was not yet over. Guards and railway police harassed the children, taking their pocket money and sandwiches, crushing tubes of toothpaste, and other spiteful acts, right up to the border crossings. The more courageous retaliated by making rude noises, and ruder gestures as these uniformed brutes climbed down on the tracks to make their exits.

Personal possessions were few. Eva Hayman,[18] who now lives in New Zealand, was careful in her choice. 'I took my teddy bear. I wore a cross, star and a little angel, so that the Almighty could choose what religion I should belong to.'

Once across the border, the children found they had entered a different world. On station platforms there were hugs from Dutch women, who brought cocoa and Dutch cakes. A child called it 'the best party ever'.

The sea voyage was the next stage of the ordeal. Impressions varied according to the season. The English Channel in winter is not particularly inviting. Many complained about the cold; others were sick. A child recalls: 'It [the crossing] was quite short but seemed very long.' A boy impressed the crew by playing *God Save the King* on a violin.

Others have pleasanter recollections. Eva Hayman has only a vague memory of getting on to the ferry in Holland, but 'a very vivid memory of waking up and seeing the sea for the first time, with the sunrise on it, and thinking how beautiful it was'.

She says: 'I can't remember if I woke Vera [her younger sister, now Vera Gissing] or if she awoke by herself. We looked at the sun on the water, and we wished our parents could see it too.'

The next stage in the drama was the arrival at Harwich. Lore Segal recalls: 'The press came on board and took pictures. I wanted my picture taken, but they wouldn't notice me. I tried looking as if I was asleep. I tried looking as if I was sad. I tried hopping up and down. I couldn't get anybody to take any notice.'

Then followed the train journey through unfamiliar English countryside to the Liverpool Street terminus in London. The next phase – waiting to be collected – was gruelling. One transportee recalls: 'I sat on my case for an hour and nobody came. Eventually this woman turned up and told me to treat her like my mother. So I put my arms around her when I went to bed. She said: "Don't do that. It's sissy".'

Others claimed a similar experience. One boy noted that the woman who came to meet him 'seemed aloof, whereas my real mother hugged me rat-tat-tat like a machine gun'. He feared it might be a prelude to being sent away.

Henry and Marion Mendelson (now Marion Beecher) had foster parents pre-arranged through a Jewish refugee organisation in London. 'Those who were unable to be "accommodated" in this way were dealt with in two ways. First, well-meaning but unsubtly discerning English people would meet the groups of children at the railway station, look them over and select one or two who took their fancy as foster children. Those who remained, immeasurably harmed psychologically by this public rejection, were accommodated in hostels.[19]

'The sight of these children being scrutinised in the cavernous hallway of Liverpool Street and Victoria Stations, eerily empty in the late evening – some selected and others discarded – left me with a mixture of shock at their plight and relief at my own destiny.'

As in all walks of life, some of the 'rescued' children were luckier than others. Jack Hellman (Hans Joachim Hellmann) had been sent off to boarding school in Frankfurt, when he was nine, to avoid the anti-Semitism he experienced daily in the German village where he was born. After *Kristallnacht*, the house-mother of the school wrote to Baron James de Rothschild asking if he would take in 26 children as well as her husband and herself and two daughters. The Baron agreed and Jack and his schoolmates left Germany on a *Kindertransport.*

Once in England Jack also prevailed upon Rothschild to provide a work permit for his father. His parents arrived in England on the day before Hitler invaded Poland and remained there for two years until the family was able to migrate to New York, where Jack continues to live.

WITHOUT EQUAL

Contrary to common belief (even the chief rabbi got it wrong) the British Government set no formal limit on numbers. This was itself remarkable. Deborah Oppenheimer, producer of the award-winning film *Into the Arms of Strangers,* has called it 'a rescue mission that had no equal anywhere on Earth until then'.[20]

A total of 9354 children had formally registered with the Jewish Refugee Committee by the time war was declared.[21] Amy Zahl Gottlieb, Holocaust historian with special interest in the *Kindertransports,* believes many more would have been saved if even a few more days had elapsed before the British and French declaration of war.

It is known that a further 132 Jewish children managed to slip into Britain via Belgium, France and Holland during the first year of hostilities. An incredible Dutch woman, Gertruida Wijsmuller-Meijer, who had earlier negotiated with Eichmann,[22] and who at border crossings bravely berated Nazi thugs, personally shipped out 60 of these children, literally as the Germans were invading her country.

Fares for the journeys were paid by parents and Jewish welfare bodies. Sponsors in Britain – churches, synagogues and numerous individuals – were asked to contribute £50 per child. This requirement was later dropped.

The British Government itself gave no financial commitment, for some a sore point in the light of references to that body's 'generosity'.

COOL CAMPERS

For some *Kinder* the initial accommodation in Britain was with a family friend or relative, perhaps an aunt who had migrated to Britain a few years before. A few 'dumped' their new charges at the earliest opportunity. Some children went direct to a foster parent. Others were accommodated in hastily prepared hostels.

Erich Cahn (now the Rev Erich Cahn, a Melbourne rabbi) found a temporary home in a Butlin's holiday camp in Lowestoft, Suffolk. The chalets which normally resounded to the summer sounds of working-class holiday-makers were now home to refugee children in mid-winter. There were no buckets and spades. Instead, Erich recalls shovelling snow from the chalet door. Snow also came in through the roof.

After a few days, Erich and several others were transferred to the larger Warner's holiday camp at Dovercourt Bay, in Harwich, Essex.[23] It was not much of an improvement. Walter Friedman recalls: 'It was one of the coldest winters in the history of England. The camp had all the sport and entertainment facilities for a good time in warm weather. But we froze, huddled around the single fireplace in a common hall where this was the only source of heat.'

Some found the English food more of an ordeal than the lack of heating.[24] The menu included kippers for breakfast, day in day out. 'It tasted like salty shoe leather.' Prospective foster parents called to view the children. A woman recalls: 'People came to look us over – it was like a cattle market. Everybody wanted a fair, blue-eyed little girl.'

For most *Kinder* the 'market' was quickly over as foster parents made their choice. Temporary accommodation was also found in boarding schools, whose students had gone home for the Christmas recess.

New trials were to follow. The 'getting-to-know-you' phase was handicapped by misunderstandings over customs, language and even dress. Kurt Fuchel (Kurt Füchsl), at seven, one of the youngest *Kinder*, recalls being taken by his host family to their home in Norwich.

'I remember walking into the house, dressed in Austrian finery: short pants, jacket, long wool stockings held up by a suspender belt, and high-rising boots, the effect somewhat marred by the grubbiness accumulated during three days of travel.

'Ahead of me were the stairs going up to the second floor. Near the top sat John, a little boy of five, shyly looking at his new "brother". I was stripped, scrubbed from head to toe, my clothes burnt, new ones provided, and then the family gathered around the table for a magnificent chicken dinner. A smile returned to my face. Here was a language I could understand.'

An older *Kind*, Walter Fulop, 15, also from Vienna, experienced a similar 'dress' problem when, a few days after his arrival, he obtained an errand boy's job at a gentlemen's outfitters in Kentish Town. 'On the first morning I reported for work, dressed in continental fashion in plus fours. I dutifully clicked my heels, bowed my head and offered my hand to be shaken. The boss looked quizzically at me, examined me from head to toe and then burst out: "You haven't come here to play golf".'

The couple looking after Kurt Fuchel hired an elderly German, who lived down the block, as a language teacher. 'He wore thick glasses, had a brusque manner and I was terrified of him. Perhaps spurred on by my distaste for the man, I learned English in record time.' Six weeks later he wrote to his parents in English: 'I no longer speak German.' 'From that day on I never have.'

Actually, most of the newcomers – having been thrown in at the deep end – learnt English with astonishing speed. Many were near-fluent English speakers within a few months of their arrival, picking up not just the language but regional accents, which they have retained.[25]

The *Kinder*, like children everywhere, were occasionally mischievous. Yitzchak Armon (Erich Podzamcze) spent his first few weeks in a disused summer camp in Suffolk, where he suffered a minor infection for which he and several companions were sent to a private hotel and quarantined.

Yitzchak and another lad – desirous of sampling the joys of England – let themselves out via a toilet window and strolled down the main street, where a sign for Cadbury's chocolates caught their eye.

As Yitzchak puts it: 'We had each been given sixpence for our German Mark.[26] After entering the shop, I turned to the sales lady and stammered that we would like to buy "schokolade". She gave us a strange look and asked us something which we did not understand. We resorted to sign language and pointed to the Cadbury's chocolate in the window. She presented each of us with a bar and, after checking our money, returned four pence to each of us".' Alas, as they turned to leave, two policemen arrived, smiled at the bewildered salesgirl, and took the boys back to the hotel.

On a positive side, children were pleased to find that to the average English person being Jewish 'didn't matter'. Jack Hellman wrote in his diary, with just a hint of surprise: 'Somebody who's not Jewish wishes to see me tomorrow.'

A British Upringing

Foster parents raised their *Kinder* as they would other English children, which meant that the newcomers absorbed features and characteristics of the British way of life.

Martha Blend arrived in England in June 1939, 'a bewildered nine-year-old catapulted from parents and everything I knew into the care of foster parents I had never met.'

'Nowadays there would be counselling for such a child, but then distraction was the name of the game.'

She recalls the near-cult status of the less affluent person's summer holiday (in her case the last before fighting began).[27]

'In England everybody who could afford it took a summer holiday by the sea – not in Goa or Palm Springs, but at the nearest coastal resort. For Londoners, Southend, with its funny hats, vulgar postcards, cockles and mussels, sticky candyfloss and a pleasure ground called the Kursaal (pronounced Kursel), was a popular choice. Jewish families preferred the more genteel Margate or, better still, Clifton.

'Preparations for this event began weeks before we were due to leave. Suitcases were hauled down from the attic and special clothes were made up or bought – a white skirt and jacket for my foster mother, a sun suit for me, and an alpaca jacket for my foster father topped by a straw hat to protect his balding crown. The cases had to be packed with two weeks' worth of underwear, clothes for the beach and quantities of suntan lotion ...

'You arrived in a different world – houses with balconies and verandas and the sound of screeching birds ducking and diving by the sea. The advertisement for the boarding house had said "a wash basin in every room", and sure enough, as you entered your allotted bedroom, there it was ...'

Kurt Fuchel, who subsequently emigrated to the United States,[28] has equally poignant memories. 'We became familiar with sirens, air raids, bomb shelters, gas masks and ration books. In school, we learned British history (and precious little about any other), and the glories of the Colonial Empire. At home, if we were lucky, we got kippers for breakfast on Sunday, porridge the other days. Upstairs bedrooms had no heating, so we took a hot water bottle to bed.

'Radio was our prime source of news and entertainment. We thrilled to the exploits of Dick Barton, Special Agent, laughed with Tommy Handley and the ITMA crew, and shivered when Valentine Dyal, The Man in Black, wished us goodnight ... and pleasant dreams. At Christmas time, we were taken to the theatre to see the Pantomime, that uniquely British entertainment in which Prince Charming is played by a girl with gorgeous legs, and the ugly sisters by men in drag.'

WHEN THE BOMBS FELL

When the bombs started falling, and the initial 'phoney' war became hot, *Kinder* became even more concerned than before about the fate of their parents who remained in Hitler's Reich.

Some of the *Kinder*, having gone through the trauma of finding their feet in a foreign land, found themselves despatched with English children to rural areas as evacuees.[29] Other *Kinder* – particularly those who had established good relations with foster parents – found the heightened conflict 'enjoyable'.

Kurt Fuchel recalls the loss of railings and then the back lawn to help the war effort. 'It was spaded over, and assorted vegetables planted on half of it; the rest was fenced in and a shed built for chickens which were expected to supplement our ration of one egg a week per person.'

Was he afraid? Not a bit. 'As a young boy the predominant feeling I had about the war was that it was exciting. Every night [Uncle] Percy[30] put on his hard hat and went up to the roof somewhere as an air-raid warden. When the sirens went off, we all went downstairs and hid in a coat closet under the staircase ...'

The Morrison shelter[31] – which offered more comfortable sleeping accommodation – was another place of adventure. According to Kurt: 'It replaced the dining-room table, and was about the size of a double bed. The top was a quarter-of-an-inch-thick steel plate, the legs heavy steel angle irons, the bottom was made of steel strips supported by springs, and removable wire netting sides completed the arrangement.

'The idea was that if the house collapsed during an air raid, the occupants of the shelter would be safe. Sleeping in the shelter was really quite fun. One could make believe that one was a caged lion or some other animal, snarling through the heavy wire mesh sides.'

In the morning there was the search for shrapnel. Sometimes, even, a downed aircraft. 'We were totally unaware of the horror.'

10
ALMOST A CLAN

'My mother told me: "We are going to meet your father on Wenceslas Square. He is in hiding now. You must not call him father. Please be very careful." And so it was that I saw my dear father for the last time, in dark glasses, a beard and a broad-rimmed hat to cover his features, while my mother discussed something with him.'

Susan Medas, about to leave on a Kindertransport[1]

THE KINDER

Some 65 years after the abrupt disruption to their lives, former participants in the Kindertransport program are a unique body of people, almost a clan, with the shared misfortune of having been born at a particular time – about 10 to 12 years before the war's outbreak[2] – which has accorded them a particular destiny. As one of them told the writer: 'I have never known Germany without Nazis.'

While most were reasonably happy in their new surroundings, the majority suffered problems associated with loneliness and deprivation, from which some still carry the scars.

Eva Hayman, who was privileged to be sent to a middle-class English boarding school, recalls meeting 'all these girls in their uniforms, very polite and very nice', though initially she could hardly understand what they said. Their 'politeness' couldn't cure the void within her.

'I was given my bed – the curtains could be drawn to give me some privacy. The first thing I did was to put out a photo of my parents so that I could say goodnight to them. Because war had not then broken out, it was still possible to write to them. She wrote in one of her letters: 'If only I could see you just for a few moments.'

Before leaving their home town of Celakovice, Eva's mother had said to her: 'If the time comes when we cannot write any more, we will send our love by the moon and the stars.' When the letters stopped, 'every time I saw the moon and the stars, I thought of them'.[3]

Children developed other ways of 'keeping in touch'. Some, including Eva, poured out their feelings in diaries; others played fantasy games such as preparing 'mother's bed'.

From her hut at Dovercourt – wearing coat and gloves to keep out the cold – Lore Segal could see a flower bed, where a single rose was still growing. It had snow on it. 'I wrote that my parents were like this rose, still alive in a winter of snow and ice, and if somebody didn't save them soon, they would die. It was not a particularly apt metaphor, but I was wonderfully proud of it. I was 10 years old and turning into a writer.'[4]

For those who had witnessed the removal of a parent to a camp, or had perhaps learnt of this afterwards, there was the agony of 'not knowing' whether a loved one was alive or dead. For some this was worse than the reality.

Eva and her sister Vera[5] remember, when peace returned, their thrill at receiving, at Vera's school, a list of those who had been liberated from Bergen-Belsen with the names of their mother and an aunt on it. The numbers tattooed on their arms were the same, except for the last digit, 'so we knew it was them and no one else'.

Alas, their mother had survived the horrors of Belsen, only to die of typhus fever two days after the war's end. Soon after, they heard that their father had been shot on a death march from one camp to another in December 1944.

Vera describes with feeling[6] her return, aged 17, to her native Czechoslovakia, the trauma of revisiting the family home – now occupied by polite strangers – and of discovering that a kitten, which she had raised in childhood, had survived.

NOT BLISSFUL

For those whose parents did survive, the post-war reunions were not always blissful. Children had become young adults, and were by now thoroughly anglicised. Many had forgotten how to speak German. Some did not wish to leave their foster parents. They found their real parents 'ugly' or were embarrassed at their 'foreign' ways.

Inge Sadan,[7] one of the few whose parents were able to get to Britain during wartime, was anxious lest the reunion be witnessed by her schoolfriends. 'The whole village was aware that they were coming. It was a tremendous ordeal. We went down to the station to wait, and I just couldn't cope with it. So I went home saying, "I'm going to put the kettle on. They'll need a cup of tea." I mean, how English can you get?'

Kurt Fuchel reacted strongly when told his parents were alive and one day he would have to go and live with them. 'I was horrified. When reunited I couldn't look at them directly. I saw their reflection in a shop window.' He hit his father when the latter affectionately put his hands through his son's hair. 'It was very sad. My parents had let go of a seven-year-old and got back a 16-year-old.'

Ruth Barnett (née Ruth Michaelis) was one of the youngest Kindertransportees, having left Germany in February 1939, when she was four. In April 1949, by now 14, she and her 17-year-old brother, Martin, both living with an English foster family, were contacted out of the blue by their mother, from whom there had been no contact since the war began.

It transpired that as a Christian, she had survived the war, unmolested, in Germany, while her Jewish husband had fled to Shanghai.

A few weeks later the mother arrived in person. The meeting was 'a disaster'. Ruth considered the older woman 'fat and repulsive'. Mother and daughter could not communicate, Ruth having forgotten her German, and the mother speaking no English. The brother and sister had suffered unpleasant experiences with foster parents, but were happy with the present couple – a Mr and Mrs Harrow – whom they loved and who loved them in return.

In Ruth's words: 'I didn't want this total stranger coming to disturb my new life. I became confused and angry. I sullenly refused to go back to Germany with my mother, and she went back alone, no doubt deeply hurt.' Martin's views were similar. He was at that time studying for a scholarship to Cambridge University, and feared his life would be 'overturned'.

Two months after the visit the children's father re-entered the scene and sued the foster parents in a British court. Agreement was reached that Martin could stay in England, but Ruth had to return to Germany.

A bad situation worsened. According to Ruth: 'It was a repeat of the original *Kindertransport* trauma. We arrived at a bombed-out shell of a vast railway station, and all around us piles and piles of rubble with planks to walk over between the few cleared paths. A lone tram took us to the half-ruined boarding house where my mother lived.

'All through the war I had been brought up on the *Beano* and *Dandy* comics, with their stories of 'nasty Nazis'. Nothing could convince me that there were not dozens of jack-booted Nazis with machine guns behind every one of these ruins.'

Ruth discovered that her father roomed in a distant city, where he had a job, and there were rows every weekend when he returned. She considered herself – falsely, as it turned out – to be the cause.

To make matters worse, Ruth missed her brother terribly. Eventually, despite the court order, her parents agreed to let her return to England and to the Harrows. Ironically, this relationship, too, was not the same, and the bonds that once existed were weakened.

During school holidays both Ruth and Martin re-visited their parents. Gradually – but painfully – a relationship was rebuilt.

Their father insisted that Ruth pursue university studies, for which she is grateful.

She now states: 'Not only did I get a degree and two silver cups for rowing, but I found the Jewish husband who helped me to realise the Jewish identity I had developed as a primary-school child to protect myself against being teased for my German origin.'

Ruth and her husband, Bernard, are both professional clinical psychotherapists. They have two sons and a daughter, and two grand-children. Martin also is happily married, and now lives in Germany. For reasons connected with her past, Ruth avoids professionally treating children.

LEDERHOSEN

During a visit to England,[8] I stayed with the couple at their London home. On one of the walls were paintings by Ruth, a talented artist from childhood. When his wife was out of the room, Bernard pointed to one of the paintings, made when his wife was about 11.

The picture showed a typical English country scene, including people loading a cart with hay, which Ruth would have observed personally from the rural property to which she was evacuated with other *Kinder*.

In the painting one of the helpers, a boy, is wearing *Lederhosen* (the short trousers with cross-strap often worn in Germany and Austria). Ruth does not remember including this, and thinks she must have done it unwittingly. Her husband – when asked for his clinical judgement – touched his head knowingly and said it repre-sented a form of regression still found among many of the former *Kinder* today.

REUNION IN LONDON

For three days in June 1999 a rally in central London marked the 60th anniversary of the *Kindertransport*. It was a happy occasion. Someone called it 'a celebration of survival'.

For this reporter, who has attended many noteworthy gatherings, and has a special interest in child and youth migration, it was possibly the most moving event of my career.[9]

Some 1200 of the original *Kinder* were present. Most were sprightly, and the years did not seem to have taken their toll. Numbers were happily augmented, as one speaker noted, by *Kinders' Kinder*, and even one or two *Kinders' Kinders' Kinder*.

The largest group, as expected, was from the United Kingdom. But only just. There were about 500 *Kinder* from the US, about 50 from Canada and Israel, and about a dozen – who received a special welcome – from Australia and New Zealand.

The reunion was organised by two former *Kinder*, Bertha Leverton and Bea Green, who have become mother figures to thousands. Their own stories would make a first-class movie.[10] A reunion committee, active for much of the previous decade, was chaired by David Jedwab, a *Kind* and former Bevin Boy (young emergency miner),[11] who also introduced the speakers.

David began by expressing the meeting's sympathy to children caught up in the Balkans conflict, then in full swing. The Chief Rabbi, Dr Jonathan Sacks, echoed this with a true story about the arrival of a group of children from Kosovo at an airport in the English Midlands. As the chairman of the British Refugee Council was waiting to meet the aircraft, word reached him that a demonstration was taking place outside.

As Dr Sacks told it, slightly tongue in cheek: '"Oy Vey", the waiting VIP said, or he would have said if he had been Jewish. "What on earth can they be demonstrating about?" He feared placards saying "We don't want you, go home." Then he went outside and saw what was written on the placards. Just one word, "Welcome".'

The Chief Rabbi contrasted the situation with 'that terrible night', *Kristallnacht*. 'On that night of shame,' he said, 'something more than synagogues went up in flames. Something human went up in flames as well. Jews knew at that moment that if they were to live they would have to leave. They were to seek the gift of life itself.'

Dr Sacks was applauded when he went on to state: 'Looking back from the perspective of 60 years we know many things. We know that the Third Reich, which was supposed to last for a thousand years, lasted for 12. Also that any power on earth that begins by destroying others ends by destroying itself.'

The theme of life as a precious gift was taken up by the nominated Australian speaker, the Rev Erich Cahn.

Rabbi Cahn said he had travelled 12 000 miles to savour a moment 'to really and truly treasure. It is a moment of solemnity and rejoicing. Solemnity because we remember the courage of our parents towards the children; rejoicing in the fact that we were rescued.

'Our parents' courage, their sacrifice in letting us go, gave us the chance to create new families, to make it possible that what they stood for and what they gave us in the few years we had with them we could pass on to our own children and grandchildren.'

Taking a cue from the title of the award-winning but controversial black comedy, then screening in London,[12] he said, amid applause and tears: 'I'm sure you will agree, whether you liked the film or not, that it is true to say, "Life for us, indeed, is beautiful".'

(The Australian penchant for giving pet names to individuals and organisations also received attention at the assembly. There were smiles when an Australian participant described Kindertransportees as 'Kindies'.)

GOOD AND BAD MEMORIES
Much of the assembly time was taken up by workshops in which people discussed their memories, both good and bad, and how to deal with them. When speaking of these events, some appeared to regress to a childhood state.[13] Participants were told this was to be expected, and probably therapeutic.

In soft focus – probably because the victims were so young – were the events of the early years in Hitler's Reich. Expulsion from school, fleeing from homes, being shunned (and sometimes helped) by former neighbours. Finding out that to be Jewish is to be 'dirty'. A woman recalls that Hitler smiled at her. This prompted the question: 'Did you smile back?'.

There were the train departures from Berlin, Munich and elsewhere. The last words spoken between parents and children. Someone asks: 'Did your parents bestow a blessing?'. Another participant, who had taken a taxi ride across London to avoid missing the session, cries as he recalls half-forgotten details of his own 'goodbye'.

Bea Green, the session organiser, remembers the kindness of Dutch women on the 'safe' side of the border handing out goodies, and the contrast this made with the behaviour of the Germans. A woman recalls the sea crossing to England: 'I threw up over my older sister.'

Some re-visit their arrival at Liverpool Street station. A mass of confusion as *Kinder* wait for their new 'uncles' and 'aunties'. A woman says she was left waiting, seated patiently on her small suitcase, clutching a toy. People looked at her and muttered, 'Poor child'. Her friends disappeared one by one. Panic set in, then her new 'uncle' arrived, apologising in an unfamiliar tongue.

A man recalls his first look at London and the English countryside. He was fascinated by the red double-decker buses. A woman remembers her surprise that 'all the trees seem to have round tops'. Yitzchak Armon (Erich Podzamcze) remembers both sensing intense curiosity about his new country, and not being able to see a thing in the fog.

LANGUAGE PROBLEMS

Learning English had its humorous side. A female *Kind* recalls being asked to help 'Auntie' to make a pudding. She was puzzled when instructed to 'use custard but not Birds'. Another girl peeked at a report about her which used the (to her) unfamiliar term 'miserable'. She consulted a dictionary and was upset to read 'contemptible, mean'. Only much later did she discover that it had a simpler meaning 'unhappy'.

Inge Sadan had a different problem. 'School was a disaster at first. Germans are terribly exact. If they say "one" or "two", it is one or two. In England, the teacher said: "One or two children are making an awful noise." Now it was the whole class that was making the awful noise, and I thought, that's wrong. I took them literally. I think that may have been culture shock.'[14]

Henry Mendelson arrived in England, in late 1938, with just three words of English. They were 'yes', 'no' and 'motor car'.

Within months – thanks to pressures of an English preparatory school and a subconscious desire to 'drown whatever had gone before' – he was not only fluent in the new language but had totally forgotten the old.

In August 1939, as Europe was about to be engulfed by war, his parents, too, fled Germany and came to England, where their children left foster care and joined them. 'My father spoke no English at all. My mother spoke some English and she acted as interpreter. More or less miraculously, while listening to them, I re-learned the German I had forgotten.'

FOSTER PARENTS

There was much discussion at the meeting on the roles of foster parents. The families – for the most part non-Jewish – were volunteers, who received no payment for their increased burden. A woman recalls the Welsh miner – a 'chapel Christian', who had little to offer in worldly goods, but gave her 'absolutely everything'.

Others speak in similar vein. In general there is intense gratitude to the British men and women who took the *Kinder* into their homes. A commemorative book, produced for the reunion, was full of such tributes. Among the lucky ones was Vera Gissing, then aged 11, who developed an instant rapport with her English foster mother, 'Mummy' Rainford. In her own words: 'When, in 1939, Mummy Rainford came to fetch me, her first words were "You shall be loved" – and loved I was. They are the most important words any refugee child, separated from home and family, could hear.'

'Mummy' Rainford died, aged 103, in 2000, having seen in the birth of the new millennium. Vera Gissing remained, to the end, the old lady's closest companion.[15]

Sadly, such relationships do not tell the whole story. And honesty demands that the truth be told. As with the British child migrants to Australia, Canada, and elsewhere, there were *Kinder* who experienced physical, sexual and emotional abuse, and were treated as unpaid labour or worse. They refrained from complaining about their experiences only because they feared retribution or that they would not be believed.

Many *Kinder* have fully or partially repressed this part of their lives, often suffering severe trauma. Susi Bechhofer (Grace Stocken) achieved temporary fame through being featured in a BBC TV documentary, *Whatever Happened to Susi?* The film, though utterly absorbing, glossed over a history of sexual abuse by her clergyman foster father. She subsequently gave a more candid account of her childhood in a book *Rosa's Child*,[16] co-authored by professional writer, Jeremy Josephs.

With incredible perseverance, Susi, who left Germany with her twin sister at the age of three, set out as a mature adult to trace her birth parents. She found she was the illegitimate child of a young Jewish woman, who died in Auschwitz, having been deserted by her loutish German partner, who subsequently abandoned several other lovers. From a half-sister she received a picture of the father she had never known. He was in German Army uniform, rifle in hand and steel helmet on his head; symbolic of all that the *Kinder* dreaded.

Having faced up to the truth about her father, Susi now confronted her clergyman 'uncle', who admitted his crimes – for that is what they were – and begged forgiveness. In this way, years of pain were finally resolved.

Rules provided that, where possible, Jewish homes should be found for the *Kinder*. In reality, these were relatively few. Quakers – remembered with particular fondness – and other Christian groups provided the main focus. Some (British) Orthodox Jews found this situation distasteful.

Nicholas Winton[17] recalls: 'A lot of them marched into my office and told me that I couldn't go on doing this. I remember saying, "If you prefer a dead Jew in Prague to a living Jew who is being brought up with Christians, that is your problem, not mine."

In an even less harmonious incident, a party of 241 Czech children arrived at Liverpool Street station on a Saturday. Some of the guarantor families, who were orthodox Jews, refused either to sign for the children or to carry their luggage. Winton's mother, who was present, marched up to them and said: 'My son has worked day and night, and done everything possible to save these children. And you say you can't break the Jewish law. What sort of nonsense is that?'

Winton now says of these and similar episodes: 'I thought the most important thing was to save the children ... Anybody who would fulfil the conditions laid down by the Home Office to bring a child over and save its life was okay by me.'

No Proselytism

Proselytism of Jewish children by Christian foster parents was forbidden. Most foster parents – including Christian clergy – kept to this rule,[18] though many children became Christian by absorption. Some children raised in clergy houses complained that ministers' wives (though not the ministers) attempted to convert them. 'Auntie thought it would gain her a place in heaven', was a comment made to me.

The situation differed from that in continental Europe where some families, having become attached to Jewish children they were concealing, had them secretly baptised and raised as Christians. Some grew to adulthood without knowledge of their Jewish roots. Pope John Paul II, when a parish priest in Poland, was involved in an incident when he insisted that a child brought to him be raised as a Jew.[19]

Some former *Kinder* now consider themselves to be both Jewish and Christian. Commented one woman: 'Am I happy with both? Yes, I choose to be. It's much easier.'

Some members of the Christian clergy had odd theories about diet, toilet habits, and general upbringing, all of which made life difficult for their charges. Petty jealousies were commonplace, and undeserved and excessive punishments imposed. However, these same people made financial and other sacrifices, for instance, sending their *Kinder* at their own expense to private schools.

Some 'uncles' and 'aunties' were well intentioned, yet temperamentally unsuited for the tasks for which they had volunteered. When rabbis occasionally called, most *Kinder* chose not to mention their problems, believing that to complain would make little difference to their lot.

JONES THE JEW

Misunderstandings arose as the result of ignorance. Justin Jones, a young Australian, unable to return to his native Sydney because of the war,[20] had much of his schooling in Wales, of which he has fond memories. In fact, 'Jones the Jew' became a distinct novelty – the first Jew that most of his schoolmates had seen. One day the lad he sat next to in class asked him back to his place for afternoon tea.

As Justin tells it: 'There was rationing; I walked into this house and the table was loaded with scones, strawberry jam and cream. I had never seen such things. This lady started to talk to me in Welsh, far too quickly for me to understand. The boy I was with said she wants to know if you're a Jew, and I said "Yes". The boy then told me: "She wants to know why you haven't got horns coming out of your head."

'I asked an adult why she thought that. I was told it was because her illustrated Bible showed Moses with horns of light coming from his head. The old lady was actually very glad that she had made friends with me, and was nice to me, possibly because I showed a love for Welsh music and singing.'[21]

Early in the war, his parents, who had started a business in Britain, had decided that their two sons would be more secure away from the UK. According to Justin: 'A week or so before we were due to sail my mother had a dream – a ship was sunk; we were on it and we drowned.' Their mother cancelled the booking, which was just as well. The ship on which the two boys were to travel was the ill-fated *City of Benares*.[22]

Young people everywhere are astonishingly resilient. Aside from the above difficulties, most *Kinder* have basically positive memories of their time 'in care', though many were – and a few still are – severely traumatised.

On the whole, the *Kinder* were treated in a civilised way and with affection – a far cry from that received in their countries of birth. A photograph of an English 'bobby' gently assisting two refugee children[23] says it all.

11
KINDER PROFILES

'I knew I could not save the world, I knew I could not stop the war from coming, but I knew I could save one human life. And, as Chamberlain broke his pledge to Czechoslovakia, and Jews were in greatest danger, I decided it must be a Czech Jewish child.'

Explanation given by a former foster parent[1]

NICHOLAS WINTON: UNSUNG HERO

Among those present at the London reunion were a handful of 'people who made a difference' – ordinary men and women who themselves took in refugee children or helped organise transports.

Chief among these was Nicholas Winton, a modest Englishman, who masterminded an operation which was to save the lives of 669 children, 90 per cent of them Jewish, from crisis-ridden Czechoslovakia.

Winton, now an active nonagenarian,[2] has been described in media reports as the Oskar Schindler of the child rescue movement. The former *Kinder*, and Winton himself, are not entirely happy with this description, pointing out that Schindler was a businessman whose main object was to keep his business going, and that he derived benefit from the slave labourers he employed.

Winton was a 29-year-old stockbroker when, in December 1938, he took a call from a friend,[3] urging him to cancel a proposed winter sports holiday in Switzerland and, instead, to go straightaway to Prague where his friend 'had something to show him'. Winton perceived a sense of urgency and did as he was bid.

Winton was appalled at the parlous situation in which Jewish children found themselves, in the wake of the Munich agreement only two months earlier. He was 'young and single', free of personal commitments, and immediately put his entire free time and effort into the cause.

He was assisted by a handful of others, most notably Doreen Warriner, who set up a refugee agency,[4] and Trevor Chadwick, who threw up his job in England as a school teacher in order to work full time for Winton in Prague.[5]

The children travelled to England in eight transports between March and August 1939. Time was of the essence. March 14, the day the transports began, was the eve of the Germans' arrival in Prague.

A ninth train, filled with over 250 children, was due to leave on 3 September, the day Britain and France declared war. The transport was halted and the children returned to their homes. Within three years all had been transferred with their parents to death camps.

'Nicky' Winton's humanitarian efforts were until recently largely unknown. Even when he married, he did not see fit to mention them to his wife, who discovered his 'secret' when she came across some old scrapbooks, while cleaning the attic, in 1988.

The scrapbooks contained not only detailed information about the *Kindertransports*, but a complete list of all the Czech and other children[6] saved. As word spread, the children themselves – by now well past middle age – learned the name of their benefactor and were eager to meet him. Winton was coerced into participating in a TV program, along with Vera Gissing, the woman largely responsible for flushing him out, and other *Kinder*.

In 2001 Vera Gissing co-authored a book about Winton,[7] and has written another book on her own experiences.[8]

Unassuming to a fault, Winton, aged 95 (when this book went to press), is self-deprecating about the achievement, which his friends point out was one act in a lifetime of charity, rather than one act of charity in a whole life.

A tireless worker for several worthy causes, he was honoured, in 1983, with the title of Member of the Order of the British Empire

(MBE) for work with the elderly and mentally handicapped. Interestingly, there was no reference to his even-more-memorable wartime activities, simply because he had never mentioned them!

His main interests nowadays are in tending his garden and the welfare of residents of a group of old people's homes called Abbeyfields. When attending one of their parties, Winton – who looks considerably younger than his years – was a little shocked when a visitor asked if he was 'one of the oldies'.

Thanks to Vera Gissing and others, formal recognition has now been given to Winton's 'rescue' activities of more than 60 years ago. In January 2003, he was knighted in the British New Year honours. In 2002 he received an equivalent award from the (then) president of the Czech Republic, Vaclav Havel.[9]

Since then he has been the subject of a film *The Power of Good*, by Slovak director Matej Minac, which has been highly praised at several European and American festivals and won an Emmy award. The narrator, Joe Schlesinger, was himself one of the 'rescued'. In September 2003, Winton was chosen to unveil a memorial to the *Kinder*[10] at London's Liverpool Street station.

His own – typically unassuming – assessment of Operation *Kindertransport* is: 'I wouldn't claim it was 100 per cent success, but I would say at least all those children were alive at the end of the war.'

'THANK YOU' FROM AUSTRALIA

As stated above, nearly 700 Czech Jewish children found refuge in Britain. There are now about 6000 descendants.

Nora Huppert (née Benjamin), now resident in Sydney, is among those who were directly aided by Nicholas Winton. In fact, so strongly did she feel about her benefactor, that she flew to England to meet the man she had not previously known existed.

Nora was a lively 10-year-old at the time of the Munich agreement and the path to war that followed. For reasons of safety – which cost her parents extra – it was decided that she and several other children should travel by air, instead of the sealed train that was customary.

Years later she was to write[11] of that experience. 'It was snowing that morning. I recall few formalities at the airport. I already missed Papa and wondered why he was not there to see me off. Mama, Fredi [her only brother] and the other children and parents provided plenty of distraction for any travel anxiety.'

As with so many *Kinder*, her last 'indelibly imprinted' memory is of her mother and brother, huddled under umbrellas with the other parents, waving goodbye. She never saw either of them again. The following day German soldiers marched into Prague, and Nora began a new life with English foster parents.

It was to be just one of five 'migrations' to five countries. In April 1962 she settled in Hobart, and later in Sydney, with her equally well-travelled husband, Peter Huppert, who had experienced an earlier sojourn in Australia as an internee in Hay with the Dunera Boys.

'SLAVE' PAYMENTS

No reference to this period would be complete without mention of Norbert Wollheim, who was 25 years old when he began organising the *Kindertransports* in Berlin. An escort for several of the transports, he returned each time to his native Germany to continue his work, which ended with the outbreak of war.

In 1943, he and his wife and three-year-old son were interned in Auschwitz. He was the only one of 70 relatives to survive. In 1951 he sued the German manufacturer I.G. Farben[12] for back pay for the two years of slave labour he spent at Auschwitz. His suit opened the way for a settlement with Farben that established a fund of $US6.43 million to compensate many other Jewish labourers. Norbert Wollheim died in November 1998 at the age of 85.

KINDERS' KINDER

In recent years a growing number of *Kinder* have felt the urge to tell their stories for the benefit of children and grandchildren. Some have participated in oral history projects. Others have produced self-published memoirs, often at considerable expense, with little or no chance of financial reward.[13]

A minority – including the wife of a well-known rabbi[14] – have shut this period totally from their lives. A few have partial mental blocks; for instance, inability to remember the arrest of a parent. Being young, it is possible they were shielded from knowledge or understanding of these events.

Several brave souls have turned detective and located the graves of loved ones, and erected memorials in their honour. A few have spoken about their experiences in Germany itself.

Sadly, in a few cases children of *Kinder* (to the hurt of their parents) either don't want to know or have reinvented their parents' origins. A *Kind* who invented his own fictionalised history was caught out when one of his grandchildren stumbled on the truth from an unsuspecting relative.

A woman at the London reunion complained that her adult children showed indifference, verging on hostility, whenever the subject of the *Kindertransports* was raised. 'I wish I had a key and could unlock it. I speak to my son and he just says "I know, I know" and goes away'.

A child of a *Kind* – one of several second generation *Kinder* present – told of this situation in reverse. 'For the first 42 years of my life the subject was never mentioned. My family tree seemed to be empty. I needed desperately to look into this black hole. There was only emptiness. If I spoke to my mother about it she would only cry.' [15]

Several original *Kinder* spoke of a general sense of alienation, and of difficulties in forming relationships with their own children. One woman said: 'As one of the *Kinder* I always felt different from my friends. It's been very special to be here with you.' Another woman said: 'I had a label. It was not on my arm but in my soul.' Yet another said: 'I was sent [by my foster parents] to boarding school. I just wanted to be exactly like everybody else. Then [after the war] I couldn't take it. It's only now in the last 10 years that I have gone on a pilgrimage to discover my roots.'

SURVIVORS' GUILT

As implied in several comments made to me, there exists an emotional division – leading to feelings of guilt – between Jews who left Germany and countries under Nazi domination before and after World War II.

The basis for this is a suggestion that those who got out are the 'lucky ones' and, therefore, their stories and experiences 'don't count'. A man who arrived in Australia in 1939 confided to me, half apologetically: 'Do you know, I have never seen a dead body.'

The gulf between the two groups was raised in a supposedly private session at the *Kindertransport* 60th anniversary reunion. In the words of a female speaker: 'I don't feel lucky. It's some luck to be torn away, perhaps interned as an enemy alien, to wave goodbye to your parents, probably not to see them again.'

One man said with feeling: 'We carry our baggage with us. We've lost that connection [with the Jewish community]. It's a double whammy. Holocaust survivors are better off.'

The word 'survivor'[16] is itself open to several interpretations. Some people apply it only to those who were in concentration camps; others include those who – though in areas under Nazi control – found hiding places or in other ways avoided capture.

Even some of those who lived off their wits – perhaps in situations requiring extreme bravery – suffer 'survivors' guilt' on the basis that 'We lived, others didn't.' Polish-born Marian Pretzel,[17] who saved his own skin, and that of several others, by becoming a successful forger (at one time wearing German army uniform), says: 'We are victors; we accomplished something that the [instigators of] the Holocaust were trying to prevent.'

A broadly based view, nowadays considered sensible, is to regard as a 'survivor' any individual or group – including those who travelled on a *Kindertransport* – who suffered indignities through Nazi policies.

Ruth Rack, an Australian *Kind*, has strong views on the topic. 'When other survivors ask "Where were you during the war?" and my answer is "England", their assumption and therefore their response is that I did not suffer. This causes me great pain as it seems to dismiss as unimportant the loss of my mother, my father, grandmother, and more than 20 members of my extended family – not to mention my home, Jewish community and secure life as I knew it.'

Ruth admits that she, too, was once a victim of 'survivor's guilt'. 'Years ago I did have this feeling, which was hard to get rid of. But I worked on it, and it's gone.'

The Australian Association of Jewish Holocaust Survivors takes an inclusive policy towards membership. As previously pointed out, it has added the words 'And Descendants' to its title. Child Survivors of the Holocaust groups have been established in Sydney and Melbourne.

'WE'VE GOT SISTERS'

A speaker at the London assembly was the film director and actor, Lord Attenborough (Richard Attenborough),[18] whose non-Jewish parents took in two Jewish children, Helga and Irene, from 1939.

Lord Attenborough, known to many of the *Kinder* as 'Dickie', explained that his father, principal of Leicester University College, was a devotee of German music and literature who had been 'absolutely devastated' at Hitler's rise to power and pre-war excesses. Likewise his mother, whose humanity had led her to care for Basque children, fleeing from the Spanish Civil War.

One day, Richard and his two brothers were summoned to their father's study, the location – since informality was the norm – suggesting that more than a routine conversation was to follow.

It was two days after the declaration of war. Their father told them that the two Jewish girls, who were already staying with them and had been hoping to be joined by their parents, would now be unable to leave. Their mother was in a concentration camp and their father was likely to go there too.

He said he would like to adopt the children, and asked the three boys for their agreement. Their response, Richard recalls, was 'Whoopee, we've got sisters!'

Lord Attenborough cried as he recalled the scene. His father said: 'We're going to suggest that they call us aunt and uncle.' His mother then chipped in: 'I have to tell you that much as your father and I absolutely adore you boys, and we will continue to give you as much love as we are capable of throughout your lives, I am sure you will understand and accept the fact that we will have to give even more love to Helga and Irene, because they have none.'

His father warned there would be times when there were disagreements, which turned out to be correct.

'There were occasions when it was difficult. Occasions when we did disagree. But we did understand. And so Helga and Irene became our sisters for eight years. When the war was over they went to America and Irene died about five years ago of cancer. Helga married; she has children and grandchildren and when she writes and talks she says I would so love Auntie to have met them.'

Lord Attenborough also spoke about his own marriage of over 50 years (to the actress, Sheila Sim), of the lessons he had learned from sharing a childhood with Jewish refugees, and of his love and respect for the Jewish people. He received a standing ovation which lasted several minutes.

A LATE ESCAPE

As previously stated, children continued to flee Hitler's Reich almost until the commencement of hostilities. Werner Oppenheim (now Bill

Oakfield), was one of the last to leave. Having opted for 'freedom' in Britain, he unexpectedly found himself an internee in Australia.

His story begins on Wednesday afternoon, 30 August 1939, when the bell rang at his home in Hamburg.

'It was a lady from the *Kindertransport* office. She told my mother: "Please take your son Werner to the Central Railway Station at 6 pm today for a *Kindertransport* to England. Only one suitcase allowed and 10 Reichsmarks. Do not tell anyone until after he has left."

'My mother started crying and then rushed to pack my suitcase. No time to say goodbye to friends and relations, just two hours left with my parents. I was an only child, a rather innocent lad of 16 who looked on life as a big adventure. I thought that in a few weeks, at most, my parents would join me in England.'[19]

Werner did not know any of the other children on the train, but was told that, as one of the oldest, he should help with looking after the younger ones. The 'escape' route was via Berlin and Cologne to Aachen. 'Trains were no longer running to Holland but our transport leader, a middle-aged, very energetic battle-axe whom we all feared, arranged for a bus and in no time at all we were rolling over the German-Dutch border.'

The journey itself is largely forgotten, 'except that we arrived at the Hook of Holland at midnight and immediately boarded the ship for Harwich'. As the ship approached the English coast, an announcement was made that Germany had invaded Poland.

At Harwich the boys and girls were separated and the boys were taken on a short bus ride to a school-cum-hostel. 'On Sunday morning, 3 September, we listened to the solemn voice of Neville Chamberlain announcing that Britain was at war with Germany.'

The next event Werner recalls is attendance at the Aliens' Tribunal which was to determine his and several companions' fate.

'Two old ladies, busily knitting and who never said a word, flanked the presiding officer, a local magistrate. 'Most of us were put into Group C – "friendly aliens of enemy nationality". The British have a talent for always finding an appropriate phrase. A few were put into Group B, who had to report regularly to the police.

'A friend, Rolf Baruch, who had come to England before me, was mistakenly put into Group A and was interned immediately. He was one of the unfortunate refugees who were drowned en route to Canada when a U-boat torpedoed the *Arandora Star*.' [20]

Werner's own seven-month stay in the hostel, which coincided with the 'phoney war', ended when jobs were found for the older boys in Wellingborough, Northamptonshire. For the first time the lad found himself among English people whom he 'liked and respected'.

'I worked in a tannery, cutting the ends of skins and earning the princely sum of 26 shillings, of which I paid 16 shillings a week for full board, including four meals a day.'

In May 1940 came the fall of France and the evacuation of the British Army from Dunkirk. The 'friendly aliens' were no longer allowed to reside in Northamptonshire The order was made that they should be interned.

Werner was asked if he had any objection to being sent to one of the Dominions. 'I had heard that many had gone to Canada, and in early July 1940 I found myself on a ship named *Dunera* and presumably on the way to that country. When we reached Cape Town we discovered that our destination was Australia.' [21]

In this way Werner Oppenheim (Bill Oakfield) became one of the famed Dunera Boys.

A NAZI FAVOUR

Walter Friedman was born into a Viennese upper-middle-class Jewish family. In his words: 'Brought up as a spoiled brat with many privileges'.

During the night of 11 December 1937, his father briefly came out of a coma and then died. It was the eve of the boy's 15th birthday and – for the father – perhaps a merciful release. Three months later Hitler came to power in Austria. As the son recalls: 'Our lives, as well as everyone else's who was Jewish, changed drastically.'

Syd and Billie Einfeld. 'Unbelievable numbers of Jewish families think of Syd as their brother, their father figure, their friend, their champion, their mainstay, their prince ...' (Rabbi Raymond Apple)

Left: Arthur Calwell, Immigration Minister, walked a political tightrope in regard to post-war Jewish migration. Some Jews considered him 'discriminatory', others (including The *Bulletin*, right) regarded him as 'generous'.

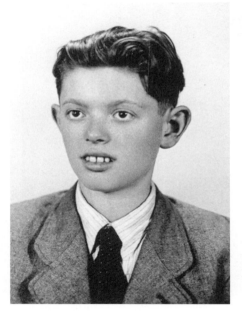

Braham Stern –
Prisoner 67957 at Auschwitz.

Braham Stern today.

Albert Halm, who was reunited with
his 'dead' mother.

Jack Schwartz, who experienced
cruelty and kindness in Bergen-Belsen.

Tom Keleman (right) is met by his appointed guardian, Julian Rose, at Circular Quay in July 1947.

Memorial to Bela Keleman and other Holocaust victims, by the railway line.

George Dreyfus: 'Richard made money and I made music.'

Jack Schwartz, Henry Lippmann and Braham Stern at the grave of their friend and benefactor, John Lewinnek.

Anita Glass – 'special agent'.

Ruth Rack on her first day of school
with *Zuckertüte* (carton of sweets).

Ruth Rack today.

Rita Newell, whose birthday fell on
Kristallnacht.

Vera Gissing and sister Eva Hayman –
Czech Kindertransportees.

Kindertransportees Bertha Leverton and sister Inge Sadan: 'People came to look us over – it was like a cattle market.'

'Horrie' Goldsmith, who 'waited 64 years' to tell his story.

Inge Sadan's German travel pass.

Nicholas Winton (1939) with rescued child, Hansi Beck.

Sir Nicholas Winton –
active nonagenarian.
(Photo: Ronald Channing)

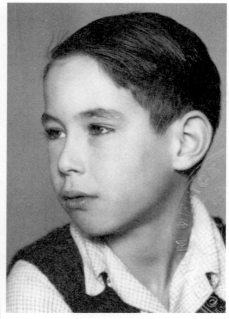

Henry Mendelson, who knew three
words of English: 'yes', 'no' and
'motor car'.

Kinder awaiting collection at London's Liverpool Street Station.

Operation Kindertransport – 6oth anniversary reunion poster.

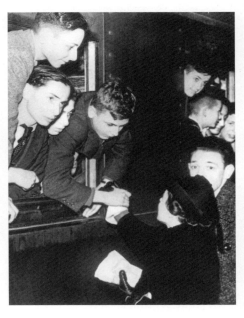

Dutch women greet *Kinder* at Dutch-German border.

Jewish immigrants to Australia on board the *Orama*.

Greta Silvers, who went to Redleaf Pool 'to meet boys and have fun'.

'Labourers in uniform', invited to fight for Australia, but not permitted to carry weapons. The 8th Australian Employment Company enjoys a smoko.

Henry James in the uniform of the 8th AEC. 'Better to be a prisoner on the *Dunera* than in a Nazi extermination camp.' Right: with wife Leah.

Lieut.-Colonel William Scott, who permitted pilfering from internees.

Lieut. John O'Neill, VC. 'Oh Man of Steel ...'

Dunera money: Five notes, originally 'worth' sixpence, one shilling and two shillings, were auctioned in Sydney recently, fetching prices from $4,200 to $8,300 each.

Capt. Edward Broughton – unconventional commander, who was 'loved' by his men.

Count Oswald 'Ossi' Von Wolkenstein, who was arrested after Mass in the school chapel.

Paul Kupfer, Lothar Markiewicz and 'Ossi' Von Wolkenstein, at Sydney Dunera Boys' reunion.

Splashing about at Balmoral. Dunera Boys at play. Left to right: Gerald Arendt, Hans Marcus, Henry Lippmann, 'Ossi' Von Wolkenstein, Henry Vollmer. (Rick Rycroft/Fairfaxphotos).

Henry Lippmann, Sydney co-ordinator of the Dunera Boys, at the unveiling of a plaque paying tribute to the Dunera Boys. 'We were refugees. We regarded ourselves as anti-Nazis. Our interests were British interests.'

Hans Marcus as a teenager, and (right) today. He describes internment at Hay as 'like an English boarding school without bullies'.

Vienna Mozart Boys' Choir – en route for Australia (1939).

Erich Troyna as a chorister (left) and today.

Ady Gravenor: 'I loved him. That was the problem.'
(Steven Siewert/Fairfaxphotos)

George Gruber –
'Nazi of convenience?'

Henrietta Marsh
(mother of Ady Gravenor),
who 'collected gentlemen'.

Willy Siesz – Australia-wide search for missing chorister.

Olav Schappacher (left) and Walter Hauser. Still singing after 60 years.

Otto Nechwatal in his Melbourne shop.

A week after the *Anschluß*, the boy's sister was taken as a hostage by the Gestapo to blackmail the widow into bringing the family's foreign bank accounts into the German Reich.

About that time, Adolf Eichmann was transferred to Vienna in charge of Jewish affairs. As Walter tells it: 'He and three of his deputies needed a place to live. They decided on four flats in a building which was owned by my family, including, through inheritance, by myself.'

The building was managed by Walter's uncle, Hugo, who thus came into almost daily contact with Eichmann in redecorating and making ready these apartments.

The man who would later administer Hitler's 'final solution' proved a difficult, though sometimes obliging, tenant. 'Eichmann, for example, had to have all of the toilets replaced because the previous tenants were Jewish and he would not sit on a toilet on which a Jew had sat.'

Walter recalls: 'It was a few days after *Kristallnacht*. Uncle Hugo was in Eichmann's office on some matter concerning the flats. Eichmann asked him: "Don't you have daughters?'. Uncle Hugo said: "Yes, I have three". "How old are they?" he asked. Uncle Hugo replied: "They are 15, 17 and 21."

'Eichmann said at that point: "The British and the Dutch are arranging for some children's transports to their respective countries. I think I can get your two daughters, the 15 and 17-year-olds, on the first transport."

'Whereupon my uncle asked: "Do you think you might also get my nephew, Walter, on this transport?". He said he would try.'

A few days later, the lad was notified that he would be leaving on 11 December 1938 – anniversary of his father's death and the eve of his 16th birthday – on a *Kindertransport*.

The lad spent the next four-and-a-half years in England, which he describes as 'a very happy period', despite hardships including brief internment as an 'enemy alien'. With some apprehension he and a sister sailed to New York, with the war still in progress, joining his mother who had emigrated two years earlier.

After serving in the US Navy, he completed studies in engineering. Later in life he headed a management counselling practice, from which he is now retired.

CRICKET

Henry Mendelson has fond memories of his 'chameleon period', when at a preparatory school in Norwich, and later at a grammar school, he was introduced to cricket.

'Never in my Teutonic dreams had I witnessed the wonders that went on by this white-flannelled brigade of young Englishmen intent on chasing a small piece of leather around what seemed square miles of green sward.

'My first encounter with this small leather sphere was when it flew straight to my face on three separate occasions on the first afternoon of my be-puzzled participation in this weird undertaking. In sheer self-defence, I caught it on all three occasions, only to be puzzled even more when my English-blabbering (who could understand a word they were yelling?) companions carried me off on their shoulders as the hero of the afternoon.

'Needless to say, after what seemed quite a short period of time, I was one of them.'

12
BRUISES UPON BRUISES

'I had come off one train and now I was going on another. Nobody would say why or where we were going ...'

Ruth Rack, Kindertransportee

Ruth Rack, now a well-known member of the Sydney Jewish community, was first a *Kindertransportee*, then – within weeks of her arrival in Britain – an evacuee; thus making her (as she calls it) a double foreigner. This is her story.[1]

'I was born in Leipzig, Germany. Little girls have no choice in these matters,' she says, matter-of-factly. The timing, April 1928, was unfortunate. It meant that she, her parents, two sisters, brother and extended family were to experience to the full the rising tide of Nazi extremism.

Her earliest memories are of a happy home. 'Mutti [mother] was very hospitable and the home resounded with laughter, music and jolly company.' Her father, Bernhard Landesberg, was cantor in an Orthodox synagogue and took his responsibilities seriously. He had been born in Brody, which, according to the shifting political sands, was variously located in Poland, Russia and the Ukraine.

In World War I, Bernard Landesberg was wounded (and decorated) for fighting on the side of the Austrians against the Russians – an irony in view of what was to come. He was, however, no stranger to racial or religious hatred. One Easter, as some form of vengeance against the 'Christ killers', Cossacks on their horses galloped into Brody. As Ruth tells it: 'My grandfather hid his wife in the wardrobe and stood guard outside it. The Cossacks broke into their home, ran him through with a sabre, opened the wardrobe and hanged my grandmother in it. She was about 37 years old.'

In 1934, at the age of six, Ruth commenced schooling at the local state school. Following a German tradition, she carried with her a *Zuckertütte*, a large 'sugar bag' filled with chocolate eggs and goodies. Her first-day nervousness was sweetened by contents of the bag.

The Nazis, in power for one year, were flexing their muscles. In winter her older brother would pull her on a sledge through the snow to school. The fun was marred by the fear of harassment by Hitler Youth and other bigots. At school the teachers separated Jewish children from the others for some classes.

Bernard Landesberg, a professional singer, who had performed with the Vienna State Opera, was forced to abandon his career, becoming, instead a successful furrier. The couple wisely removed the telephone from their house, so that neighbours who had previously asked to use it 'and had spied on us while in the house' lost the excuse to visit.

Life at school became progressively harder. One day the students were lined up as usual to shout *Heil Hitler* (Ruth would mouth the nonsense words *drei Littler*)[2] and sing the German national anthem. 'We were in the big hall, with all the teachers on stage. All the Jewish children were called up in front of the entire school, disgraced and then expelled.' She moved to a Jewish school, which she actually preferred.

The home itself was no refuge. One day while the family was having lunch, a rock was thrown through the window into the room with the message *Juden Raus!* (Jews Out!).

Thoughts turned to 'getting out' and, in particular, the possibility of a new life in England. Ruth herself was already fascinated by the two 'little princesses', Elizabeth (now Queen Elizabeth II), and Margaret Rose. 'I used to fantasise about their lives. I wondered if they had set bedtimes and had to eat their crusts. Princesses live in castles and I visualised them sitting on little thrones wearing beautiful dresses and silver or sometimes golden crowns on their heads.'

Then came November 1938 and the events of *Kristallnacht*. A few days earlier an order had been given that Jews of Polish origin (which included Ruth's mother) living in Germany were to be expelled. What those departing didn't know was that Poles at the frontier were not allowing them to enter, resulting in vicious fighting – with armed police with dogs on both sides – in which many Jews, trapped in a kind of No Man's Land, died.

On the day of *Kristallnacht* Ruth was 10 years old. Her school had already been attacked by the Nazis when she arrived. She quickly ran home to warn her parents. It was decided to leave the building immediately and to walk, in pairs, but within sight of each other, to the Polish consulate, far enough apart to prevent the whole family being wiped out if one pair was attacked.

Her father told the children: 'We are Jewish and if we are caught on the way to the Polish consulate, we will not deny this. We will never pretend and hide our religion – we are proud to be what we are.'

She was warned not to look to the left or the right or to make herself conspicuous. 'Not to panic, just to keep going until the destination was reached.' The journey to the consulate is engraved in Ruth's mind. 'There were wild crowds of jeering people everywhere, among them the woman who ran the local corner grocery store, and who sold me lollies by the single piece. I had regarded her as a friend, and was deeply wounded to see the hostility in her face.'

The little group passed the synagogue, where her father was cantor, and which was in flames. They walked on, outwardly unconcerned, inwardly in turmoil. At the entrance to the consulate was the worst mob of all. Her mother whispered: 'Yell with them,' which she did with feigned enthusiasm as they edged ever closer towards the wire gate. Having reached the gate, 'we positioned ourselves so that we could slip in when it opened from inside without letting the mob in as well.'

Inside this imagined 'sanctuary' Ruth fainted. The events which followed have been largely blanked out. In her own words: 'I've got a blackout between *Kristallnacht* and May. It was too horrible.'

Ruth knows, either first hand or from what others have told her,[3] that the family returned home to find the carved walnut front door of their fourth-floor apartment had been smashed with an axe, and nearly every piece of furniture which they owned, every piece of cut crystal, the beautiful chandeliers and the whole Dresden china collection smashed, slashed and in ruins.

Pools of blood suggested that one or more of the vandals, in their enthusiasm, had injured themselves. Mr Landesberg noted wrily that strips of white fabric torn from the Shabbat cloths appeared to have been used as bandages. He said: 'I hope they hurt themselves.'

The child's 'blockage' of these events extends, mercifully, to the disappearance of her own father, who was taken to Sachsenhausen[4] concentration camp, briefly released, then cruelly re-interned.

Her only recollection is of being in some sort of hiding place, 'where we had to be very quiet and not to flush the toilet'.

For those who remained, the desire to leave the country gained panic proportions.

At one time (before *Kristallnacht*) both parents had had the opportunity to escape to London on adult visas. However, they would not even consider this option before all four children were safely out of Germany.[5]

WISH ON AN EYELASH

Early in 1939, Ruth's two older sisters went to the airport outside Leipzig to fly to England and safety. They had been lucky enough to obtain student visas. Her father's two sisters in London, Becky and Fanny, set aside personal differences and jointly guaranteed 100 pounds for each niece.

Ruth at that time had two firm wishes. The first was to live in England without Nazis and in peace. The second was to survive long enough to grow up into a sexy woman with big bosoms.

'One of our funny little customs was to make a wish on an eyelash. When a loose eyelash tickled my cheek, I gently picked it up between my thumb and first finger and blew it away. No magic carpet arrived to carry me to freedom, so, to help fate along and give me more wishes, I started to pull out my eyelashes, one by one, making frantic wishes.'

On 3 April 1939, Ruth had her 11th birthday – 'filled with guilt, fear and emotions that no child should have to bear'.

Four weeks later, in May, came a furtive opportunity for Ruth and her brother, the remaining children of the Landesberg family, to leave Germany. Ruth carried a small, brown, leather suitcase. 'It was packed tight and I could barely lift it.' She struggled to make it look effortless to handle, as they walked nonchalantly to the station. She wore layers of extra clothing, which made her feel conspicuous.

Her mother and Aunt Gina [her mother's sister] came on the platform to see them off. 'It was all smiles, pretending to be casual as they hugged and kissed us and said goodbye. For the 10th time Mutti reminded us to take care of ourselves and to stick together. She maintained the fiction that she and Papa would follow us to England in a couple of weeks.'

In a carriage with other children Ruth opened the packet of rich food, lovingly prepared for the journey. She ate it all but was sick with anxiety. The only money allowed to be taken out of Germany was a small coin, one *Groschen*, about the equivalent of a shilling.

The train pulled out and chugged towards the Dutch border. It stopped on the German side 'and so did my heart'. A lot of activity – shouting, opening and closing of doors, stamping of boots and whistling. 'We sat very quietly, holding our breath.'

At last they reached the Hook of Holland. They were shepherded onto a boat, which was a new experience for Ruth. She dimly recalls going to bed on a strange, flimsy stretcher, covered by a thin, woolly sheet. She was sick over the Dutch female attendant who looked after them.

It was dawn when they arrived in Harwich. A group of Jewish women gave them sandwiches and put them on a train for London where her Aunt Fanny, their father's younger sister, was to meet them. Ruth was given a nice bedroom with three single beds in it. The other two were for her parents, who she continued to believe would join them shortly. Her brother was sent to stay with Aunt Becky's son.

On her first full day in England Ruth was put on a tram to the local school, where her progress in English was remarkable. Within weeks she had joined a children's library, where she took out the maximum three books a week permitted. 'I liked to read aloud, so people could tell me if I pronounced the words correctly.'

At school assembly they sang the British national anthem, *God Save the King*, and other patriotic songs. She joined in wholeheartedly, unlike in Germany. Like her father, she had a fine singing voice. During her first term she was picked to represent her London school in an all-England schools choir under the baton of Sir Thomas Beecham.

Though physically safe, and outwardly calm, she suffered internally. She had a number of recurring nightmares.

'In the cold light of a winter's evening, there is a sheltered spot in the forest. Under a big tree, there is a very large, luxurious, upholstered velvet armchair with a person sitting in it. In front is what looks like a large pond full of people with their arms stretched up above their heads. Their mouths are wide open as if they want to scream, but no sound comes out, as they are slowly swallowed in the quicksand. The figure sitting in the chair tries desperately to get up but is not able to move. Most nights the same nightmare returned. Ruth awoke crying and screaming.

In August 1939, three months after their arrival, and in the first school holidays, Aunt Fanny, her Irish maid, cousin Leonard (Fanny's son) and Ruth took a holiday in a cottage her aunt rented in Brighton, Sussex, a popular coastal town. She was upset when told she must share a bed with the maid, whose personal habits she found offensive.

As compensation the house was minutes from the sea and to Ruth this was paradise. Her cousin Leonard, on whom she had a secret crush, played a ukulele in the manner of George Formby.

'One day[6] we were all on Brighton beach, enjoying the sunshine, when a loud wailing filled the air.' It was the air raid warning. 'With loudspeaker blaring, a van drove up and down the seaside announcing that Britain and France were at war with Germany.'

She recalls people grabbed their clothes and rushed off the beach, as if 'expecting an immediate invasion from the sea and instant bombs to hurtle down on the unprepared population'.

Her aunt was hysterical. 'She packed my little brown suitcase and instructed Mai [the maid] to take me back to London by train.' Arrangements were made for Ruth to stay with a male relative – who molested her – and his wife in London. Mercifully, the stay was brief. Within days she was packed off to begin yet another, totally unexpected, chapter in her life, this time in the company of British children as an evacuee.

GAS MASKS AND LABELS

The new phase in her life began at Paddington Station, the main terminus for trains to the south-west of England. Platforms were lined with children – a cross-section of the London working-class population – most carrying gas masks and wearing large identity labels. None seemed to be Jewish. The scheme aimed to remove children from areas likely to be targeted for German bombing.

The problem was nobody had explained this to Ruth, who was nonplussed and traumatised by it all. She calls the double uprooting 'getting bruises on my bruises'.

'I thought the Nazis rejected me, the schoolteachers rejected me, and now my Aunt Fanny had rejected me.[7] Nobody loved me or wanted me. There must be something wrong with me.

'I had come off one train and now I was going on another. Nobody would say why or where we were going. It was horrible. I thought, when I get off this train they're going to kill me.

'Additionally, I was separated for the first time from members of the Jewish community, which was a cultural shock to me. I was a strange child to these English children, committing the sin of being different. I had the distinction of being a refugee from Germany as well.'

The train took the evacuees to Paignton, in Devon; a charming seaside town, close to the major resort of Torquay, to which her school had also been moved. After alighting, the children were marched crocodile-style to a church hall, where on the stage a number of grown-ups stood and looked searchingly at the assembled children, pointing to the one or more they wanted to take away with them to their home.

Most of the children were selected and left quickly for their billets. Ten children – including Ruth – remained. A woman in a grey uniform then took the 'leftovers' to a grand house, with several lawns, a fish pond, apple trees and strawberry beds. The lady of the house, a gracious woman who was clearly an aristocrat, welcomed them warmly and, without hesitation, offered a home to all ten.

For Ruth and the others it was actually a stroke of luck. Mrs Stafford Northcote, whose daughter was a lady-in-waiting to the Queen, had a home to match her generous disposition. From the house, a short walk led to the golden sands of a long, completely deserted beach. Soon after their arrival Ruth had kicked off her shoes and ran her feet through the inviting sand before sampling the water's edge.

Curiously, the very comfort of their new surroundings was to create problems. Ruth befriended a cockney lad whose father was a 'barrow boy'[8] in the East End of London. He was a happy child who was enjoying his new life immensely. When his parents visited and saw the type of home he was living in, they were jealous and immediately took him back with them to London.

Ruth was now 12 years old. The film *Pinocchio* was screening locally, which she and several of the other children wished to see.

Lacking pocket money, Ruth organised and presented a concert party in Mrs Northcote's garage. It was an early example of her entrepreneurial skills. The other children were eager performers. Tickets were sold to the neighbours, from whom chairs were also borrowed. A local air raid warden provided material for a stage curtain. Songs were planned and rehearsed. The children made enough for the cinema outing with money left over.

Gradually the other children, too, returned to their parents or moved elsewhere. Even the maid left to join the WRAC,[9] leaving Ruth alone with her benefactor.

Theoretically, throughout this period her education was uninterrupted. A problem arose when she sought transfer to a selective grammar school. Ruth sat for the exams and gained one of the two places available, but her headmistress disallowed the placing on the grounds that she was not British and priority had to be given to 'our own people'. Appeals were lodged, but a supposedly successful outcome was spoiled by the fact that she was now too old to catch up on all the lessons she had missed.

Meanwhile, her two sisters were no longer living with their Aunt Becky but had been evacuated to the seaside town of Bournemouth. She wished they could be together.

Near Mrs Northcote's house was a splendid mansion, belonging to the Singer sewing machine family, that had been taken over by the RAF to train new recruits. There were thousands of young men on the estate. One night there was a bombing raid, but the main target was missed.

Mrs Northcote's house was also damaged by the blast, which hurtled Ruth out of bed, smashed all the windows, and killed the two dogs, cats, bird and the goldfish. Mrs Northcote herself suffered shell shock and went into rapid decline. Ruth – who by now loved her dearly – nursed her for several weeks.

The local Women's Voluntary Service (WVS) billeting officer, a kindly woman known to Ruth as Mrs Paige, came to the house and decided this situation was not right. She invited Ruth to stay with her until a new billet could be found. Just three days later Mrs Stafford Northcote died. Ruth was to write later: 'I grieved for her as I would for a relative. She had been a kind and dear friend.'

Rosa Paige, like Mrs Northcote, was to become another close and reliable friend. She was a widow whose husband had been gassed in World War I and ultimately died from the effects. 'She was a remarkable woman, always ready with a cheerful smile, never complaining, when she must have been very tired. She was sincere and accepted me without trying to convert me to her religion.'

Mrs Paige belonged to the WVS. 'She wore a trim grey wool uniform and serve she certainly did. It made little difference if it was day or night – any hour around the clock she was ready to answer the call to service.'

Ruth and her new companion would go for long walks in the Devon countryside. Retired people who lavished attention on their gardens and pampered dogs occupied the immediate area. 'Soon we would leave the suburbs behind, cross fields dotted with black, white and brown dairy cows and walk into the woods. Here unfolded a vista of endless bluebells and whole hillsides covered with yellow daffodils.'

Ruth found comfort in the solitude and stillness. 'My hope of ever seeing either of my parents again was fading, and yet I could not give myself up to grieving for them as the uncertainty of their fate still haunted me. I prayed that I might know how they had survived or, alternatively, that they had perished.'

SPIES AND FIFTH COLUMNISTS

By this time, fearing spies and Fifth Columnists (traitors), the British Government had begun internment of enemy aliens. 'It was freq-uently said, "There is a war going on". As I had recently escaped from Germany, I started to be treated with suspicion and mistrust.' In Devon even Londoners were 'foreigners'.[10] Ruth was a 'double foreigner'.

Her problem was 'how to convince them that I was not a German spy but a victim of Nazi persecution'.

She was now 14 and, as an alien, had to report at intervals to the local police. The police station was manned by two young women. They were sisters and kind to her. 'As winter deepened, and it was snowing and I had no overcoat, I came in shivering and blue with cold in my thin white school blouse and navy uniform tunic. The women must have noticed my plight and soon presented me with a warm navy-blue woolly jumper which one of them had knitted for me. Then the other sister knitted me a snug navy cardigan, which buttoned up to the neck and kept me cosy and warm to go to school in winter. I was touched by their gesture of kindness and have never forgotten it.'

Britain was now fighting back. Ruth would lie awake counting the bomber planes passing over the house – 'the drone of the engines still haunts me.' When they returned some hours later there were usually fewer engines to count. 'In the morning we would silently and intently listen to the radio news when an announcer would speak of a raid over Germany or France or wherever and end by giving the number of planes lost in operations. It became a grim game to see if I had counted the number of missing planes correctly.'

Ruth's next billet was with a Miss Bull, retired headmistress of a girls' high school. She was a worshipper at the High Anglican parish of Christ Church. Once or twice Ruth accompanied her to services, thinking of herself as a spectator rather than a participant. She was a pleasant enough woman. But Ruth came to realise 'this dutiful, religious spinster lady had cared for me out of a sense of duty, while what I needed desperately from another human being was love'.

At about this time Ruth heard on a wartime radio broadcast a reference to the anguish of European Jews. 'I fervently wished I could be with my parents in their suffering, even in the face of death.' She tried to draw comfort in prayer and in Jewish rituals that she only slightly understood or remembered.

She was to write later: 'This was the lowest point of my wartime isolation. I developed a prisoner's mentality, keeping record of time, trying to keep a mental diary of the times when the Jewish holidays and the festivals occurred. But I was all muddled up about the correct sequence.'

Additionally, the Devon beaches were being blocked off with barbed wire. It seemed that a shooting match was likely to begin.

Ruth joined the Sea Rangers where she was befriended by an older girl called Millicent. 'She asked her mother if I could come home with her and this became my next abode. I decided not to tell them I was born in Germany because I guessed (correctly) they would not understand. I just said my parents were lost in the war.'

One day they invited her to attend Midnight Mass, which she did. 'After the service we strolled home chatting. "Mum" confided how she hated the Jews. Spontaneously, I replied: "I am Jewish." The words spilled out. She then said something along the lines: "I hate the Jews, but you are different", "Some of my best friends are Jews." I had heard it all before.'

Soon after this incident, Ruth returned home one afternoon to find the front door, which was otherwise never locked, securely bolted. 'My open brown leather suitcase, with clothes spilling out, was lurching on the doorstep. All my precious books were strewn about in the snow.'

With nowhere to go, Ruth headed vaguely in the direction of town. She trudged through the woods, her feet getting heavier. She stopped for a rest, leaning her back against a tree. She dozed off, woken by snow falling on her head from a branch. She remembered Mrs Paige's offer of friendship. 'You can always call on me in an emergency. I am your friend, dear.' I trusted her. She was as good as her word. Without fuss, she welcomed me and I was warmed once more by her friendship.'

Ruth continued to be active in the Sea Rangers and was thrilled when Princess Elizabeth and the Rangers' chief, Princess Margaret, visited the troupe at Paignton and Brixham. Her ambition, at the time, was to join the WRNS.[11] She also volunteered to work during school holidays to assist on the farms where women from the Land Army were bringing in the harvest.

'I worked wherever I was needed. We lived under canvas and were paid one shilling an hour, from which charges for accommodation and food were deducted. We milked and herded cows and picked up potatoes churned up by a mechanical plough. We were woken at dawn and taken in trucks to the fields.'

CUB REPORTER

At 16 and waiting for the results of the Commercial School Certificate, Ruth took a job as cub reporter on a local newspaper. This was a rare opportunity for a girl, only offered because all the men were at war. 'I earned three pounds a week, as well as the choice of a travel allowance or help to purchase a bicycle. I chose the latter.' She was delighted when her articles appeared on the front page of the *Paignton News*.

Not all her journalistic tasks were pleasant. 'Lists and lists of obituaries of servicemen killed or missing in action had to be followed up. Most of them were too young to die.'

One assignment was of particular interest to her. When the examination results were to be announced at the South Devon Technical College, Ruth was sent by the paper to cover the event. With notebook and pen on her lap she recorded in rapid shorthand the events of the day and, as a student, listened anxiously for her own results.

Ruth had managed to get a place in a special matriculation course for ex-servicemen and women whose education had been interrupted by the war. She was delighted to have a 'real opportunity' at last, compensating for her inability to get into a selective grammar school.

It was possible to take examinations through either Oxford or Cambridge University, but in order to matriculate to university it was necessary to have five credits, including English and Maths. Lacking confidence, she took extra subjects – English Literature, German, Hebrew, Geography, Commerce and Shorthand. When the results were announced she found she had not just 'passed' – she had gained four distinctions and four credits. 'That night I dreamt I had wings and was flying through the air. It was a glorious, exhilarating feeling, floating around in the sky.'

'My exam results easily qualified me to enter Cambridge University, and I had it in writing from the university. However, I did not go. Exam results alone were not enough. Money is necessary to support a student at college. I had no idea how to apply to a college and nobody came to my assistance.

'In the mid-1940s it was unusual for a woman to have such an opportunity and it burnt me up that I could not use it because of circumstances beyond my control. To this day it is an unfulfilled ambition.'

It was now 1945 and the war was over. As the evacuation scheme had also ended, Ruth was no longer entitled to a billet. For a while she was subsidised by her sisters, who were now married, and briefly went to live with one of them in their London flat. Her brother was, by this time, also married and living his own life.

The arrangement with her sister didn't 'work out'. Instead, she moved into a hostel supposedly for government white-collar workers. She shared a room with another four girls and women, ranging in age from 20 to 25. She was to become good and lasting friends with two of them.

Ruth got a job with a secretarial agency and was sent all over London to fill temporary positions when someone was suddenly ill or on holiday. This led to a permanent position with London Rediffusion in Baker Street. Ever the sporting type, she cycled from Earls Court across Kensington Gardens, across the main road, across Hyde Park, across the main road and into Green Park. In the summer she sometimes swam in the Serpentine in Hyde Park.

In 1947, when she was 19, Ruth received an invitation from the Home Office to take up British citizenship. 'I accepted joyfully. I treasure my British passport and always keep it ready to use at short notice.'

Her brother-in-law introduced her to the Unity Theatre in London. 'I loved acting and associating with other actors. I had a part in one play that ran six nights a week for six months.' Many famous people were interested in and associated with this theatre – Dame Sybil Thorndike, George Bernard Shaw, among others who later became well known through London shows and British television productions. Two whom Ruth recalls are Alfie Bass and Bill Rowbottom.

It was here that Ruth Landesberg met her future husband, Peter Rack. 'Since he was the front-of-house manager, we saw each other every night. On the one night off, he took me to lovely restaurants, including Leon's, where I had my first Chinese meal.'

Peter, a native Londoner, was a diamond setter, who had served in the RAF during the war. He proposed on his knees in the grounds of Dover Castle. 'He made me a beautiful diamond ring, which I still wear and which is still admired.' On 27 November 1949, they were married. 'We had a fancy wedding in the West End.' Six days later the couple sailed on board the P&O liner *Ranchi*, as British migrants to Australia.

In the post-war years, and after many contradictions, Ruth gradually discovered what had become of her parents after her own arrival in England, in 1939. Much of this was discovered during an extensive, and somewhat stressful, visit to her original home town of Leipzig in 2001.

Her father, Bernhard Landesberg, died in Sachsenhausen concentration camp on 7 June 1940. The death certificate gives cause of death as pneumonia, the standard explanation at that time. The Germans, ever thoughtful, sent an urn containing his ashes to the Leipzig Jewish community.

His widow, Anna Landesberg, being now aware that she could do no more for her husband, filled out a Jewish association survey in a vain attempt to emigrate.

'She was a slave labourer. She had to live in a *Judenhaus*. They took away her warm clothing, everything that she had. This woman of 42, who'd had five children in seven years, and had never worked in her life except as a mother. She was the last surviving member of our family in that horrible, hostile place.'

In May 1942, Mrs Landesberg was deported with others to Belzyce, a ghetto near Lublin in Poland. The *Encyclopaedia Judaica* gives the following information about Belzyce during the Holocaust period:

'The German army entered the town in September 1939, and the Jewish population became subject to persecution and terror carried out throughout Lublin Province ... On May 12, 1942, several thousand Jews from central Germany (Saxony and Thuringen) arrived. The town's Jewish population grew to about 4500 at which point mass deportations to death camps began. On October 2, 1942, the Germans conducted an *Action* to liquidate the remaining Jews in Belzyce.'[12]

15
'KEN FISCH, KEN FLEISCH'

'There were things about my childhood I liked, and things I didn't like, such as being taunted at school and so on. But, basically, if you're brought up in the slums and you haven't got enough to eat, you don't like it, but you don't feel deprived. I guess you just feel, well, this is life.'

'Horrie' Goldsmith, Kindertransportee

'Horrie' Goldsmith is a warm, easy-going man with a philosophical approach to life. 'I've been waiting 64 years to tell my story,' he says with a chuckle as we meet for the first time.

He was born in Meiningen, in Thuringen (Thuringia), central Germany. He was four years old when Hitler came to power in 1933.

His father worked in a bank. When forced out through the Nazis' anti-semitic laws, he did a variety of menial jobs, ending up selling coffee, tea and chocolates door to door.

He had a brother six years older than himself. An asthma sufferer, he had been sent to Switzerland for health reasons, a move which probably saved his life.

On *Kristallnacht* in 1938 his father was rudely roused with a knock on the door at midnight, arrested and sent to Dachau. His wife went to the local police station, where a friendly policeman offered the advice: 'Go to Dachau, and tell them you want your husband out because you're going overseas.' To her response that she didn't have a visa, he told her: 'Just buy a ticket; they'll accept that as evidence.'[1] This approach succeeded.

The desire to escape became desperate. In December 1938, a month after this event, Horrie recalls being taken by train to Hanover, where they spent the night before he and a large number of children were to be taken by ship to England.

He remembers little of the sea voyage, other than an older boy being instructed to look after him, but he vividly recalls – in a role reversal – saying to his father: 'Don't come to the ship because it will upset YOU too much.'

On arrival in London the children were given cardboard placards with their names on them. Two great-aunts, who had already migrated to Britain, came to pick him up. They looked at his card – it said Horst Goldschmidt – and declared: 'We can't call him Horst, we must call him Horace.' 'That was in 1938. And I've been Horace or Horrie ever since.'

Like many other *Kinder*, his stay with relatives was brief. The next two or three months were spent at a disused holiday camp in Deal, Kent, converted into a hostel. The hostel had its own school for the younger children. Horrie, who was nine, was duly enrolled, but soon afterwards transferred to a local school. 'I sat at the back of the class, crying my eyes out, because I couldn't understand what was going on.'

In Germany some of Horrie's relatives had belonged to a radical socialist movement, which had fallen foul of the Nazis, and was now operating in the British Isles. It was decided that the boy should attend a school run by the movement, which meant moving to Wales. He recalls the juniors lived on one side of a mountain, near Abergavenny, and the seniors on the other.

'All the other kids were German. I hardly spoke English at all. We were also taken to the boy scouts. And of course our mob kept speaking in German to each other. So they didn't want us any more.'

Both the senior and junior sections of the school then moved to Bristol. Just as Horrie had settled in, the war hotted up and the teachers were interned as enemy aliens. Horrie was sent to a children's hostel in High Wycombe, Buckinghamshire, which was run by a pleasant Church of England couple.

'They knew we were Jewish and on Sundays they gave us a choice. Either we went to church or we could stay at home and learn the psalms. So very often we decided to go to church because it was too terrible to learn the psalms. If we made this choice it meant that the night before we had to find out where we could get a farthing. We only got threepence pocket money, and we had to fish out a farthing for the plate.'

After about a year, Horrie and several others were transferred to a hostel and school in Lincolnshire, which also had refugees from the Spanish Civil War and a small number of boys transferred from the school in Bristol.

When he was about 13 someone 'discovered that I needed some Jewish education'. He was transferred to a Jewish hostel in Oxford, where he spent the remainder of the war.

Many years later Horrie was to hear of the unpleasant experiences of so many of the children farmed out to foster parents. He considers himself lucky, therefore, to have spent most of his time in hostels. His greatest stroke of fortune, however, was the knowledge that his parents were safe.

Thanks to a relative, who was already living in Australia, Horrie's parents were accepted as refugee migrants in Australia, a proviso being that they came as domestic servants and were not accompanied by children. Before undertaking the journey they were even able to pay a short visit to England, where Horrie visited them at a relative's house.

His parents' voyage to Australia was hardly uneventful. The German cargo ship, on which they were travelling, reached Fremantle, offloaded a certain number of passengers, then set off around the coast for Adelaide, Melbourne and Sydney. By an unhappy fluke, war broke out soon after the ship had left Fremantle, so the skipper, fearing internment and the seizure of his vessel, changed course for South America.

Happily, passengers bound for eastern Australia – including Horrie's parents – were able to disembark in Batavia, where they waited for another vessel in which to complete their journey.

The knowledge that his parents were safe and sound in an English-speaking country affected his attitude to his surroundings. 'There was this constant feeling that one day I'm going to be reunited with them, which is a good thing. At the same time it's a burden, because you're not living in the moment, you're living in the future. This creates confusion, and that's not good for a child.'

'Another problem was I wasn't English, wasn't German. I was stateless. An in-between. As they say in Yiddish, *"Ken Fisch, ken Fleisch"* (neither fish nor fowl).[2]

'It's a bit like the Englishman who emigrates to Australia. He comes out here and he's a Pommy. Then he goes back to England after many years and finds he's not an English person any more; he's an Australian.'

Horrie himself came to Australia, when he was 18, in 1947. He sailed from Holland, with other young Jews, in the *Johan De Witt*. In Marseilles a large number of displaced persons were picked up. This and similar voyages were the subject of controversy.[3]

The ship docked at Wharf 13, Pyrmont, on 16 March. 'It was a typical Sydney hot summer's day. From the rail, before disembarking, I could see my parents waiting on the quayside. It brought a lump in my throat.

'Somebody drove us to the place where my parents were living in Ashfield. It was a difficult time. We had to get to know each other. They were expecting little children. But we were grown up. My brother, Werner, who also migrated, was 24 and already married.'

The course of his parents' lives had also changed. They were no longer domestics. In fact, they had a 'very Australian' job, making – from their home – the puggarees (hat bands) worn over their slouch hats by the Australian Army. 'My father used to cut the cloth at night after finishing work and my mother would sew them up in the morning.'

As for Horrie, he had trained as a dental mechanic and initially took this line of work in Australia. 'I wasn't bad at it, but I used to get eczema with all the water and the plaster and everything. Somebody suggested I'd do better as a jeweller. So I got appreciated to a jeweller to learn the trade.'

JEWELS AMORE

In 1955 Horrie started his own business, in the city, as a manufacturing jeweller and designer. 'It is mainly rings, but we do brooches, earrings, pendants as well. It's called Goldsmith and Amore. I had one partner for 19 years and then I went into retail and had another for 10 years. Then I was on my own again for 15 years. A few years ago I thought well, I've got to wind up somehow and see whether the business can be kept going. I got this young Italian bloke and I went into partnership with him. And, honestly, he is the best partner I could have wished for. A wonderful fellow; he's a pleasure to be with.'

Horrie went into partnership of another kind when, in 1961, he met Betty Popov, an Australian-born physiotherapist at Sydney's Rachel Foster Hospital. They were married two years later and now have an adult son and daughter.

Since this interview was given, Horrie has retired. With more time at his disposal, he is often reflective about his past. 'I don't talk much about the *Kindertransport* and my early life. Probably people wouldn't understand what it means. I've often thought I should write it down for my children. I've started a few times but get on to other things. Then you came along and jogged me. Perhaps now that I have a bit more time ...'

He finds it difficult to assess his own childhood experiences under the Nazis. 'The problem for children of my age is that we never knew anything else. For myself I was reasonably happy and didn't understand what was going on.

'However, as a grown-up, and particularly in my later age, I have pondered the unbelievable and the terrible things that actually happened. I dwell on the fact that my grandparents didn't get out, my uncles didn't get out. And what terrible sufferings they must have gone through.

'It has become a reality that gives me a feeling of ... [Horrie pauses] It's akin to guilt, yet it's not guilt. Because I couldn't have done anything. These awful things would have happened to me too, if I hadn't got out. At the same time I'm aware that I've lived a life of physical safety and, by their standards, luxury. And to think ... they bore the brunt of all this absolute terror and they perished.'

RITA NEWELL: BIRTHDAY GIRL ON KRISTALLNACHT

'My mother was in the room with me when my father came racing up the stairs, breathless and ashen faced, exclaiming "Hitler ist Reichskanzler geworden!" (Hitler has become Chancellor!). I remember being puzzled by all this excitement, which meant absolutely nothing to me.'

Rita Newell, Kindertransportee

The date was 30 January 1933. Rita Newell (née Braumann) was six years old and confined to bed with scarlet fever. Until then her life in the city of Cologne had been uneventful. 'I was a rather spoiled little girl, with Heinz as the older, forever teasing big brother. I started school at a local primary centre in Cologne at Easter 1933 and soon after was moved to a Jewish school because Hitler made it clear that Jews were to be segregated from Aryans.'

About mid-September 1938, Rita came home from school one day and instead of lunch being served there were dark-suited men seated around the dining room table. 'Later my parents told me that they were bankers and had told my father that his account had been frozen and that he would have only limited access to his funds.'

The child was more interested in her approaching 12th birthday. 'I wondered if there would be enough money for the long-promised bicycle, the very latest three-speed model. A very selfish thought, as I realised much later.'

Mr and Mrs Braumann were friendly with a non-Jewish couple, an English lady who had married a German, Mr Westhoven. 'They were very good friends and he insisted on visiting us even after he was forced to join the Nazi party.' They had a small holiday house in the country where the two couples spent many happy weekends.

In the small hours of the morning of Thursday, 10 November – her birthday – the phone rang. It was Mr Westhoven who said: 'Braumann, get out of town, go to Ruhrberg [the weekend house]; you know where the keys are hidden.' He said synagogues and Jewish schools had been set ablaze during the night, and homes ransacked.

'But we did not go. My usually pessimistic father was full of confidence, maintaining that nothing would happen to us because he had fought in the Kaiser's Army in World War I and had even been decorated.'

By 9 am the family discovered that their friend's warning was well-founded. Rita's own school and two neighbouring synagogues were burning fiercely, while the fire brigades were merely standing by to prevent Aryan properties from being damaged.

As Rita tells it: 'Obviously, I did not go to school that day. My best girlfriend, Helga, who lived nearby, came to wish me a happy birthday and was still at our place when the doorbell rang at 10.30 am. My father, who had meanwhile pinned his wartime decoration to his lapel, opened the front door.

'There stood five Stormtroopers, who politely asked him: "Are you Braumann? Is this house your property and is this your family?". When told that Helga was my friend, they turned to this blonde and blue-eyed girl and said, *"Du bist doch kein Judenkind?"* (You couldn't be Jewish too?) When she nodded they yelled: *"Mach daß du nach Hause kommst!"* (Get yourself home!). She burst into tears and ran.

'To us they said, "Go upstairs to your bedrooms!" and *"Grüß aus Paris"* (Greetings from Paris) (a reference to the incident which had allegedly sparked *Kristallnacht*.[4] We then heard the systematic destruction of all our furniture with tools they must have brought up from the cellar, because they were not carrying anything when they arrived. The noise was deafening. We went out on the balcony; neighbours were on theirs and wanted to know what was happening, but we were too frightened to reply.'

Finally, there was silence. The sight which awaited them downstairs was unbelievable. 'Absolutely everything had been demolished. Shattered glass made it dangerous to walk anywhere. Bottles of wine had been poured over Persian carpets, homemade jam had been emptied all over the place, making a sticky mess everywhere. Valuable paintings had been slashed with an axe or knife.'

Suddenly the telephone rang. According to Rita: 'When we eventually located the receiver it was the mother of one of my school friends to enquire whether the scheduled birthday party was still taking place that afternoon.' Amidst the debris stood the promised new three-speed bike, only slightly damaged, but never to be used by her.

The next few nights were spent with relatives. 'My parents woke me on a very cold, foggy morning on Thursday, November 17. Outside stood a car which had been sent by friends from Holland to take me and their young nephews and nieces out of danger to their home near Amsterdam. My parents had packed a few of my clothes. I did not have time to be afraid. It was all done so quickly.'

She found the parting painful. Tears were shed. 'I said goodbye to my parents and they just melted into the fog as the car drove off.

'Only when my own children reached that age did I realise what an enormous sacrifice they had made by sending me away.'

Rita was to spend seven months in Holland, living in a children's home, during which time two unsuccessful attempts were made to send her to England to join her brother.

Each child in the home had a type of cupboard fixed to the wall with their earthly possessions in it. One day Rita went to get a handkerchief, to discover that her possessions had gone. She went to tell the matron, who replied calmly: 'You're leaving in one hour.'

She was put on a train to the Hook of Holland, where she linked up with a *Kindertransport* from Vienna. It was 22 June 1939 – a pleasant sunny day. She recalls being asked to wear a nameplate of rough cardboard. In England she was reunited with her brother.

Her first foster parents were an English Seventh-Day Adventist couple with their own child aged four. They were poor but affectionate – 'a lovely family. I'm still in touch with them now.' As devout Christians, they expected her to go to church with them. 'I went three times a day. I knew all the hymns, the Lord's Prayer and everything. I learnt it all very quickly and still remember it today.'

She later went to live with a rabbi and his family in Sheffield, and finally in a Jewish girls' hostel in London.

She was sent to a state school, where she was expected to attend scripture. 'I didn't want to go to scripture really, but one morning a teacher took me aside; her name was Miss Danziger. She said: "Rita, I'm also Jewish. You're going to scripture classes won't do you any harm. You are one girl out of 500 here. You don't need to show you're different".'

Like other *Kinder*, being thrown in at the deep end ensured that she learnt English very quickly. 'It was very embarrassing – I was the only non-English-born child and kept walking off with the prize for essays.'

The separation from her parents lasted seven years. She missed them, but 'mercifully they survived the war'. Her parents had travelled illegally from Germany into Belgium; guided on foot by good people for a lot of money. Almost their first act was to send a postcard to their children. Rita still has the card, which she cherishes.

When the Germans invaded, they fled in turn to France, which was in turn quickly overrun. They then returned to Belgium – being strafed by enemy planes on the way. They spent the rest of the war in hiding, under the noses of the enemy, in Brussels.

Her brother, meanwhile, had left school and joined the British Army. In June 1944, he was sent to Belgium with the Liberation Forces after D-Day. In what may have been a fluke, he later met his own parents. According to his sister: 'It was May 8, 1945 – VE Day. It was not entirely by accident. He went looking for them, but they saw him first. It was in liberated Brussels and they were taking their very first walk. They just found each other in the street.'

Before World War II, Rita's father and a brother had lived in adjoining houses in Cologne. In 1938 both had applied to emigrate to Australia. One brother was accepted, the other – Rita's father – was not. 'We watched whilst their container was being prepared and all their possessions packed away.'

After the war the 'Australian' uncle badgered the authorities and got permission for the others to come out as well. 'We travelled on the *Johan De Witt*, with more than 700 Jews, all survivors of the Holocaust. We arrived in March 1947.[5] We lived in Melbourne first, which was where my uncle lived.'

Rita took up needlework and worked in the garment industry, forming her successful, modest business. She gave it up on her marriage in October 1954, and removal to Sydney, where she and her husband, Alan, raised a family – as she puts it – 'in the old-fashioned way'.

Like many others she found the reunion with her parents difficult. 'First of all there was the language. I understood German, but I couldn't speak it any more. It took a while to get my German back. My father spoke fluent English, my mother did not. In fact, she never learnt English very well at all.

'It was interesting to suddenly have parents again, who wanted to protect me. They thought of me as still being a child, whereas I was 19 years old when we met again in Europe. My brother, as I have said, was in uniform. People thought the soldier was going out with his landlady.'

Like native-born Britons who have been through the war years, Rita has memories of the Blitz, doodle bugs, gas masks (which were not needed), and life on the 'home front'. She still has her ration book.

Rita does not share the 'I survived but they didn't' complex common among many *Kinder*. 'I don't have those feelings of guilt but my husband does. Because he is the only one out of his entire family who survived. His two sisters, his brother, his parents, they all perished.' Alan Newell, Rita's husband, migrated from Poland in 1948.

Rita has returned three times to her native Cologne. 'The first time was simply by chance while I was visiting my brother who has made his home in Belgium. I was standing on the platform waiting for a train – he lives in a rural area – when an express train to Cologne pulled in. I decided that the next morning I would be there to take it. And I did.

'I found my way to our former home, rang the doorbell and explained who I was. The lady who came to the door was quite nice about it and let me in. She had her sick mother upstairs so I couldn't look at my room, but I looked in the main living area, and I bawled like a baby. I went into the garden and then walked in the park, around the corner, where I used to go rowing with my father on Sunday morning on the lake.

'The next visit came when my husband and I were on a Rhine cruise and we stopped in Cologne for the day. I swore him to secrecy. I said: "Don't let anybody know that I speak or understand German." And I reacted just like any other tourist. I felt nothing. I didn't feel upset or anything.

'The third visit was to go to a reunion of my school in Cologne, where they honoured the late headmaster. He had led a sort of Scarlet Pimpernel existence. He went backwards and forwards across the channel, taking children from the school to safety. But in the end he was caught. His whole family perished. They renamed the public square after him. I attended that reunion with my cousin and her husband.'[6]

BERTHA LEVERTON: TO LAND OF KINGS AND PRINCES

In 1989 and 1999 Bertha Leverton organised reunions to mark the 50th and 60th anniversary, respectively, of the Kindertransport. She remains the movement's guiding figure and inspiration.

Bertha Leverton (née Engelhard) arrived in Britain, from Munich, on 6 January 1939. She was nearly 16, older than many *Kinder*, but young and somewhat immature in outlook.

She had been raised in 'a loving Orthodox family', originally from Poland. She was the first of three children.

Around 1935 her parents lost their business. 'They had a small leathergoods company, manufacturing sports articles like rucksacks, which sold very well in Munich because of its location near the Alps. But the Germans were greatly discouraged from buying from the Jews, so the business collapsed.'

Various lesser business ventures followed, her parents, like many others, failing to appreciate the scale of the Nazi horrors which lay ahead. 'They thought, "The Nazis haven't got it against us. We're just ordinary people, small people, working people. They just mean the rich Jews with the big firms and the big, big businesses. We'll stay put. It will all blow over."'

Of course, it did not blow over, which explains how – following some deft negotiations by her father – Bertha and her 12-year-old brother Theo, came to be placed on a *Kindertransport*.

Bertha had her own ideas about the land to which she was travelling. 'I thought of England as a land of kings and princes. It was quite thrilling.

'A year or two before we had seen pictures in newspapers of the coronation,[7] and those people with their ermine robes and crowns on their heads. We really thought in England that's how people got dressed – perhaps not every day, but sometimes on Sundays.'

Her identity document (they were now considered stateless) shows a smiling teenager, described on the form as a 'young person ... admitted to the United Kingdom for educational purposes under the care of the Inter-Aid Committee for children'.

She was, in fact, sponsored by the Dean and Chapter of the (later razed and re-built) Coventry Cathedral. This noble gesture by local Christians was diminished by not-so-fine treatment from the family initially chosen to look after her.

She was to work for the couple as a maid. She refused to wear a uniform – her one, solitary protest. 'Auntie Vera', as her employer liked to be known, tormented her, but Bertha charitably puts this down to the fact that she was a semi-invalid, and possibly resented her own good health. Vera's husband, 'Uncle Billy', had the reverse problem of undue 'friendliness' – a tactfully chosen word to denote amorous advances which Bertha successfully fought off for five long years.

On the plus side, Bertha was not alone, but had her brother's company. Her nine-year-old sister Inge (now Inge Sadan) joined them after about six months. All three were looked after by the same couple.

If a local Jewish refugee committee existed, the children knew none of it. They occasionally attended Sabbath service in the nearest synagogue (a two-mile walk). Not one of the congregation even noticed the three youngsters who would have dearly liked to have been part of Jewish life.

One day, Theo came home crying and limping from school. He had fallen into a bomb crater. For several days he was made to continue to go to school and told not to be a cry baby. Only when his foot swelled like a pumpkin was he allowed to see a doctor and the discovery made that he had a compound fracture of his leg.

Many times Inge's little arms were full of bruises from being punched by auntie for some minor naughtiness. When the children were banished to the kitchen for their meals, they did not mind in the least.

Being above the minimum school-leaving age on their arrival,

Bertha never went to school in England. To this day she finds it a disadvantage.

'The people I came to not only didn't encourage me to pursue a secondary education like night school, they actively discouraged me. The way I learned English was from the radio and the one woman's magazine in the house. For me it was traumatic – a house without a book. Some children came to families who were more cultured than theirs; with others it was the opposite – the luck of the draw.'

'OUR WORD AGAINST THEIRS'

After the blitz on Coventry, the children were evacuated with the family to the village of Delph, near the Yorkshire-Lancashire border. Twice a year they were visited by a young rabbi, whose job it was to visit children in non-Jewish homes. According to Bertha: 'There was no point in complaining to him about our treatment. It was our word against theirs, and by that time we were so cowed, we just accepted our fate.'

Bertha was sent to work in a cotton mill, doing the housework at night and at weekends. She was happy because it took her away from 'home' and the girls were kind and accepted her. She was on piece work and was soon earning top rates. Theo, by now 14, was sent to work in a factory. Inge went to senior school and won a scholarship.

Though she earned good money for the time, Bertha was to see very little of it. She and her brother were required to hand over their pay packets to auntie intact, getting half a crown back from each pound earned. But that was in theory only. For even that small sum was likely to be 'borrowed' back, a day or so later, never to be returned.

After a while Bertha was taught by other factory workers how to steam open the envelope, remove one pound and falsify the amount on the docket.

There were other occasions when all three children rebelled and did unheard-of things like asking for their sweet coupons. Then auntie would 'fall into a faint', accusing them of impairing her health and being ungrateful.

Uncle and auntie liked playing Monopoly, but it wasn't much fun just played by two, so the children were usually invited to play with them. They developed a skilful strategy of losing. This made the adults happy and earned treats like tea and biscuits, or some sweets.

Bertha recalls 'one wonderful week in January'. As she tells it: 'Auntie and uncle went to visit her mother in Coventry and we were given permission to open our wage packets and take out our allowance and a little extra for food.

'It was my 21st and Inge's 14th birthday during that week. We went to Oldham, the nearest town, lunched in a cafe on eggs, beans and chips, saw the sights and then went to the swimming baths where I taught Inge to swim and then had our photographs taken. The happiness and freedom of that birthday will remain for ever in my memory.'

More happiness was in store. Unknown to the children, both parents had managed to flee Germany in 1940 and, by semi-legal means, travelled to what is now Yugoslavia, from which they eventually reached neutral Portugal. It was still wartime. A law had been passed in the British Parliament permitting close relatives from neutral countries to travel to England, providing they had children under 16 there. Inge, the youngest, qualified on that score.

WOODEN CLOGS

Auntie's mother, who ran boarding houses, had bought another house in Coventry on hearing about their parents coming. It was intended to install them as housekeepers there so that they could earn their keep. However, when the parents arrived and saw the state the children were in – Bertha had no shoes, only wooden clogs which had left her shinbones horribly raw – there was a terrible rumpus.

According to Bertha: 'We had decided not to say anything bad about auntie and uncle, but during the night our mother had wormed the whole story out of me. Inge had lost all and Theo most of his German.

'Parents are not deceived and I shall never know how, but Papa, via the village telephone, and not speaking any English, managed to contact the nearest refugee committee, in Manchester, and within hours they arrived by car and we were taken away.

'My parents insisted that I should be bought a proper pair of shoes along the way. This was a few days after my 21st birthday.'

A new, happy era started. The family settled in Birmingham. Bertha married and raised a family, with two daughters and several 'wonderful grandchildren'. She was also no stranger to tragedy, experiencing the death of her son, Danny, at the age of 21. Also her brother Theo died when he was 43.

She finds consolation in the knowledge that, unlike many of the *Kinder*, she can at least visit their graves.

POSTSCRIPT

Recently Bertha obtained her records from the refugee agency. She found that she, her brother and sister had been officially labelled as 'troublemakers'.[8]

IV

THE DUNERA EXPERIENCE

14
THE 'THIRD FLEET'

To the Prime Minister of Australia:

Honourable Sir,

I have heard on the wireless the news that Australia would be willing to receive internees from England. I beg to protest; we have enough of the scum here already, too many in fact.

I am not a vindictive woman; these aliens are God's creatures just the same as we are. All the same, I sincerely trust that a U-boat gets every one of them.

Faithfully yours,

M. Gibbs, Shenton Park, Western Australia

Letter in Australia's National Archives

In September 1940, a stir was caused with the arrival in Australia from Britain of some 2000 category C civilian 'enemy aliens',[1] mostly German and Austrian Jews,[2] together with a smaller group of German and Italian seamen and military prisoners,[3] on the HMT (Hired Military Transport) *Dunera*.

Like the convicts of old, the passengers were not exactly volunteers. Some have jokingly called themselves 'The Third Fleet'. They were officially considered 'friendly', though it suited the authorities in both countries not to know. In common with the wartime child evacuees,[4] their stay was intended to be temporary, but about half ultimately settled in Australia.

They had left their homelands to avoid Nazi persecution, and undertaken new lives in Britain,[5] only to be rounded up under legislation introduced by the Home Office at a time when the mother country feared invasion.

They were taken into custody by local police, and sent to internment camps – one was on the Isle of Man, another at Huyton, near Liverpool – or 'tent cities' with only the most basic amenities. Several *Dunera* Boys spent their first nights in 'captivity' under the stands at Kempton Park Racecourse, near Hampton Court.

There was a degree of confusion. A Jewish soldier sent to guard internees in the Isle of Man found his own father on the other side of the wire. Wives of internees became objects of suspicion. A young internee, whose father was also interned in Britain, recalled how every time his mother used her typewriter, a neighbour called the police, accusing the woman of sending Morse signals to the enemy.

There were lighter moments. The Huyton camp post office received a parcel with the outer wrapper torn, and the name and camp number missing. The sergeant who opened the parcel picked up a small paper bag on which was written 'raisins for Apfel Strudel'. He took the bag into the room where all the camp records were kept, and said to the two clerks working there: 'See if you can trace this chap Apfel Strudel.' [6]

The policy of transportation got off to a terrible start. On 2 July 1940, the commandeered Blue Star liner, *Arandora Star*, was torpedoed on its way to Canada with 1500 German and Italian internees. The same submarine, U-47, had earlier attacked and sunk HMS *Royal Oak*, pride of the British fleet,[7] inside the Royal Navy's almost impenetrable anchorage at Scapa Flow. For this attack the U-boat's commander, Gunther Prien, had been awarded the Knight's Cross in a public ceremony by Adolf Hitler. It is not known what the Führer thought of the second attack.[8]

Most of those on board the *Arandora Star* died. About 200 survivors were picked up off the coast of Ireland by warships and returned to Liverpool. Wartime censorship, and media bias, impeded accurate reporting of the sinking. The tenor of the reports was that the Nazis had killed their own kind, so it didn't really matter.[9] The survivors then joined other detainees on board the *Dunera*.

The '*Dunera* Boys', as the travellers came to be known, sailed from Liverpool on 10 July 1940. The association with Liverpool, their sea voyage and the word 'boys' has caused them to be confused with English child migrants or with child refugees. The group included genuine boys – records show that 22 per cent of internees (the highest bracket) were under 20 – and 'boys' of pensionable age. The youngest were 16, the oldest over 70.

As if their enforced departure, let alone earlier misfortunes, weren't enough, these victims of Hitler, who were undeniably pro-British, were abominably treated by their British military escort – a shameful episode which surviving *Dunera* Boys, with innate decency, are inclined to play down.

THE JOURNEY

From England's coast

So far away

They took us on a trip.

To see the world,

On a pleasure cruise,

From a pick-pocket battle ship.[10]

The *Dunera*, launched in 1937 for its owners, the East India Company, was not a 'broken-down old tub', as is commonly claimed. It gained its reputation because of indignities deliberately imposed, and crowded conditions – nearly 3000 people including military escorts and ship's crew – in a vessel intended to hold a maximum of 1600.

Internees falsely assumed that the *Dunera* was headed for Canada. Mike Sondheim recalls: 'We first headed west, as we could glean from observing the sun through the portholes. Then after a few days the ship turned south. In mid ocean – on July 17, according to my diary – we learned that Australia was to be our destination.'

Most realised, immediately they boarded the vessel, that they faced annoyances other than the threat of U-boats. Suitcases (pierced by soldiers' bayonets) were taken from them, and the contents rifled. Watches, rings, money and personal valuables confiscated. At one stage the deck was littered with empty wallets.

Moritz Chlumetski, 58, stumbled up the gangplank carrying a violin case. He explained to the guards that it contained a valuable instrument belonging to his son, also an internee. The guard responded by bashing Chlumetski's foot with a rifle butt. Rene von Podbielski, a Junker nobleman, was carrying the manuscript of a novel on which he had been working for years. It was seized and thrown overboard.

Karl Koenig recalled that he was 'asked in a friendly way by two commissioned officers to hand over all my valuables. When I requested a receipt, I was smilingly told that I could trust a British officer, and this was for my own protection. I never saw valuables or baggage again.'

Fred Gruen hid two English pound notes in his tie. He wore it even in the tropics. Another internee tied his watch to his testicles.

Henry Lippmann recalls an incident near the end of the voyage, when he was fingerprinted and asked to sign an identification card. An officer handed him a fountain pen, which he immediately recognised as his own – a bar mitzvah present from his father, and of great sentimental value. When he tried to claim it back, the officer just growled: 'Get going'.

Indignities were not confined to stealing. A survivor from the *Arandora Star*, who was deliberately put down below the water line, was told: 'You won't get off this time if the boat sinks'.

The *Dunera* was at one point struck by a torpedo. Or two torpedoes. Or a near miss. Accounts differ on what actually took place. The incident occurred 24 hours after the *Dunera* had left port. Several of those on board report hearing a loud bang, which was followed by violent rocking, but which produced no serious damage. General opinion is that the ship received a glancing blow from two torpedoes, which failed to explode, or that the missiles passed under the vessel.[11] There is an interesting theory that, in taking a zig-zag course to avoid further attack, internees' luggage was knocked overboard. It is claimed some of this luggage was retrieved by the U-boat skipper who, on reading letters in German, told other German u-boat crews in the area to 'lay off' the *Dunera*.

Memories of the voyage are not all of hardships. It is claimed Professor Peter Meyer, a talented composer and musician, wrote a *Dunera* Mass, celebrated by a German-born Jesuit priest, Father Walter Koenig (one of two Christian ministers among the internees). Most of the choir were Jews.[12]

'CAPTURED' IN PICCADILLY

The ship's first port of call in Australia was at Fremantle. Here the internees were fingerprinted[13] and subjected to further indignities based on a continued misunderstanding about who they were. Even the paperwork created difficulties, internees objecting (understandably) to being asked to fill in forms headed 'prisoner of war'. Several angrily scratched through the question: 'Where were you captured?'. One man allegedly wrote down 'Piccadilly Circus'.

Italians and military prisoners were offloaded at Port Melbourne. On 6 September, after 50 days of being hungry, unwashed, unclean, without even a change of clothing, the *Dunera* and the majority of its human cargo finally reached Sydney, berthing at Wharf 21, Pyrmont.[14]

Henry Lippmann recalls the event. 'The entrance into Sydney Harbour I shall never forget. I managed to come on deck. There was a small enclosure behind barbed wire where we could stand for a few minutes. A meal was being served, I forgot about that. I could see little houses on the shore. It was beautiful. I thought, this isn't a bad place, one day I might stay.'

Not that the *Dunera* Boys saw much of it. At least, not then. They were to spend the next 18 months in camps in Hay, in the Riverina, south-western New South Wales, and Tatura, in rural Victoria.

Upon disembarking, internees were pleased to find the British guard troops replaced by Australian soldiers, who, having established that the people they were escorting were not 'spies and Nazis', swapped yarns with their 'prisoners', and shared fruit and sandwiches with them during the long and otherwise tedious train journey to their place of internment.

There were five trains. From the windows the captives saw kangaroos and a bushfire. But what they remember most is the behaviour of the Australians. Henry Lippmann quickly convinced a guard he was not a dangerous criminal. 'The contrast was unbelievable. They treated us like mates.'

Mike Sondheim recalls: 'They were middle-aged men, including World War I veterans, some of whom had been in Palestine. They were surprised when we spoke to them in English. They believed what we told them, and were not going to take unconfirmed rubbish from other sources. Their discipline didn't stultify their judgement.'

A scene in the 1985 TV mini-series, *The Dunera Boys*,[15] also available as a feature film, shows an Australian escort asking an internee to mind his rifle while he rolls a cigarette. Another guard, on hearing of ill-treatment by the Britons he had replaced, remarks: 'Never did much care for the Poms m'self.'[16] Whether true or false, both incidents have become part of *Dunera* lore.

TWO VILLAINS
Every war story has its particular villains, and the *Dunera* had two. The first was a member of the escorting party, Lieutenant John

O'Neill, probably the only junior officer in the entire British Army to have had songs written about him – the only way victims could let off steam – by those he tormented.

A portrait of O'Neill (ironically in a panel dedicated to heroes) in London's Imperial War Museum shows a thickset, bull-faced man with slightly wild eyes. He is there because in World War I, as a Sergeant in the Leinster Regiment, he won the Victoria Cross.[17]

He was born in Airdrie, Lanarkshire, in 1897, and initially joined his father as a coal miner. He was 17 when war was declared, and immediately volunteered. He was clearly a brave man, gaining the Military Medal and French Medaille Militaire, in addition to the VC. For these acts he received considerable recognition, including an invitation to ride with the Prince of Wales during a peacetime awards ceremony.

In 1922, after the disbandment of the Leinsters, O'Neill returned briefly to the coal mines, but soon afterwards enlisted as an aircraftman in the RAF, working up to sergeant's rank with his skill as an armourer. In July 1939, after 16 years' service in the RAF, O'Neill was discharged – but not for long. When war was declared, in September, he volunteered once again and was commissioned in the Pioneer Corps. One of his first military duties was to escort passengers on the *Dunera*.

His World War II career was less glorious than the first. O'Neill personally robbed and assaulted detainees, and encouraged those around him to do likewise. He reacted to minor misdemeanours by devising punishments that would not have disgraced the Gestapo. During a routine search, Jewish religious vestments, some of them rescued from burning synagogues in Germany, were seized. When an internee, Rabbi Ehrentreu, complained, O'Neill allegedly grabbed him by his beard, and threatened to throw him overboard.[18] A sketch of this encounter, a prized *Dunera* relic, has been featured in several displays.

One wonderful Dunera night
the moon was shining low
You came to look
What was inside
That's how we came to know

Oh oh O'Neill, my dear O'Neill,
I wish you'd only know just how we feel;
You don't know how much we love you
For the kindness we got from you,
Man of steel; Oh oh O'Neill.

Watches, chains and fountain pens,
And even wedding rings.
We never knew, quite how much,
the bastard liked these things.

Oh oh O'Neill my dear O'Neill ...

Lyrics and music, Ray Martin

Possibly an even greater villain – in terms of neglect of duty if not in the actual acts performed – was O'Neill's superior officer, (Acting) Lieut-Colonel William Patrick Scott.

Scott, another World War I veteran, had been a peacetime officer in the 14th London Regiment, Territorial Army, who was called to the colours (and transferred to the Pioneer Corps) with the substantive rank of Major.

Many, though not all, the other guard crew members were also from the Pioneer Corps. There is a theory, advanced to explain their brutality, that men in this lowly regiment have either 'done time' or have something in their pasts which makes them unsuitable for service in other formations. Another explanation offered is that the soldiers were veterans of Dunkirk, who ill-treated prisoners to retaliate for the horrors they had seen.

Scott tried to avoid verbal communication with internees, believing, in the manner of senior officers, that this was a matter for subordinates. Ironically, an address to his own men subsequently brought about his downfall. In it, Scott referred to internees as 'our guests', and said that if roles were reversed (ie. aliens were searching British soldiers) 'we would be lucky if we had our belly buttons left'.

He appeared to believe this justified thieving by his men, and went on: 'I am an old soldier, and I know that the British Tommy looks upon a time like this as an opportunity to help himself to any unattended trifles.'

On arrival in Sydney, Scott received hero treatment, including a flattering write-up in the *Sydney Morning Herald*.[19] The newspaper described him as 'an impressive kilted figure, and quoted him as stating: 'The internees were better fed than any British troops. By the time they reached Australia they had filled out and were dashing round the deck like two-year-olds.'

The (Sydney) *Daily Telegraph* showed journalistic licence when writing about the internees. 'Tragedy and wild excitement marked the voyage to Australia of a British troopship carrying German and Italian prisoners which reached Sydney yesterday,' it stated. 'Among the internees were parachutists, other prisoners of war, and hundreds who had been carrying out subversive work in England. There were no women.'

Happily, other voices were at work. An officer who disliked Scott had instructed a soldier (a professional shorthand writer) to take down the 'belly button' speech. Because of this and the actions of two medical officers,[20] Scott and two others appeared before a court martial, on 20 May 1941, which sentenced Scott to be 'severely reprimanded'.

Some *Dunera* Boys believe that the action of the authorities in pursuing such a matter in wartime does credit to the British Army.

Others feel the affair was glossed over. No charges were brought against Lieutenant O'Neill. The *Dunera* Boys – the victims – were considered unsuitable people to give evidence.

The Australian Archives contain damning material about both men, including a memo from Scott that he preferred Nazis to Jews.[21]

Attempts by writers over the years, including myself, to locate William Scott have all failed. He did not claim a war service gratuity; nor does his name appear in British social security or taxation records. His death has not been officially recorded. If still alive, he would be 95.[22]

Lieutenant O'Neill died suddenly, of an unspecified heart condition, in Hoylake, Cheshire, on 16 October 1942. His death was reported by his wife. He received a full military funeral, and (in the 1980s) a second commemorative headstone, courtesy of the Commonwealth War Graves Commission. His grave, which had been neglected, was restored recently by the Hoylake unit of the Air Training Corps.

Good Guys

The *Dunera* saga is not without its complement of good guys, among whom must be numbered the ship's doctor, Lieutenant Alan Brooks. Brooks was a Scotsman, officially attached to a field hospital in northern England. In 1940, at the invitation of his commanding officer, he volunteered for a secret mission, 'destination undisclosed'.

When he boarded the ship, he was scandalised by what he saw – in particular a bizarre incident in which an internee nearly lost his finger while having his ring forcibly removed.[23] Despite stifling conditions, prisoners were denied permission to open windows and portholes. Brooks rigged up an emergency ventilation shaft which saved many lives. Because of him, there were only three deaths – two from natural causes and one suicide – during the voyage.

Another interesting player in the *Dunera* saga was an Australian military doctor, Major Alan Frost, who had the title Deputy Assistant

Director of Medical Services (DADMS), Eastern Command. His duties included giving a health check to incoming military personnel and to their vessels.

Major Frost was the first person to board the *Dunera* after it berthed at Pyrmont. He told me:[24] 'It was appalling really. I inspected the ship with the purser. I had a chat with the ship's doctor [Alan Brooks], a very nice fellow, who had done his best under difficult circumstances. I met the colonel in charge of prisoners [Scott] and the ship's captain. I had the impression that the real skipper was the colonel. I don't know what the captain was doing.'

Frost quickly realised that something was wrong. An internee was being led towards the side of the ship with little more than a towel around him. 'I said, "Where are your clothes?". He pointed to the guards and said, "They got them".

'Anyway, we started walking around and I saw one of the guards with two watches on. I thought that's a bit unusual. Most of us can only afford one. I then saw another young bloke being taken off the ship with little more than a towel around him.

'I thought there's something odd here, so I asked to be taken to the holds. I saw suitcases, bags and things had been ripped open, presumably with bayonets. Clearly, there had been thieving.'

'I wrote a long report, which went through Eastern Command to land headquarters in Melbourne. I'm glad the Colonel was punished.

'These people were not criminals in any way, nor were they prisoners of war, though they had some of the POW entitlements. They were a gentle group of people, who had been lifted out of England because of a scare.'

After the war both Brooks and Frost returned to normal medical practice. In Brooks' case this was in the Welsh valley town of Ebbw Vale, where he became a legend. He was still practising medicine, though stone deaf, at 91. He visited Australia in the 1980s as guest of the *Dunera* Boys, and died soon after his return.

15

DUNERA: HAY DAYS

Hay days, Hay days,
Make the Hay days your play days,
Sing on every day,
Doodle oodle ay,
Hay days.

Lyrics and music, Ray Martin

Towards noon on a clear September day the trains carrying the Dunera Boys reached Hay. It was early Spring, but according to Walter Kaufmann:[1] '... the singeing sun had reached its summit and the ground reflected unsparingly the heat and the brightness that engulfed [us] like a burning blanket.'

They had never seen such country in their lives. 'One step from hell, hot and dusty, but you'll get used to it,' said one of the friendly guards from the train. On leaving the station, the internees marched – with more troops lining the road – to their new 'home'. They saw few townspeople. Henry Lippmann spotted some workmen, who seemed 'well dressed, with good shirts and hats'.

Mike Sondheim recalls: 'There were soldiers all over the place, with fixed bayonets. We carried what little earthly goods we still had. We must have seemed a bedraggled lot. To us the camp looked like it was on the edge of the desert.'

Walter Kaufmann later wrote in the literary quarterly, *Meanjin*: 'Behind the last of the column three barbed-wire gates closed slowly ... A dog began barking as a bugle sounded. Inside the roll was called by a sergeant with a face burnt the colour of earth. He counted by stepping swiftly along the flank, two men for every step. One more,

194

one less, what matter; none would go missing – for where in this desert could they go?'.

They were fed almost immediately upon arrival. According to Horst Jacobs: 'Although we were not starved we had until then been always hungry – there was never quite enough. Now it was different. There was this total abundance of food, which actually made a lot of us sick.'

There were originally two camps at Hay, each with accommodation for about 1000 inmates. A third, on the far side of the town, was added later.

For some detainees, especially after the *Dunera*, life at Hay seemed – despite the oppressive heat – 'like paradise'. To the younger ones like Lippmann it was an adventure. 'I felt like a boy scout coming to camp.' Others found it 'unjust but bearable'.

Detainees allocated themselves specific chores. Lippmann recalls: 'We had an army of potato peelers, dishwashers. My job was to make hot water. A friend was in charge of latrines. Somebody else chopped wood.'

Food was not just abundant but of high standard. 'We had among us professional cooks who could make out of army rations meals that you couldn't find in the finest restaurants in Sydney.' And they had all day to do it.

Sleeping arrangements were interesting. There were huts for Catholics, others for Orthodox Jews, even a 'communist hut'. These arrangements were informal. In the words of an inmate:[2] 'People just gravitated towards where their friends were.'

According to Peter Huppert:[3] 'From the beginning it had been made clear to us that we could have self-government, provided we could show that we could run our affairs in an orderly manner. I never saw an armed guard inside the camp [but] recall the appearance of a tall, self-possessed, bronzed Aussie sergeant-major, who treated us as equals and impressed on us the need for a creative occupation in view of the approaching summer. "It will be 110 in the shade," he predicted, "and will drive you crazy unless you find something to do".'

His advice was hardly needed. Detainees formed their own 'parliament', with communist, left, right, religious and anti-religious factions. Meetings were lively. 'Where you had 10 people there were 15 opinions.'

Classes were run; there was no shortage of teachers. The camp complement included 14 lawyers, several with degrees in British law. There was a journalist formerly with the *Berliner Tageblatt*, two theatrical agents, medical doctors, a world-famous psychologist, a circus acrobat and strong man, and several people addressed by the others as 'Doctor' or 'Professor' – though of what is uncertain. There was an excellent debating society. One motion was that 'Ladies should be admitted to the Debating Society'. According to Bill Oakfield (Werner Oppenheim): 'As we had not seen any "ladies" for many months, that motion was acclaimed with great enthusiasm and a lot of unprintable witticisms.'

Oakfield was briefly a Hay internment camp 'policeman'. 'Our job was to patrol the camp at night and prevent the interminable squabbles which were going on all the time. One bloke made a big fuss because he had not been addressed as *"Herr Doktor"*. We solved that problem with true Jewish wisdom and it was decided that from then on everybody would be addressed as *"Herr Doktor"*, even 17-year-old boys like myself.'

Leisure pursuits included bridge, chess, handball and soccer. Mail was sent and received using the POW service, confirming, in a curious way, that they were indeed prisoners rather than 'guests'. They refused an offer, via the Swiss Consul, to receive 'wages' allocated by the Germans to POWs.[4]

With the connivance of the publisher of the *Riverine Grazier*, the camp briefly produced its own currency, designed by an internee, George Teltscher, who was a skilled graphic artist. Notes were issued in denominations of two shillings, one shilling, and sixpence. The design included a border pattern of barbed wire with the camp motto: 'We're here because we're here because ...'

Internees claim the notes were 'legal tender for one week'. Then the authorities clamped down. The TV mini-series improved on the joke by calling the notes 'Goodonyas' – i.e. one Goodonya, two Goodonyas etc. (At the 1995 Sydney reunion each participant received a Goodonya.[5] This time there was no fear of arrest.)

In the mini-series, internees were shown breaking out at night, and having affairs with local women. In reality, 'two or three went into town, and they did so legally. The film said many silly things.'

Within a few weeks of their arrival, the Dunera Boys received a visit from Colonel Scott and Lieutenant O'Neill, who had not yet returned to Britain. Scott attended a town sports meeting, giving away as prizes watches his men had stolen from internees.

On another unpleasant note, the weather, as predicted, turned hotter – very much hotter. According to Huppert the huts were 'almost unbearable' to enter during the day; the walls too hot to touch. 'One gasped for breath in this dry atmosphere, wondering how to survive. Water from under the shower was lukewarm, a mere trickle and barely refreshing.'

The flat landscape, disappearing over the horizon, and absence of vegetation, gave the appearance of a moonscape. There was drought, dust and sandstorms. Says Lippmann: 'At home I used to like sugar and cinnamon on my porridge. At Hay the porridge started to look like it had sugar and cinnamon. Then I realised it was dust.'

Huppert and others 'craved for the sight of a cloud'. When the clouds did come, the downpour was such that the camp was quickly two feet under water.

Internees did their best to remain cheerful, some seeking refuge in song. Kurt Kohn, an accomplished musician, who had studied at the Vienna Conservatorium, composed the music and words for the ditties (which came to be known as the Broadhay Melodies) featured in this and the preceding chapter. In post-war Britain, having changed his name to Ray Martin, he became a popular band leader, composer and arranger, with over 1200 original works to his credit.

Say Hay for happy

When you feel snappy

And you don't want to cry;

Say Hay for happy

When you feel snappy

And you don't want to die.

'MOST LOYAL' INTERNEES

We have been Hitler's enemies,

For years before the war.

We knew his plan of bombing and

Invading Britain's shore.

We warned you of his treachery

When you believed in peace,

And now we are His Majesty's

Most loyal internees.

The story of the Dunera Boys – in particular the confusion about their identity and allegiance – combines pathos with black humour. It is claimed, though difficult to prove, that the Australian Government itself shared the 'misunderstanding' that the internees were hardcore Nazis, and was unaware that Britain itself had reversed its policy in regard to lesser categories of aliens.[6] Another theory is that the Australians were wise to the truth, but found the situation 'embarrassing' and continued the deception through fear of releasing them into a community which would not take kindly to the thought of a 'bunch of reffos' jumping the immigration queue.

Both governments would have been aware that to return the internees to wartime Britain would be expensive as well as hazardous, and in any case the required shipping just was not available.

In a scene from *The Dunera Boys*, the Hay camp commander rings the Prime Minister, Robert Menzies, an old school friend, and says 'There's been a cock up.' That part, at least, is an understatement.

MAJOR LAYTON

In June, 1941, the internees in Hay had a welcome diversion in the form of a British visitor, Major Julian Layton, who came to inform them that Britain's policy on internment had been reversed.

Of all the people featuring in the entire *Dunera* saga, none had a more extraordinary role than this Jewish civilian, accorded military rank to facilitate his extraordinary mission.

Physically and in other ways Julian Layton was larger than life. He came from a rich and influential family, known throughout Europe for their work among Jewish refugees.

In October 1940, the government issued a white paper which formalised the release of thousands of those interned in the general round-up, who were now free to assist the war effort.

Like Chamberlain, Layton arrived in Australia brandishing his white paper. A scene in *The Dunera Boys* shows him being fobbed off with questions about his laundry, and this basically is what occurred.

After showing the internees his document, Layton returned to Sydney and Canberra to take up the fight for their release. Other groups and individuals also came to their aid, notably the Australian Student Christian Movement, the Religious Society of Friends (Quakers), and Anglican Bishop Venn Pilcher. These groups also provided textbooks, pens and pencils, enabling younger internees to matriculate within the camp.

Meanwhile, with Layton still lobbying, a compromise was offered. Basically this was that Australia would release the detainees if Britain organised ships to send them home, and physically provided the escorts. The scheme foundered, apparently because transport was not available.

As consolation, there was good news on another front. Because of the unsuitable climate at Hay, the 'boys' were to be transferred to Tatura, near Shepparton. Not only was the climate far more agreeable, but there were opportunities to work outside the camp. In this way several Dunera Boys became hop pickers.

A scheme was also announced whereby fit detainees were offered a chance to return to Britain. There was a catch in it. It entailed joining the British Army's Pioneer Corps, the same regiment (the only one to take non-British nationals) to which most of their oppressors had belonged.

Several accepted the offer, which would ensure returning to England and liberty. Some of those who joined the Pioneers later transferred to other regiments for Intelligence and active duties. Some were killed in action. At least two Dunera Boys were taken prisoner – this time in British Army uniform[7] – and experienced captivity once again.

Meanwhile, Major Layton, undeterred, continued to bombard British and Australian authorities, surfacing again with another offer – this time too good to refuse. The Dunera Boys who volunteered would be released *and* enlisted into the Australian Army.[8]

'A DEPLORABLE AND REGRETTABLE MISTAKE'

According to historian and academic, Paul Bartrop, who has written widely about the topic,[9] claims that the British and Australian governments acted 'unjustly' in regard to victims of Nazism need to be seen in a historical context.

'In 1940, the British Government panicked, within the context of the time quite reasonably. Much of Europe was under German occupation. Infiltrators and fifth columnists, some of them planted years before, had helped bring this about. Britain now had 60000 refugees, technically enemy aliens, some of whom, it was thought, were security risks. There was no time for a proper assessment. The Prime Minister, Winston Churchill, issued the order, "Collar the lot".'

This explanation did not then, and does not now, cut much ice with those affected. Henry Lippmann says: 'We always regarded ourselves as anti-Nazis. Our interests were British interests.'

It should be stressed that public opinion in England supported the British Government's policies. For weeks before it acted, newspapers published strident editorials, suggesting, virtually, that every 'foreigner' was a fifth columnist.[10] Australian public opinion endorsed Churchill's line concerning the internment of aliens – provided it was temporary – as a reluctant duty in support of the war effort.

Interestingly, when the British Government did as the newspapers bid, and the first shock waves started to erupt, virtually all of Fleet Street demanded the practices be reversed.

As the threat of an invasion diminished, internment – let alone transportation – of lesser categories of enemy aliens was no longer deemed necessary. With the war still in progress, Churchill himself, responding to complaints by the National Council for Civil Liberties and other bodies, was to call the *Dunera* episode 'a deplorable and regrettable mistake'.

When the war ended slightly under half[11] of the Dunera Boys accepted an offer of citizenship and permanent residency from the Australian Government. Two Queensland RSL branches condemned the offer as 'disgraceful', complaining of 'enemies' 'queue jumping'.

A 100-year ban on the release of certain material relevant to the *Dunera* issue is still in force in Britain, and has handicapped researchers. However, much useful information has been released by the Australian National Archives, and was helpful in the preparation of this book.

FROM DUNERA TO NUREMBURG
Bill Oakfield, then still Werner Oppenheim, was one of those who took the 'Pioneer option'. He was inducted into the British Army

at Huyton – the same base where so many of his friends were first interned.

'We had to take the oath of allegiance: "I swear to bear true allegiance to His Majesty, the King, his heirs and successors." One inductee (not a Dunera Boy) was unable to speak English so the officer conducting the ceremony got impatient and made him repeat the oath in a mixture of German and Yiddish.'

Basic training was performed at Ilfracombe, Devon. He recalls a certain corporal (not a Dunera Boy), who, 'unable to forget that he had owned a café in Vienna, when saluting an officer, also bowed down at the waist at the same time'.

In 1943 rules were changed to allow those deemed suitable to volunteer for combat units. Bill undertook infantry training,[12] but hurt his knee and was sent to an Artillery training camp in Yorkshire. This led to an invitation to join the Jewish Brigade, which was then fighting in Italy.

The end of the war did not mean an immediate end to Bill's military service. He became a translator at the Nuremberg Trials. 'I arrived there in December 1945, and was plunged into the most harrowing experience of my life. I had just found out from a friend of my mother's, who survived Theresienstadt, that my parents had been transported to Auschwitz in September 1944 and had not been heard of since.'

He found himself in court facing down Goering, Kaltenbrunner, Streicher and other Nazi thugs. He can still hear in his mind the sombre voice of the president of the court as he pronounced the sentence of death over many of the accused.

He was happy to receive orders to return to England for demobilisation at the end of October 1946. 'The train steamed out of the station just as the blood-red sun was setting over the accursed city of Nuremberg. At last I was able to look forward to a normal life after the most terrible seven years of the 20th century.'[13]

16
INVOLUNTARY MIGRANTS

'My brother and I were taken, I don't know why, possibly because our school was only 15 miles from the coast. It was Sunday morning during term time.'

'Ossi' Veit Von Wolkenstein

Count Oswald Veit Von Wolkenstein – 'Ossi' to family and friends – was 16 when taken from the well-known English public school, Ampleforth, with his older brother, Christopher, after Mass in the school chapel.

'A policeman just walked up and said, "I'm sorry. You've got to come with me." I did as I was told. It was a shock. I don't know if you can blame anybody.'

According to another version of the story,[1] the policeman left without taking the two boys, instructing them to report to the police station later in the day. They cycled to the station, left their bikes outside the door and did not emerge – other than as prisoners – again.

It was an abrupt downturn for boys whose lives had begun with silver spoons. Oswald, who dropped the 'Von' in deference to Aussie egalitarianism, was born in Vienna on 8 April 1924; the second of five sons of Fortunat Graf Zu Wolkenstein-Rodenegg (*Graf* is a title roughly equivalent to Earl), and his Italian wife, Margit Locatelli. The family had two castles, the main one at Rodenegg, now part of Italy.

The countess died in 1932, when 'Ossi' was eight. His father, a government Minister, wrapped himself in his work, gradually falling foul of pro-Nazi elements, who were then emerging. Like the Von

Trapp family, with whom they are sometimes compared, the older man formed a family musical group – Oswald's role was to play the flute.

In March 1938, a few weeks before Oswald's 14th birthday, came the *Anschluß* – the union of Germany with Austria. His father, who did not wish to see his sons in the Hitler Youth or serving in the German Army, decided to quit the country. He did so, in July, taking his sons with him. The group travelled to Britain via Italy, to which they had valid tourist visas, and Yugoslavia.

In Britain they were given refugee status, their sponsor being the historian and historical philosopher, Arnold Toynbee. Through Toynbee, all five sons found places at top-drawer English Catholic boarding schools; Oswald and Christopher going to the Benedictine college, Ampleforth, and the other three to the rival Jesuit-run Stonyhurst. The separation would unexpectedly influence their lives.

The decision to intern enemy aliens, in some cases followed by transportation, was carried out haphazardly. Though 'Ossi' and Chris were interned, their three younger brothers, at Stonyhurst, were untouched.

Incredibly, their father, who should have been interned, was left totally free. In a scenario of classic comedy, he was invited to do 'war work'; first as a butler – surely the most well-bred gentleman's gentleman of all times – and then in a munitions factory.

'Ossie' and Chris Wolkenstein were not the only schoolboys to be interned and transported to Australia like the convicts of old.

Lothar Markiewicz, also 16, had a similar experience – in his case whilst a boarder at Sherborne School, Dorset.

To Lothar's young eyes the place 'seemed more like an institution than an educational establishment, with its ancient buildings, archaic rules and spartan life'.

He soon adapted to the regimen, but a problem arose during holidays. Lothar, unlike other boys, had nowhere to go. The organisation which brought him to England had a 'getting-to-know-you' scheme whereby refugees were welcomed as house guests.

Arrangements were made for him to participate in this, spending ten days or so with one family, then moving on to another.

Sadness clouded what should have been happy occasions. As Lothar tells it: 'There was no heavy wartime activity anywhere and yet, whilst staying with one kind family, they were advised by the War Office that their son had been killed in action. However much I tried to convince myself that it was not my fault, deep down inside me there was a feeling of guilt that the country where I was born, brought up, nurtured and partly educated was responsible for what had now happened to these decent people.

'If that was not enough, exactly the same thing happened during my stay with another family. I felt there must be something evil inside me which brought about a situation like that not once but twice. I must say that both families were as nice and kind to me after they had received the shocking news as they had been before.'

For this particular newcomer there was greater turbulence in store. On 10 May 1940, while lessons were in progress, he was summoned to the headmaster's study. 'Markie, they have it in for you; they think you are a spy!' said the headmaster, Canon Ross Wallace, a man who exuded joviality in sometimes inappropriate circumstances.

The headmaster continued in similar vein. 'They're coming to collect you tomorrow at 11 o'clock. Just a formality, nothing to worry about. You'll be back by the end of the week. Get matron to get you a clean pair of pyjamas; take a toothbrush and whatever else you need for a night or two. No point in taking more than a few essentials!'

The next morning, as arranged, a police car drew up by the quadrangle. Lothar still recalls every detail. 'At the windows of the classrooms I saw countless faces staring out, as both driver and escort came out of the car, saluted me, one of them opening the door for me to get in; at the same time carrying my little case for me and sitting himself beside me. Both men called me "Sir".'

The police treated him well, but events took a turn for the worse when he was transferred to a holding cell in Dorchester prison. The youth's arrival coincided with that of troops rescued from Dunkirk. 'They were in a terrible state; I quite believed the prison officer who told me I was lucky to be in protective custody.'

Within weeks of being taken into custody, Lothar, together with 'Ossi' and Chris Wolkenstein, were on their way to Australia. The voyage on the *Dunera* was followed by the shared experiences of life in the Hay and Tatura camps.

All three boys had their internment cut short through help from different quarters. Being Catholic – a minority among the internees – and still of school age, the situation of the two Wolkensteins aroused the attention of Father Walter Koenig, a Jesuit priest who was a fellow internee. Father Koenig wrote to the Archbishop of Melbourne, Daniel Mannix, who pulled strings to arrange their early release.[2]

On 12 January 1942 'Ossi' (still only 17) and Chris were collected from Tatura by the Jesuit provincial, and driven to Xavier College, Melbourne, where Mannix – now officially their guardian – had arranged for them to complete their education. They were taken to see him the same night. Oswald wrote in his diary: 'He was very kind, tall and has white hair. Went to bed and slept very well in a decent bed again.'

Lothar Markiewicz had even better luck. An English visitor, related to the person who had arranged Lothar's sponsorship to Sherborne, heard about his unusual situation and notified Eleanor Rathbone,[3] Independent MP for the Combined English Universities, who had a reputation for helping underdogs.

Rathbone, who enjoyed a good 'stir', raised the subject in the House of Commons, telling the House (which included at least three Old Boys of the school in question) that a boy from a top-drawer school had been nabbed as a Fifth Columnist (traitor) – 'he probably doesn't understand the word' – and transported to the colonies.

Her presentation was effective. Within days the British Government officially sought his freedom. He was released on

29 September 1941 – three months before the Wolkensteins – and returned to Britain on board the *Stirling Castle*.

WEEKEND IN THE SAN

Back at Sherborne, the headmaster, true to form, treated his absence like a weekend in the sanatorium: 'Good, you're back. Now you can get on with your studies.'

All three boys were to have interesting futures. At the end of the war 'Ossi' took a range of Melbourne University courses, but – according to the man himself – was 'more interested in revelling', and did not advance very far. He worked for a radar equipment firm, motor-car distributor and as a bank clerk before returning to Austria to rejoin his father, who was engaged in post-war reconstruction, and other family members.

In Austria he found work in wool classing and processing, becoming a successful wool buyer, and later wool futures broker, upon returning to Australia some four years later. Meanwhile, his brother Christopher became a successful medical practitioner in Canada.

In 1959 Oswald Wolkenstein married Jacqueline Morath, a member of a well-known Mosman (Sydney) sporting family. On their honeymoon he decided to call on Archbishop Mannix, and to introduce his bride. An aide said: 'You can have five minutes.' The meeting lasted three hours. The couple have two sons, a daughter and four Australian grandchildren.

In 1967 'Ossi' changed careers once again, becoming an insurance representative for the AMP Society. He was still 'in harness' in that role – albeit on a part-time basis – some 36 years later.

An avid sportsman, and follower of Australian Rules Football, 'Ossi' twice broke his self-imposed rule about not using his title. The first was when he wanted to see his beloved Richmond play in an important game. Finding that tickets were sold out, he gave his full name and 'handle', to be immediately offered two excellent seats, moreover without charge. He tried the same ruse, successfully, at a boxing match. Then conscience got the better of him.

For Lothar Markiewicz, like the Wolkenstein brothers, the future was to prove eventful. In July 1942, six months after his return to Britain, Lothar sat for the School Certificate, achieving the required five credits to obtain matriculation exemption.

The war brought mixed tidings concerning his parents, who were Jewish. His father died in the Holocaust. His mother survived, under the noses of the Gestapo, by moving from house to house in Berlin, assisted by the mainly Communist underground movement.

In 1950 Lothar married Margot Berndt, a fellow refugee. Lothar himself pursued a successful career in business. In 1981, their son, Michael, emigrated to Australia. In 1993, some 50 years after his first visit on the *Dunera*, Lothar returned with his wife to live in Australia.

He now states: 'Looking back on it, as a boy of 16 years of age, I considered it all an adventure. I could truly say I had been round the world entirely at His Majesty's expense.' The couple, who became good friends of the Wolkensteins, have three Australian grandchildren.

MODEST ARISTOCRAT

Oswald Wolkenstein died at his Sydney home on 17 May 2003. He was a warm-hearted, perpetually smiling man who enjoyed a beer and a joke. Given the contradictions in his life and circumstances this was just as well.

Unlike some other Dunera Boys, this modest aristocrat never showed anger either about the cruelties inflicted aboard ship – which resulted in several courts martial – or the indignities of incarceration. 'I was young,' he said, 'and looked upon it as an adventure.'

His one grouse was about the 'friendly enemy alien' tag. As he once told me: 'Friendly? Yes. Alien? I suppose so. Enemy? That's a bit rich. I don't like that at all.'

'BOARDING SCHOOL WITHOUT BULLIES'

Hans Marcus has good reason to remember his 18th birthday – 2 July 1940. His father was a passenger on the *Arandora Star*, sunk on that day with great loss of life.

Hans was in Liverpool, where he would shortly board the *Dunera*. 'They asked for volunteers for an overseas transport, and I was happy to go. I volunteered for the *Dunera*, thinking it was going to Canada.

'We were told that one transport had been torpedoed and sunk, but were not given its name. I said, "Well, lightning doesn't strike twice. If one ship was sunk, the next one will probably get through".'

He did not then know of his father's death, nor that he had been on board the doomed ship. 'The thought hadn't occurred to me. Dad was interned in Paignton, in Devon, and he had written to me two or three times from there. I didn't know he had been transferred to Liverpool and from there to the *Arandora Star*.'

He remained in ignorance even when the *Dunera* sailed, and was joined by survivors from his father's ship.[4] He discovered the truth after receiving a letter from his mother (who was not interned), that was awaiting his arrival at Hay.

Hans, a youth of happy-go-lucky disposition, had finished school the previous summer and had begun architectural studies at London's Regent Street Polytechnic.

Hans and his parents, who were originally from Düsseldorf, had left Germany voluntarily in 1933 at the start of the Nazi era. His father was not a religious Jew and had been in partnership, as a solicitor, with an Aryan. The latter had Nazi leanings, and 'Father realised, early on, that they were up to no good'. The family moved first to Holland, then, after a little over three years, to England.

When the war broke out, Hans and his parents moved to Wales – a kind of 'voluntary evacuation', as he calls it. Then, 'when nothing happened,[5] before the bombing started, we came back to London'.

Soon after their return, his father was interned. Hans assumed correctly that his own turn would quickly follow. 'Whether sooner or later, it didn't bother me. I had been to a boarding school, Tonbridge, and I thought internment was just another boarding school without bullies.'

In a book of memoirs, *Their Service Our Heritage*, published by Hurstville Council, Hans Marcus expanded on this view. 'One of the few things I am in debt to my English public school is that they made both internment and the joys of the *Dunera* a lot easier to live through ... I'd been in the officer training corps, boy scouts and all this sort of thing; an English boarding school is practically as rough in some ways as the ship.'[6]

When the police came he went to a glass showcase in the dining room and removed 'a few knick-knacks of sentimental value' and took them with him into captivity. One was an 18th century leather notebook with inscriptions from family members, some of them in Yiddish. Another was a miniature bronze baby shoe. Curiously, despite the *Dunera* guards' reputation for thieving, the items were not taken, and remained in his possession. The notebook is now in the rare books collection of Sydney's Mitchell Library.

For social reasons, the boy had been baptised, and raised, albeit nominally, as a Lutheran. On arrival at Hay, when it came to selection of sleeping quarters, Hans found himself in the 'Catholic' hut – his bunk was above that of Chris Wolkenstein – about 30 per cent of whose occupants were non-Catholic.

'I don't know how I got into that hut. I was a mixture of Lutheran, in which I was baptised, and Church of England, in which I was confirmed at Tonbridge. I didn't know very much about Judaism and found the more Orthodox and narrow-minded section of it unappealing.'

The Catholics had a choir which practised regularly. 'There was nothing to do in the camp so you went to everything. I remember going to Communist lectures. They were the most dominant group in our camp parliament. Some of them went to East Germany after the war.'

Whilst older people found internment stressful, Hans Marcus solved it by applying his theory about 'boarding school'. In his imagination the guards were 'prefects' and the sleeping huts 'dormitories'.

Early in his incarceration Hans took up calligraphy as a hobby. 'I wrote a letter as neatly as I could and addressed it to the sergeant-major of the guard company, who happened to be a nice bloke. I asked him whether there was any work to be done in writing things out in decent script. They didn't have too many typewriters in those days, and of course there were no computers.'

The result was that Hans obtained a job in the guard room, which was outside the camp confines, creating the impression of greater freedom. 'The people I worked with in the guard room were from the last war. They were elderly, but had an Australian sense of humour and I enjoyed their company.' It meant I only had to be inside the camp proper at night time, when I could read books or go to concerts and lectures. As a result I didn't go through the mental disturbances which many people exhibited.'

Hans later joined the 8th Australian Employment Company and, when the war was over, opted, like many others, to remain in Australia rather than return to Britain.

'I suppose I wasn't that friendly to English ideas, especially after they interned my father, which led to his death. And I decided I wasn't on very good terms with my mother. I had been in the Australian Army for four-and-a-half years, and I had acquired a girlfriend while on leave in Melbourne.

'I had other friends – some Australian, some English, some refugees who had come here before the war. All in all, I had more connections in Australia than in England, so I decided to stay here and give it a go.'

Study benefits were an additional factor. 'Because we had been in the Army we got government assistance under the post-war reconstruction scheme to go to university and receive other higher education. So I commenced my architecture studies again.'

Having recently turned 80, Hans Marcus combines a quiet, thoughtful personality with a droll sense of humour. He has a photograph of the *Dunera* in his bedroom, and reflects periodically on how the one ship changed his life.

He is aware of the 'apologies' given by the sending organisations to former British child migrants and of the return air tickets they have received to be reunited with relatives and family in Britain.

He has suggested, half-seriously, that the British Government might do likewise in respect of the surviving Dunera Boys. If this is impractical, perhaps a letter from the Queen or Prime Minister, similar to that sent to people on their 50th wedding anniversaries or when they become 100 years old.

The Dunera Boys are now part of the Australian mainstream. Indeed, the very name evokes reactions of warmth and affection. A few years ago I attended a function at the Australian National Maritime Museum to honour migrants who had arrived by sea.

The British diplomat, who was guest of honour, made special mention of the Dunera Boys, their role as 'involuntary' migrants, and the part they had played in building a modern Australia.

17
A SHARED EXPERIENCE

'Welcome to the Dunera crowd. We're neither special, nor extraordinary, it's just that our experiences are extraordinary.'

Henry Lippmann, Dunera Boy

Mention the words 'Dunera Boys' at certain social gatherings and the name Henry Lippmann will be uttered in the same breath. The convenor of the Sydney Dunera 'Old Boys' reunions – the main association is run from Melbourne[1] – and the founder of the quarterly *Dunera News*, he admits that 'keeping the flame alive' is important to him.

I met Henry Lippmann for the first time at a house party in the 1980s. Extending a hand in greeting, he uttered the words quoted above.

Words like 'boys' and 'crowd' have overtones of club, clan, or brotherhood. Not all former internees advertise themselves in this way. Indeed, some never want to hear the name 'Dunera'.[2]

According to Henry Lippmann: 'It depends whom you are talking to. We have had a shared experience. Some people want to run away from it, others want to come closer to it, and to be more aware of it. I belong to the ones that are aware of it, indeed are very conscious of it and have drawn certain conclusions from it.

'At various times we have all wanted to get away from it. From the fact that we were once persecuted for our identity, for having been opposed to a regime, for our race and religion. That experience you can never forget, and you don't have to, though some have tried. They're running away from it, which I think is wrong.'

Lippmann was 17 when he arrived in England on 29 August 1939 – five days before war broke out. Two days earlier he had said goodbye to his parents and younger brother on the platform of the Charlottenburg railway station in Berlin. It was the last he saw of them. 'I had no idea that I would never see them again.'

He was one of 100 youths, who arrived in Britain under the auspices of a trade school run by the Jewish educational organisation, ORT.[3] The organisation, founded in Tsarist Russia, aimed to teach young people a trade or profession that would enable them to earn a living wherever they might find themselves, without resorting to charity. In 1930s Europe, amidst a resurgence of anti-Semitism, the emphasis was on acquiring technical skills

Having been booted out of Nazi Germany, the school was in the process of re-establishing itself, with British Government approval, in the north of England. Five ORT teachers travelled with the boys. Sadly, the manager of ORT Berlin, Werner Simon, who had organised their visas, chose not to accompany them, believing that he had unfinished work in Germany. Somehow, he kept the office going until 1941, when it was closed by the Gestapo. Werner Simon, his wife and small child, were sent to the Theresianstadt concentration camp, where it is assumed they perished.

After a few nights at Kitchener Camp, near Dover, the youths and their teachers found lodgings in a large Leeds hostel, where all went well for several months. Then came Dunkirk and a shift in official attitudes. 'I think the government's view was, "We don't know who these people are, so we'd better intern them".'

Thirty[4] of the original 100 were subsequently 'transported' to Australia on the *Dunera*.[5] During his first year in England, Lippmann was still receiving letters, via the Red Cross, from his parents. 'They were living miserably, but they were alive.' The correspondence continued, even after his internment, through a censored POW service. After about a year the letters stopped. He received a message via the Red Cross that they had been moved into the Warsaw Ghetto.

Henry assumed that they had died there – perhaps following the famous uprising. (Some 30 years later he discovered from a West German Government document, that his parents and brother, Kurt, had died in the Trawniki extermination camp.)[6]

On the *Dunera* Henry suffered the deprivations, described by others, and had several personal items stolen. Ever the gentleman, he prefers not to dwell on these and other acts of misconduct, which he considers untypical of British officers and military men.

He was, and still is, annoyed that internees were considered, at least initially, to be little different from Nazis. 'We were refugees. We regarded ourselves as anti-Nazis. Our interests were British interests.'

Like others in his age group, Henry Lippmann was later able to exchange confinement in Hay and Tatura camps for military service in the 8th Australian Employment Company. He is proud of this period in his life and still remembers his service number V377661. Some years ago I suggested at a reunion that former members of this unusual corps should seek permission to march in Sydney's Anzac Day parade. Henry's hand shot up in agreement. Other hands stayed firmly down.[7] He has instead joined the National Association of Jewish Ex-Servicemen (AJEX), of which he is a board member.

THE REAL HURT

On 17 November 1994 a plaque was unveiled at Darling Harbour honouring the Dunera Boys. After the ceremony an onlooker complimented Lippmann on the way – 54 years earlier – the 'boys' had withstood their ordeal. He later told me: 'It was nothing being a Dunera Boy. It was losing my family which hurt.'

In times of loss, mementos of loved ones are important. In 1949, while he was working for the Sydney businessman, John Lewinnek,[8] Henry was delighted, and a little surprised, to receive a letter from a woman in Germany. In his own words:

'My uncle, who was a banker in Berlin before the war, had a secretary, a non-Jewish lady, with whom we never had any problems.

She lived close to our place in the west of Berlin. When my parents were notified that they would be taken from Berlin and transported to the east, they feared, correctly, that they might lose their lives.

'They contacted this lady and asked if she would be willing to keep for the duration of the war certain pieces of jewellery, which they wanted me to have as their son. And she did just that.

'Mr Lewinnek, who was a good friend as well as my employer, visited Germany on business, as well as on Jewish communal affairs, and was himself originally from Berlin. I asked him if he would be kind enough to call on this lady, and he agreed.

'He found her quite easily – a fine, decent type of person – and she gave him a parcel. He opened it and offered her some item as a reward for her good deed. She took something small; I don't recall what it was.

'When Mr Lewinnek came back to Australia and gave me the parcel I was in tears. It was not the monetary value, but the sentimental value. There I was holding my parents' wedding rings. I was confronted with these items which had meant so much to them. They were the only things I had, after all these years, which had belonged to my parents.'

The story has an unhappy ending. 'I got married a year later and wore my father's wedding ring as my own. My son Michael was born, and then my younger son Eddie.'

One summer's day the family went to Bondi. 'We had a kind of small surfboard. I threw it down on the water with a bit of force. The ring slipped off my finger and fell into the sea and the sand. I dived down many times. I tried to keep my eyes open. It was hopeless. I remember I got out of the water and cried like a baby.'

BACK TO BERLIN

In the 1960s Henry and his wife, Julie, returned to Germany and re-visited the flat in Berlin where his parents had lived.

It was a bittersweet occasion. According to Henry: 'I had loved that place. I mean, you do not love only people; you love music, sounds, and other things. Even the smell on the stairs was familiar.

I rang the bell and this elderly man opened the door and said "Come in".

'I looked around and I was nearly crying. Julie knew how I felt. Here was my little brother and here was my grandmother and here was this and that; it was all very vivid. I could see it all in my imagination.

'The man who lived in the place was very nice; indeed he had no need to let us in. But there was that degree of unease. I thought to myself, "They are of the right age group. Did they have anything to do with the atrocities?". There's always that suspicion. Who are they? What did they do, and how did they behave?

'But I go further than that. I think, what would I have done if I were not Jewish? And I have to tell you the answer is not good. I'll give you an example. I attended a good school, a *Gymnasium* (high school), and one day they showed a film about the Hitler Youth.[9]

'It had good actors, and was well done. The theme was the beautiful things in this scout type organisation for the Fatherland, the Führer and the German race. I was drawn towards this glamorous outfit. Of course, young people are most impressionable and are easily misled. I'm glad now that, as a Jew, I could not have joined.'

APOLOGY

Henry Lippmann and others[10] have suggested in the past that the British Government 'apologise' for transporting the Dunera Boys. In 1987 he proposed that the Old Boys' association write to Mrs Thatcher[11] about it. Others on the committee disagreed.

His view at the time was: 'If somebody is imprisoned wrongly he has the right to be exonerated. Not that I personally suffered. But it would be a nice gesture.'[12]

The 50th anniversary of the arrival in Sydney of 'the first convict ship since penal days' was celebrated on 6 September 1990.[13] Celebrations were organised by both the Sydney and Melbourne committees, and included a return to the original internment site at Hay.[14]

The shire council, which now considers the Dunera Boys almost as 'family', thoughtfully provided a few strands of barbed wire, with which to decorate the tables. Actually, there is not much to see. Only a part of the foundations remain, together with a former observation tower, rebuilt to serve the racecourse.

The consensus view is that by and large Australia has been good to the Dunera Boys.

Lippmann himself shares this view. At the golden jubilee celebration at the Australian National Maritime Museum, Lippmann told the assembled gathering: 'We didn't intend to come here, we had no wish to come here, we came to an unknown destination. We didn't receive a terrific welcome at the time. But as it happened we stayed here, many of us served in the Australian Army, and we were accepted by the Australian Government. Fifty years have gone by; the majority of our people have passed away already. Those who remain welcome the opportunity to say "thank you" in the presence of the Governor General.'[15]

BETTER THE DUNERA THAN A DEATH CAMP
Henry James (then Heinz Jacobius) came to England as part of the group of 100 ORT youths mentioned previously. Like Henry Lippmann, he was 17. He recalls the crowds at the station and the sense of imminent danger. He had to board the train by climbing through a window.

His first night in Britain was spent at the Rowton House hostel in the poor London district of Whitechapel. A bed for the night cost one shilling.[16] The view from the window was 'like a scene from Dickens'. He and the other new arrivals then moved to the relocated ORT school in Leeds. The hostel was run in military, no-nonsense style by a strict, but kindly man, whose list of 'rules' dominated daily conduct.

An introductory note to the list stated: 'Although you have all passed the [immigration] Tribunal, you are, in the eyes of the Leeds Christian people, members of an enemy country at war with England.

Do nothing at any time, to arouse the slightest hostility, and do not attract attention.'

The 'rules' themselves, which say much about prevailing community attitudes, are printed in the Appendix on pages 269-71.

Normal educational studies were combined with apprenticeship as a mechanic and toolmaker. What seemed like the start of an orderly life was interrupted when plain clothes police contacted Henry at his workplace.

'The policemen were very polite as the English usually are. They said: "Would you mind going back to the hostel to collect your things." They didn't rush me. They took me in a black limousine to Leeds Town Hall, where I found others in a similar situation. We were led away again. This time there were police in uniform, buses and tommies with their bayonets. I suppose they were worried we might run away.

'They took us to an internment camp at Knavesmire racecourse in York. After about two weeks we were taken to Liverpool and from there by ferry to Douglas in the Isle of Man. The British Government had commandeered all the hotels and boarding houses along the beach. We lived in the rooms upstairs and took our meals in the dining rooms. We had ocean views and it was quite pleasant. We almost forgot the guards and the barbed wire along the sea front.

'After another few weeks the officer in charge asked if we would like to join a transport to Canada. I thought about this. Maybe it would be wise to leave England at this time, so I volunteered.

'Back in Liverpool harbour I saw two big boats. I could see captured Luftwaffe people with their kit bags boarding one of them. The other was the *Dunera*. Of course, I did not know then that the destination would not be Canada.

'The guards treated us roughly, but as a young fellow I didn't take it too seriously. Better to be a prisoner on the *Dunera* than in a Nazi extermination camp.' He laughs at the comparison.

GOOD GERMANS

Though he lost his parents in the Holocaust, Henry James was aware, more than most, that there were 'good' Germans who did not conform to the anti-Semitic behaviour, as well as Germans who conformed.

When his parents' business collapsed, through Nazi discriminatory policies, a woman whom he remembers as Frau Schulze, offered food and accommodation when others were ideologically opposed, or perhaps 'too terrified' to be seen to be helping Jews. She later advised him – as did the village postman in a discreet fashion – of his parents' arrest and transportation to the Warsaw Ghetto.

Rather more dramatic was the action of a teacher at the state school he had attended until the age of 15, when he quit to attend an establishment for Jews only.

This teacher, Herr Lehmann, an older man, was unfazed by the Nazis. He was not only bold but had a liking for black humour. 'When the Nazis came to power we had racial lessons about the superiority of the Aryan race. They were depicted as blond, blue-eyed, Nordic types. Studies were made of the human face, with charts and diagrams to show the desired type.

'Herr Lehmann, knowing full well that I was Jewish, but also that I had fair, wavy hair, called me to the front of the class and used me as an example, saying, "This is Heinz Jacobius. He's got many of the desired features".'

The same teacher took the boys swimming in a nearby lake. Local Nazis erected a sign saying 'Jews forbidden'. It was the day of a swimming carnival where prizes were to be awarded.

As Henry tells it: 'I saw the sign and hesitated. The teacher called out: "Forget about that, just come in!". I swam in a race and came second. This was embarrassing because the prize was a big picture of Hitler. He felt he couldn't give that to me, so he gave me the first prize, which was a book. The real winner got the picture of Hitler.'

In 1988 Henry James re-visited Halbe, about 50 km from Berlin, and had his photo taken, with another former classmate, in his old school. Herr Lehmann's daughter still lives in the village.

No 'Shame Ship'

If an apology is in order for the *Dunera* internees, perhaps their ship, too, deserves an 'apology' for its badge of shame.

HMT (Hired Military Transport) *Dunera* was initially a passenger liner, specialising in educational cruises, built for the British India Company. Though not a 'classy' vessel, it was not a 'broken-down old tub', as some accounts maintain.

At the beginning of World War II it was converted into a troop carrier. Officially it could hold 1600 people. On the voyage to Australia it held some 50 per cent more.

After taking internees to Australia, the Dunera accredited itself well in several areas of combat. It took invasion forces to North Africa, Sicily and France, occupation troops to Japan, and participated in the colonial wars in Cyprus and Malaya. In 1960, the *Dunera* reverted to its original use as an educational cruise ship. It was finally sold to Spanish interests and broken up in 1967.

18
LABOURERS IN UNIFORM

'He spent 24 hours a day looking after our interests, sharing in a deep personal sense our triumphs and failures. He was shocked that we were considered "enemy" aliens, and fought to get it changed to "friendly" status.'

Horst Jacobs on the Commanding Officer of the 8th AEC,
Capt. Edward Broughton

They were invited to fight for Australia – but were not allowed on combat duties. Conditional upon release from internment (in 1942) was an agreement whereby Dunera Boys of military age, other than those repatriated for war service in Britain, could join a specially created military unit, the 8th Australian Employment Company (AEC).

It was nicknamed 'Enjoyment Company'. Certainly, it was an unusual entity – the only military body exclusively made up of 'foreigners'. They wore Diggers' hats, dressed and drilled like other soldiers (substituting shovels for rifles), but were, in effect 'labourers in uniform'. The youngest were barely out of their teens.[1] The oldest had served in World War I.

The 8th AEC had about 700 members. Strictly speaking, they were volunteers. About 50 of the recruits (like the talented musician, Werner Baer) had come to Australia via Singapore and other threatened regions of the Far East. The great majority were Dunera Boys.[2]

'Navvies' they may have been, but well-educated. Certainly, no military unit in Australia, and possibly the world, had a higher percentage of accountants, lawyers, professors, *Herr Doktors* and other men of academic distinction. They may be forgiven if their drill was lousy and discipline not up to scratch.[3]

Military orders and conversation when on duty were conducted in English. Off duty it was more difficult. 'Among ourselves we would fall back into German. Of course, we wouldn't do it on buses and trams.'

Somewhat unkindly, the regulations barred promotion beyond the rank of sergeant.[4] Nor, officially, could men be transferred to other formations.[5] To some this irked. According to Henry Lippmann: 'Officially, we had the same rights and duties as any other Australian soldiers, but it was difficult to transfer to any other unit, and certainly not to a fighting unit. This was odd, because we, of all people, had a reason to oppose Hitler.'

There was pride in service. According to one former member: 'We worked on wharves, railways, shifting supplies. That was our job, we did it well.' Said another, lightheartedly: 'In the Army six people do the work of one. At least it kept us fit.'

In what some saw as a contradiction, men who were not allowed to carry arms (though some did so on sentry duty) spent much of their days loading bombs on trucks.

The existence of the 8th AEC was not widely known. Members met with reactions from surprise to cordiality when 'discovered' by soldiers from other units.[6] An article about them in an army magazine said: 'Although these people speak with funny accents, and you may think they are Germans, they've been through hell and are decent blokes and they are on our side.'

EDWARD BROUGHTON

The Company was commanded by an officer even more unusual than his men. He was Captain Edward Renata Mugunga Broughton, a Maori half-caste, known to his family as 'Tip'. He was thought to be one of only two 'coloured' officers in the Australian Army.[7]

His background is interesting. His father was an English (or Scottish) farmer, with a holding, Ngapuke, near Hastings. He was descended, on his mother's side, from one of the chieftains who had signed the Treaty of Waitangi, in 1840.

His paternal grandparents had considerable wealth, but the fortune was lost in circumstances which are unclear.

Educated at the pukka Wanganui Collegiate School, Edward Broughton quit at 16, and by falsifying his age, fought with the New Zealand Rifles in the Boer War. After discharge, he returned briefly to farming, later becoming private secretary to the Chief Judge of the Native Land Court in Wellington.

He married a Maori woman, about whom little is known, and (in 1908) they had a son. In World War I Broughton re-enlisted, serving with the Maori Battalion at Gallipoli. He served with distinction in France and was mentioned in despatches and commissioned. He was discharged with the rank of Captain. His movements between the wars are a mystery. It is thought he came to Australia, living in both Victoria and NSW, working as a professional punter or bookmaker.

In 1940, by now a widower, Broughton again saw military service. This time he reduced his age by 16 years to join the 2nd AIF in Melbourne as a private soldier. He was promoted to Corporal, posted to the 2nd 14th Australian Infantry Battalion, where (after three months) his deception was discovered. He was transferred to the CMF, and regained his commission. Somehow he wangled his way back into the 'real' Army, was promoted to Captain and given charge of the embryonic Employment Company.

He loved his men and they loved him. According to Mike Sondheim, president of the Hay–Tatura Association: 'He was a father to us, especially the younger ones who by now had guessed what fate had befallen their parents. He knew everybody's first name and personal details, and was concerned about their welfare.' He told one recruit: 'You're a musician, I want to save your hands.'

Hans Marcus recalls a young member of his troop fronting up to Broughton and asking for a weekend pass. The conversation went something like this:

Broughton: Is it to go out with your girlfriend?

Soldier: Yes.

Broughton: Is she married?

Soldier: Yes.

Broughton: In that case, no leave.

Life in the 8th AEC was not all slog. The unit had talented artists and musicians. (Sgt) Kurt Sternberg, already a film producer in Germany, re-created a camp show, *Snow White 53828*, first performed at Tatura. Such was the standard that it had several repeats at the Union Theatre, Melbourne, with an appreciative top brass among the audience.

The company was based at Camp Pell, in Royal Park, an inner Melbourne suburb. The 'Boys' now had freedom to go into the big city.

Henry Lippmann recalls: 'The lights in Melbourne were dimmed, but the atmosphere was amazing. We were shy, the feeling of someone coming out of prison is a bit awkward. We were among women and girls, there was jazz music, Glenn Miller style bands, and everywhere soldiers on leave. It was like a carnival.

'I remember the first time I went out in uniform. I was very proud, but not very sure of myself. Some of the 'Boys' spoke very good English, but there was a language handicap. A strong accent would give us away. People would say, "My God, what kind of people are they?"'

DOUBLE DUTCH

Anxious to meet girls, Lippmann and others spent much of their time at dances. 'I approached one girl, she asked me where I was from and I said I was Dutch. "Oh," she said, "that's interesting, because my friend has just has just met another Dutchman, I'd like you to meet him." I protested furiously, but she pulled me over to the corner where that other supposed Dutchman was. It was another Dunera Boy.'

Their Commanding Officer had other charming idiosyncrasies. Younger members, in particular, were impressed by his spartan lifestyle. He liked to sleep in the open air and used a brick as a pillow. He wore a Private's rough serge uniform (with officer's pips) and rarely wore a tie.

Raised as a Catholic, he was fascinated by Jewish customs and ritual. He held synagogue parades on the Sabbath. 'They were not compulsory, but he made sure we all went.' When members of his 'flock' were married, he ensured he was a guest at the wedding.

The men under his command were uncertain what to call him, when off duty. Some chose the term 'Skipper', which seemed to reflect the right blend of respect and friendliness.

Horst Jacobs recalls: 'He was reasonably formal, we saluted and called him Sir. He had none of that ethnic or racial prejudice that was so common at that time. Outside the camp, anyone with an accent was immediately treated differently. He would have none of that and wouldn't tolerate it in any of his sergeants either.'

He had a sharp wit, demonstrated in an unconventional speech when one of his officers, an Australian Lieutenant, died. Wearing for a change a smartly pressed uniform and tie, he said a few words about the departed officer and concluded: 'He ate too much, he drank too much, he didn't exercise and now the angels have him.'

KAMARADEN

Broughton was also, according to former internee, Walter Pollak, a bit of a 'ham actor' and showman. Probably the most novel incident occurred when Broughton returned from inspecting a detachment on the Victorian–NSW border, ignored the 'English-only' rule and decided to address the troops in German.

Calling an elderly German-born NCO[8] by his side – a man who had been an officer in the Kaiser's Army – Broughton bellowed to the parade-ground throng: *'Ich bringe Ihnen Grüße von die* [sic] *Kameraden!'* (I bring you greetings from friends). Then turning to his companion: 'Correct, Sergeant Fischer?', at which point the elderly man clicked his heels and replied: 'Von *den* Kameraden, Sir.'

He played each part with panache, sometimes displaying an out-of-character insensitivity to the feelings of hapless subordinates. One day on the parade ground at Camp Pell he addressed the troops on a routine subject and ended with the words: '.... and anyone with the perspicacity of a grasshopper can see that this would not be helpful.'

He then turned round and looked at his Australian Sergeant-Major, a man by the name of Stone. 'Sergeant-Major, do you know what the word "perspicacity" means?'. The old Sar' Major, never a threat to Einstein, looked perplexed. 'No Sir! Can't say that I do.'

Broughton pointed to Henry Mayer (later a well-known Sydney academic).[9] 'Private Mayer, do you know what "perspicacity" means?' 'It means,' said Mayer, looking smug, 'the same as perspicuity or the power of perception.' The Captain turned back to the old warrior, his eyes scanning the heavens in typical Broughton fashion: 'Did you hear that, Sar' Major? And he is only a Private and a foreigner to boot.'

MISFIT

It is interesting to speculate, as many have, how a man like Broughton came to be given his unusual command. One theory is that the Army was embarrassed at having an officer who was (a) demonstrably brave, (b) of mixed race, (c) eccentric. In military terms he was a misfit.

According to this theory, what better solution than to put him in charge of other 'misfits' – German and Austrian Jews, until recently interned as 'enemy aliens'.

It is likely that his own racial tensions affected his approach to his duties. According to Lippmann: 'With hindsight, I think he needed us as we needed him.' Walter Pollak once heard him remark, casually and without rancour: 'It doesn't matter how many years I've been in this country and what I did for it; in the end I am, and will always remain, a bloody Maori.'

In May 1944, Edward Broughton was discharged prematurely from the army. Another CO was appointed. 'He thought he would make a Guards unit out of us but he wasn't very successful.'

Allied victory brought about the disbanding of the Employment Companies. It was generally considered that these 'foreigners' in Aussie uniforms had done a good job and earned their spurs.

Edward Broughton worked for a while in Darwin (apparently as civilian manager of the officers' mess), then settled in the Melbourne suburb of Middle Park. Here, he continued to be a part of the lives of the men formerly in his care. 'He wrote to us, followed our careers, came to our weddings and our children's bar mitzvahs.'

He was known as a person who could hold his grog. According to Hans Schaye: 'He could carry his liquor all right, even at 60. I learned what that means and to appreciate the line, "Not drunk is he, who from the floor, can rise again and drink once more".'

On 9 May 1955 he suffered a massive heart attack after swimming with the winter swimming club, Brighton Icebergers. He was attended by a local doctor – coincidentally a former Dunera Boy – but died the same day. A requiem mass was held at the Church of Our Lady of Mount Carmel, Middle Park.

The army has no testimonial archives to Captain Broughton. If anything, the records show him as a troublemaker. Yet 50 years on, grown men shed tears at the mention of his name. He was a father figure par excellence.

For over 35 years Edward Broughton lay buried in an unmarked grave, in the Catholic section of Fawkner Cemetery, near Melbourne. It was re-discovered in 1991. The 'Boys' of the 8th Australian Employment Company paid for a suitable plaque.

Mike Sondheim said in a statement of tribute: 'He was an extraordinarily sympathetic and understanding man. He had a very difficult task in dealing with a mob of people with different backgrounds, and helped us find our feet. We shall never forget him.'

Says Henry Lippmann: 'I was only 20, and had been for some years without my home and parents. It was heartening to have someone not just bossing you around but taking a personal interest. He made us feel like human beings again.'

A bust of Broughton, by the Melbourne sculptor, Karl Duldig, paid for by former members of his troop, is in the Australian War Memorial, Canberra. A replica[10] is in the Jewish Museum, Melbourne.

DUSTING OFF MEMORIES

At the end of the war, some 900 of the original *Dunera* internees returned to England and a similar number accepted permanent residency in Australia. About 150 went to other countries. There had been 13 deaths.

With peace restored, the Dunera Boys followed a variety of occupations. There were musicians, academics, an actor, judge, wharf labourer, butcher, author, sports coach, glamour photographer and an agricultural economics adviser to the Federal Government. Others followed technical trades and 'normal' occupations, becoming quiet achievers in various ways.[11]

In 1992 I accompanied Dunera Boys Mike Sondheim and Horst Jacobs on a visit to a regional office of the National Australian Archives, where they were allowed to inspect, for the first time, their personal files.

Mike, who was 23 when interned, was an engineering student, whose father was also interned. He was learning English with a view to joining his brother in the United States.

Blowing the dust off his file made the years roll back, and he was in Hay once again. He was interested to see that, 50 years on, his weight was unchanged. His name was originally Gunther. A sympathetic officer had told him: 'That's not a good name for you in wartime. Mike would be better.'

As a new arrival, he had worked on the baggage party, responsible for going through internees' luggage, recording the condition in which cases were found and where possible, returning items to their rightful owners. The report which he prepared was used against those involved in looting. Mike himself had lost a watch and minor valuables. Modest compensation was awarded. 'I think I got nine pounds.'

The file triggered other memories. Before internment he had lived in Richmond, Surrey, and had frequented a local pub, the Roebuck Hotel. At Hay he started a handball team, naming this and his sleeping hut after the hostelry.

Horst Jacobs, now a retired dental surgeon, arrived in Britain in 1937 in order to take up a scholarship at an English public school. Like Mike Sondheim, his father was interned also, and they had become separated.

Horst, like other internees, disliked the term 'enemy alien', the use of which – staring at him from his file – was a reminder of the offence. 'We were classified as refugees,' he says, 'in a category in which we could move around freely. Then all at once, without any tribunal or re-hearing, we were made enemy aliens. It was in response to a panic measure at that time, and it still grates.'

Opening further pages of his file, he saw his 'prisoner' number, 39827, and 'place of capture', Manchester. Personal effects are listed as 'chromium watch and suitcase'. There is a pencilled note in which he asks that information about him not be sent back to the German Government. In the same page on another file, a colleague had drawn a Union Jack. There's no doubting where loyalties of the Dunera internees lay!

V

THE VIENNA
MOZART BOYS' CHOIR

19
SINGING FOR THEIR SUPPER

The calendar, like a flick of the switch, sometimes determines fate. In the case of the Vienna Mozart Boys' Choir, a gap of a few days changed the course of several young lives for ever.

They were mere children, but their status was obscure. How should they be treated? As refugees? Illegal migrants? Enemy aliens? Victims? Or just kids in need of tender loving care?

On 1 September 1939, German troops invaded Poland. The Australian Government immediately barred the departure of commercial shipping bound for European ports.

On 2 September, 20 members of the Vienna Mozart Boys' Choir were scheduled to give the final performance, in Perth, of a highly successful US, New Zealand and Australian Pacific tour.

It proved 'final' in more ways than one. On 3 September, Britain and France, their dominions and territories, declared war on Germany. Overnight the choristers and their adult escorts lost their celebrity status and became exiles. Most were never to see their homeland – other than as tourists – again.

The choir itself was an independent (or breakaway) group formed at the end of 1936[1] by Dr Georg Gruber, formerly senior conductor with the famed Vienna Boys' Choir.

Gruber's resignation from that position came at the end of a tour, which he led, to South America. Also on the South American tour was a woman called Henrietta Marsi (Marsh). According to former chorister, Leo Steger: 'She was the nurse and governess, who came along to look after the boys.' It appears she also looked after Gruber.

Gruber himself was a remarkable man, whose musical gifts were matched by personal charisma. He had an extraordinary ear for tonal quality and was said to be a 'magician' on stage when conducting. The choristers' eyes were riveted on their leader, who used facial expressions and dexterous manual signs unseen by the audience. Physically he was tall, dark, handsome. Women fancied him; to the choristers he was a father figure.

The first overseas tour by the new group was to England, Ireland, Canada and selected northern cities in the US. Each concert was an enormous success, many considering the Vienna Mozart Boys' Choir better, even, than the Vienna Boys' Choir, some of whose members had made the switch along with Gruber.[2] The group also visited various cities in Europe.

When travelling, it was the custom to sing the National Anthem of the host country at the end of each performance. A man watching the performance in Derry grimaced and pulled his hat down below his ears as Gruber had the choir sing *God Save the King*. Some of the audience stood. Others remained, defiantly, seated. Gruber, always the diplomat, followed immediately with the anthem of the Republic of Ireland.

In Berlin, none of the former choristers can remember which, if any, Nazi leaders witnessed the performance,[3] but all remember the female gymnast dancer, actually from Canada, who lost her skimpy costume while doing the splits. There was also an Italian girl violinist with whom several of the impressionable young singers fell madly in love. (She made a paper hat for all 20 of her admirers.)

The choir returned from its first trans-Atlantic trip in February 1938. A month later, on 12 March, there came the *Anschluß* – the forced union of Germany and Austria and the latter's incorporation into Hitler's Reich. For most of the boys the *Anschluß* itself was a non-event. Erich Troyna recalls: 'We were away in school, in a big building in a place called Mauer. We were trying to catch up on our schooling and were quite isolated.'

On 18 December the group left by train from Vienna, travelling overnight to Hamburg, where they stopped for two days. On 21 December 1938, they embarked on the SS *Hamburg* for the choir's second major overseas tour – this time to the far side of the globe. There were 20 children, only 11 of whom had been on the first overseas tour, and four adults.

The vessel was the pride of the Hamburg-Amerika Line. Its skipper was Captain Gustav Schroeder, subsequently skipper of the *St Louis* and hero of a major drama involving Jewish refugees.[4]

The boys spent Christmas Day on the high seas. The group landed in New York, but gave their first concert in Boston, where a huge Christmas tree, three-storeys high, dominated the interior of their hotel. Alfred Ziegler recalls that the younger boys played an elaborate prank, stealthily chopping off more and more pieces from the tree, which they re-assembled with wire and glue, in a room occupied by one of the boys. Meanwhile the hotel's tree gradually diminished in size.

American audiences were delighted by the boys' singing. The *Chicago Tribune* critic noted: 'They put the birds to shame.'

Accompanied by Gruber, the boys visited a Red Indian reservation, where they were made blood brothers of the tribe. Ernst Koller remembers that Stefan Haag – later to become executive director of the Australian Elizabethan Theatre Trust – disappeared. Ernst, who was travelling in the same car, went looking for him. 'I found him holding hands with an Indian girl. They were lovestruck. She gave him her headband as a memento.'

Some 40 years later Koller told the story to a group of adults. Haag confessed: 'I've still got it. My daughter wears it.'

The choir left San Francisco for Hawaii on 31 March 1939. A dock strike had delayed the departure of their new vessel, *Lurline*, for two weeks. Tour organisers decided – rather than to disappoint audiences through cancellations – to reschedule the remainder of the tour by a similar period. The decision was to have unexpected consequences.

In Hawaii, which they reached on 6 April, the choir gave one concert. According to Leo Steger: 'The whole island was magic.' Two days later the choir left Honolulu on the *Monterey* for New Zealand, which they reached – via stops in Fiji and Samoa – on 18 April. Concerts, many of them repeated, were given in Auckland, Wellington and numerous smaller venues.

On 1 June 1939, the group – weariness kept at bay by excitement at what was in store – left New Zealand on the *Aorangi* for Australia, arriving in Sydney on 3 June. Concerts were given in Sydney Town Hall and St Mary's Cathedral. In Melbourne, the critic for the *Argus* was impressed with the way the boys sang *Valtzing Matilda* (sic), with German accents.

The choir gave 14 performances in Melbourne, including six at the Town Hall. At one of these, the boys were supposed to be presented to the governor-general, Lord Gowrie. Gruber instructed the boys to march up, bow, shake hands with the governor-general and kiss the hand of Lady Gowrie. Leo Steger, by mistake, kissed the governor-general's hand and shook hands with his wife. The next followed suit. Gruber was furious.

As in the US, the choir gave repeat performances at many of the Australian venues. In Queensland the choir visited country towns such as Ipswich and Toowoomba. Rural centres in Victoria included Geelong, Warrnambool, Hamilton, Ballarat, Ararat, Horsham, Kerang. In the era before television, the performances created great excitement.

In Adelaide the children were very well received. In Western Australia they enjoyed performing in Kalgoorlie, where each child was given a tube of gold dust. The tour ended in Perth, which was appropriate, since Fremantle was to be the port of embarkation.

SOUVENIRS BUT NO JOURNEY HOME

It was customary for the boys to keep mementos of their travels, each vying with the other for the largest or most novel collection. Olav Schappacher explains: 'When we stayed in hotels we were all souvenir hunters. Each one collected something. I collected brochures, matches and small cakes of soap.'

Two of the boys collected bathplug chains. Herbert Strommer linked his together until they were several metres long. Alfred Mayerhofer fancied them as a kind of watch-chain. The boy carried his case – which seemed to weigh a ton – to the docks at Fremantle. It was 2 September; the ship was to depart the next day.

The Aberdeen and Commonwealth Line vessel, *Moreton Bay*, was waiting in its berth, tantalisingly close, but Alfred and the bathplug chains were destined not to leave Australia.

That same night the choir was due to give its final performance. Olav Schappacher noted, as did his friends, that the audience was smaller than expected. The choir ended as usual by singing *God Save the King*. The next day Olav saw crowds milling around in Perth. The family with whom he was staying tuned into the Prime Minister's announcement and told him that World War II had begun.

To most of the boys the phrase had limited meaning. According to Leo Steger: 'I knew that war was on, and that we wouldn't be going home, but it didn't sink in. We were all in the group together; nothing seemed to be different.' To Olav Schappacher it meant: 'One day we were important, the next we were nothing.'

On the other side of the world, the boys' parents were devastated by the separation. Later, as older brothers and relatives were killed in action and even civilians were at risk, most parents revised this opinion.

In the weeks before the tour, the voices of four choristers had broken, preventing them from participating and effectively ending their careers.

One of the four was Franz Urbanek, who had participated in the first overseas tour. Says Leo Steger: 'We called him "Gucki" (Freckles). I took his place and wore his uniform. I had been a member of the choir for only three months.'

In Frank Heimans' excellent SBS two-part documentary, *Class of 39*, Walter Hauser (Schopfhauser) mentioned the episode as one he will always remember. 'Gucki was running alongside the slow-moving train, tears in his eyes, waving us goodbye.' The swap was fortunate. For Leo Steger, but not for 'Gucki', who died while fighting on the Russian front.

With war declared, the 20 members of the Vienna Mozart Boys' Choir found themselves in a kind of limbo. Though 'enemy aliens', they were, after all, children. It would be hardly civilised to intern them. Repatriation by the Red Cross – assuming it could be arranged – could take months or even years.

The oldest of the choristers, Otto Nechwatal, was 15. The youngest, Kurt Schuster, nicknamed 'Floh' (Flea), was eight. Clearly, someone or some organisation would have to take responsibility for them. But who? And how?

SANCTUARY

The choirmaster, Dr Georg Gruber, remembered an off-the-cuff remark by the Catholic Archbishop of Melbourne, Archbishop Daniel Mannix, while the choir had been in that city. He had stated: 'Why don't you stay and sing with us?'.

Gruber telegrammed Mannix and received the reply: 'Come immediately.' Gruber left immediately, ahead of the others, who were accommodated privately in Perth. En route for Melbourne, he was arrested in Adelaide, but released almost immediately when proof was provided of the offer from Mannix. The boys returned to Melbourne on the *Manunda*. Ernst Koller recalls the ship was blacked out during the voyage, which added to the excitement and sense of unreality.

In these novel circumstances the Vienna Mozart Boys' Choir became, for the major period of the war, the official choir of St Patrick's Cathedral, Melbourne.

Archbishop Mannix, always headstrong and accustomed to getting his own way, aroused a degree of controversy by his move. Most saw it as simple generosity – the tradition of 'sanctuary' extended by the Church throughout the ages. Others detected a desire to get back at the British with whom, as an Irish patriot, he had often crossed swords.

Papers in the National Australian Archives inspected by the author support the 'sanctuary' theory. It was also a shrewd business transaction – the boys literally sang for their supper.

They sang in Latin and 'very funny' English, which they hardly understood, and occasionally in French or Spanish. They were boarded with Catholic families who had come forward in response to requests from the pulpit for foster parents. Many of the participating families were poor. Many assumed mistakenly that the arrangement was for a few weeks only. The boys received free schooling from the Christian Brothers. Within a few months the youthful 'enemy aliens' found themselves participating in a St Patrick's Day parade.

Lack of a sound working knowledge of English created problems. Olav Schappacher remembers bringing breakfast on a tray to his foster mother, who asked for her glasses. He returned with two empty drinking glasses instead of her spectacles.

One choir member went to live in East Melbourne with a 'lovely elderly couple', who treated him as their son. One day, after returning from school, he was told he would have to go. No reason was given. He was then quartered in a room above a pub in Fitzroy. It had no window, just a skylight, and homework had to be done by the light of a candle.

Leo Steger and Stefan Haag shared the same foster parents, the Doyle family in Richmond, who owned the Lord Raglan Hotel. According to Leo: 'They looked after us famously.'

Erich Troyna and Ted Menhart went to live with a schoolteacher in Abbotsford called Myrtle Carrodus, of whom they became immediately fond. Regrettably, she found it hard to cope financially, and the boys had to be removed. Erich spent a 'not very pleasant' couple of months in a Christian Brothers' boys' home, at the end of which 'Aunty Myrt' decided she could cope with one boy and selected him.

She taught Erich to swim in the Yarra and gave him English lessons. She did this so competently that Erich (despite having spent much of his life overseas) still writes faster and more grammatically correct English than German. His friendship with 'Aunty Myrt' was to last 55 years. She died, aged 93, in August 1995.

The boys felt the absence of their parents severely. According to Erich Troyna: 'It must have been very hard for my mother, as I was an only child, and we could exchange only 25 words at a time, every six months, through Red Cross letters. We never dreamed we would be separated for so long.

'Of course, I still had another family, when I think of it, the boys in the St Patrick's choir.'

This view was shared by others. Walter Hauser used to say at choir reunions: 'I belong to the most exclusive club in the world.' Ernst Koller concurs: 'I still do consider them nearly as brothers.'

Herbert Strommer received a letter with a difference from his mother. Tucked into the envelope his mother had inserted 'an invitation from Hitler's men' – call-up papers for the armed forces of the Third Reich. 'There were a couple of small forms, instructing me to report to such and such a place, and bring this and that. I wish I still had them. I was only about 15, which seemed young for military service. Perhaps I would have been sent into the forest to shoot Russians. It was a good thing to miss.'

For this and a variety of reasons the former choirboys have 'no regrets' about their enforced stay in Australia. At the same time they reject and resent the rosy, schmaltzy *Sound of Music* image which many outsiders hold of the boys' formative years.

Erich Troyna is strong on this point. 'It was not rosy. I was interviewed by a journalist, who quoted me as saying, "We were all so happy". I did not say that and it is untrue. Many of the boys weren't happy at all. They had no choice.

'The people we stayed with were poor before the war and they were poor after the war. Everyone more or less had a roof over their head but that was it. Some of the boys managed to be sent out to three, four or five different families.'

The boys had high IQs – a factor in their original selection for the prestigious choir – but a combination of circumstances prevented most from receiving a higher education. Troyna says without bitterness: 'It was a traumatic experience, staying with completely strange people. And it was even more so going through *that* school.'

'That school' was the Christian Brothers' Parade College, East Melbourne. In Austria they had been used to discipline, which was necessary to combine lessons, choir studies and travelling. But the Christian Brothers were different.

According to Troyna: 'We knew discipline in a sensible way – without it we wouldn't have been able to cope. But the Christian Brothers, oh my God, I've never seen anything like it. There was a Brother called "Waddy" Ryan. He would line you up and say, "All right boys, just come along; you're all going to get six of the best." All this and the class hadn't even started.'

Ernst Koller, too, remembers Ryan. 'He had a particular way of carrying his strap. He curled the top around and tucked it into his sash. He came in, opened the door. You know the advert where people flap their elbows like chooks. He would sing, "Chirichiribin, Chirichiribin", and if anybody laughed, he'd say, "Who laughed? Come out here, boy!". And you'd get a couple. His favourite saying was, "Are you hankering for a couple?".'

Koller laughs at his recollection, and believes little harm was done. Erich Troyna disagrees. 'As I said, we were accustomed to discipline, but not to these idiotic beatings just to enforce their power; to browbeat the pupils so that they would be quiet and sit properly and pay attention in class.'

At Gruber's instigation, the four oldest boys – Otto Nechwatal, Willy Siesz, Leo Steger and Stefan Haag – went to St Joseph's Technical School, in Abbotsford. This, too, was run by the Christian Brothers, but the boys' experiences were more pleasant. Steger recalls: 'The headmaster, Brother Hanley, was marvellous. He looked after us, did everything for us; we couldn't do anything wrong.'

According to Steger, St Joseph's was 'more or less a trade school for students who were not academically gifted'. In contrast, the school he had attended in Austria, run by the *Schulbrüdern*,[5] was a high school equivalent of considerable reputation. The school had been forcibly shut down by the Nazis, giving him – unlike the other choristers – good reason to remember the *Anschluß*.

ORPHANS

Leo Steiger, unlike the others, was an orphan (or as he puts it 'half orphan') in his homeland. In 1930, when he was six, his father had died in a train accident. His mother, who was unable to support him, put him into a Catholic orphanage, which was also shut down by the Nazis.

After both the school and orphanage were closed and he was once again living with his mother and attending a state school, he joined the local church choir, from which he was recruited into the Vienna Mozart Boys' Choir.

Herbert Strommer, like Leo, had an unsettled home life. His parents separated when he was a toddler; he grew up in the care of his mother and other relatives, in poor circumstances, and spent time in a boarding school and in an institution.

In Australia Strommer, by then 12, was put in the care of two sets of foster parents, the second of whom were 'very decent – I was given piano lessons at their expense; we had a very warm relationship'. Just as he thought his luck had changed, he was removed from the couple and placed in St Vincent's Orphanage in South Melbourne.

He still doesn't know the reason for his removal. 'I played up a little, but no more than any fellow of my age. I wouldn't say I was a problem child. The war had by then been on for a year-and-a-half or more and I suspect things were just getting difficult for them.'

The orphanage was run by the Christian Brothers. 'Some of the Brothers were quite nice and some weren't so marvellous. It was a regimented life and frankly not so pleasant.' He was later transferred to the same Order's St Augustine's Orphanage, near Geelong. Ted Menhart, another chorister, went with him.

In both institutions minor infringements brought violent solutions. Herbert remembers one incident at the St Vincent's Orphanage. 'You were supposed to pray in chapel for the repose of the souls of the faithful departed. Ted and I were spotted whispering to each other. As we filed out in single file this huge fellow, a big Irish Brother, "Donger" Daly, punched me so hard in the solar plexus that I thought I was going to die.

'I was a skinny kid, about 12-and-a-half then. A couple of months later the fellow himself died and we had to file past his coffin which was lying in state. I couldn't help remembering what had occurred previously, and I gloated – you're dead now and I'm alive.

'Another brother used to run his hands down the inside of boys' trousers and rub their bottoms. He'd do it quite openly. We would see him walking along the veranda with some lad alongside. He'd have a smile on his face which would be very reddened as well. He also had this tick; he used to jerk his shoulder upwards with the hand that he wasn't using. Believe me, it was quite a sight.'

After leaving the institution, Strommer occasionally raised the subject of the Brothers' conduct when speaking with older people. It was a time when such discussion was taboo. 'It was communicated to me right away: "Don't you dare talk like that about these wonderful men who give their lives to a good cause." You were immediately silenced. There was nothing else you could do.'

20
NAZI OF CONVENIENCE

In a waste bin the searchers found a torn-up photograph, which they pieced together, of Gruber wearing a Nazi lapel badge. More damaging to Gruber were claims that, at the time of the Australian tour, he was being groomed as a kind of musical mastermind of Hitler's Third Reich.

A year or so after their arrival, the presence of 20 Viennese youngsters as the official choir of Australia's second major Catholic cathedral ceased to have novelty value.

Cathedral authorities found an unexpected hazard – girls. Word got around that the older boys, in particular, were good lookers. The choir stalls were at that time close to the front pews. Seating was rearranged and a curtain strategically placed to obscure the boys' knees. Some of the boys dated, and subsequently married, girls who ogled them in this way.

It was not the only romantic interest. The visit of the (then) recently formed Vienna Mozart Boys' Choir to Australia was sponsored by Henrietta Marsh, mentioned previously in connection with the Vienna Boys' Choir's South American trip, who had switched allegiance with Gruber from the larger and established body. Once more, she travelled with the choristers, joining the party in New York. She was a naturalised Australian, so the voyage was in essence a homecoming.

'Henny' Marsh, formerly Marsi (the name of her Italian husband from whom she was separated), was one of the more interesting women to grace Melbourne society in the 1930s. She had been in her younger days a beautiful but unconventional member of Viennese society. At the age of 36, she went deaf, conversing with those around her in a kind of shorthand. The handicap neither affected her lifestyle nor her love of music.

Her daughter, Adrienne Gravenor, known as 'Ady' or 'Bobby', says her mother's main hobby was 'collecting gentlemen'. One of the gentlemen she collected was Dr Georg Gruber.

Having secured his appointment as choirmaster at St Patrick's Cathedral, Georg Gruber at first enjoyed what seemed like a comfortable war. He had various teaching posts in addition to his role at the cathedral. Dick Hughes, the prominent journalist and jazz musician, remembers Gruber visiting the Christian Brothers' schools and teaching them how properly to sing *Waltzing Matilda*.

Gruber moved into Henny Marsh's Brighton home, and appeared to live well, becoming a noted member of the Melbourne musical scene. Apart from his role as choirmaster he was given various additional teaching tasks at schools and seminaries in the archdiocese.

Things abruptly changed on 3 March 1941, when – at 6.30 am – military police went to the Brighton home and arrested Gruber, who was accused of being a Nazi.

Henny Marsh, having opened the front door, led them first to his bedroom, which was empty. She then nodded in the direction of her daughter's room and withdrew. They found Gruber under Ady's bed.

It would appear from the above that his political leanings were not the main factor that caused Henny Marsh to dob him in to the authorities. Of more pressing concern was that her lover had transferred his attentions to her teenage daughter.

This act of revenge was not carried out immediately. Ady, who had led a sheltered life, and had only recently left school, claimed later that she overheard a conversation between Gruber, who had a wife and two children in Austria, and her mother in which a fee was offered – an increase of £15 in the rent – for overlooking the new situation.

As Gruber was being led out of the house, he told Ady to ring Dr Patrick Lyons, Administrator of St Patrick's Cathedral. Lyons immediately lodged a formal complaint about the arrest, stressing the Archbishop's annoyance that as 'guarantor for Dr Gruber's conduct', he had not been consulted. A flurry of letters followed, the last of which states: '... in the light of certain circumstances of this distressing case which are now known to the Archbishop, but which were not known when the requests [for release] were submitted, His Grace does not propose to take any further action in this matter.'

That night several of the choirboys – unaware of the nuances involved – visited Mannix at his residence to ask that he intervene to obtain Gruber's release. They concluded (correctly) that the Archbishop had 'lost interest' in the affair.

The Evidence

When the police arrested Georg Gruber they found in his room various items regarded as incriminating. Much was made of a letter from a Sydney-based German newspaper, *Die Brücke* (*The Bridge*), whose editor, A. Von Skerst, had addressed him as 'Dear Party Member Gruber'. The letter was of a routine nature, saying that a story and photographs about the main Sydney concert had been sent to newspapers in Berlin.

In a waste bin the searchers found a torn-up photograph, which they pieced together, of Gruber wearing a Nazi lapel badge. More damaging to Gruber were claims that at the time of the Australian tour he was being groomed as a kind of musical mastermind of Hitler's Third Reich. A document in his security file refers to an alleged proposal to establish a new academy (headed by Gruber) which would teach military music, flute and concertina playing, choir singing, folk dancing and – 'since the political will of the people is expressed in ceremonial activity' – instruction in Nazi ritual.

According to Gruber, the claims made for his role were exaggerated. 'I was engaged upon the revision of the musical education program of youth. I chose the songs the children were to sing. It was necessary to see that the songs were suitable in the eyes of the government.'

Apart from the boys, there were few in public life prepared to speak up for Georg Gruber. An exception was Dr Herman Schildberger, musical director of Melbourne's Temple Beth Israel. Otto Nechwatal took a message to the house in Brighton where a party was in progress. He found Gruber seated on a piano stool playing a duet with Schildberger.

Two members of the choir, Stefan Haag and Olav Schappacher, actually sang in Dr Schildberger's synagogue. It was the cathedral authorities, not Georg Gruber, who objected.

Certainly, Gruber had other prominent Jews among his friends – an unlikely situation for a committed Nazi. Though it is not mentioned in the security files, it is generally believed that the boys' tutor on the tour, Otto Sternberg, who had sailed with them from Europe, was Jewish. (At least, that he had one Jewish parent or grandparent, which was enough to damn him in Nazi eyes.) There is a theory that Gruber appointed him to help him escape.[1]

Some say that during the long voyage to the Antipodes he and Gruber told them to 'forget about Hitler'. Certainly their lessons contained no political slant.

Ady Gravenor says her mother was a strong Anglophile who pinned flags on maps to mark the British Empire, and who 'nearly had a fit' when she heard Chamberlain's 'peace in our time' appeasement speech on the radio. It would have been out of character for her to take an admirer of Adolf Hitler as her lover.

Otto Nechwatal, who was closer than most to Gruber, believed his mentor was probably a 'Nazi of convenience', a man without ideological convictions, but who joined the party – many would have done at that time – to advance or prevent disruption to his career. Erich Troyna believes Gruber was 'simply an opportunist'.

Georg Gruber was sent to the Tatura prison camp, near Murchison,

Victoria. A report by his first commandant described him as a 'model prisoner' who gave little trouble. A later commandant took a different view, describing him as a 'plausible liar' and 'rabid Nazi', considered to be 'the real power behind all the Nazi clique in the compound'. This was denied by Helmut Becker, founder of the Nazi Party in Australia, who was a fellow internee.

The same commandant grudgingly acknowledged Gruber's gifts, describing him as 'the well-educated, polite, aesthetic type, interesting himself deeply in musical matters, in which respect he is brilliant'.

The hapless Otto Sternberg was also interned in Tatura. His security dossier contains the odd statement that 'though an anti-Nazi at the beginning of the tour, his embitterment turned him pro-Nazi'.

Henny Marsh discovered early in Gruber's imprisonment that her daughter, who was denied the right to visit, was secretly writing to Gruber. Her solicitor wrote to the camp commandant, resulting in an order that Ady's letters not be passed on.

Later, the daughter received an offer of marriage from an English officer. She told him, 'I love Georg Gruber, but I will marry you if you visit him on my behalf.' He agreed, making several visits to Gruber. The marriage did not last and her husband returned to England. She does not know if he is alive or dead.

GUEST OF THE GOVERNMENT

As the war dragged on, the choirboys, granted sanctuary and a job by Archbishop Daniel Mannix, found their situations changed. Their voices broke; even the youngest became teenagers, while the oldest left school and had to fend for themselves. They queued for clothes at charity shops, ran errands for butchers. In the words of one of them, Olav Schappacher: 'We lived on our wits.'

Meanwhile, their former choirmaster, Prisoner V2127 Georg Gruber, remained a guest of the government, resident conductor of the Tatura prison camp orchestra.

When hostilities ceased, Gruber made formal application to stay in Australia. The request was endorsed by several former choristers, now Australian citizens, who wrote a barrage of letters referring to Gruber as 'my guardian'. After a long delay the application was rejected on the grounds that he 'might preach National Socialist philosophy in Australia.'

Gruber appealed against the verdict, and came up with an attractive and unusual bait. He said he had come to the conclusion that Australian boys had naturally the world's finest voices. If released, he offered to form an Australian equivalent of the Vienna Mozart Boys' Choir, which would achieve equal renown. He appealed directly to the Immigration Minister, Arthur Calwell, who was apparently sympathetic. Henrietta Marsh got wind of it and put in her oar. The application to stay was once more rejected.

Two years later – by now it was 1947 – Gruber was still in confinement. First with two others; finally he was alone – Australia's 'last Nazi', guarded by at least a dozen men.

To alleviate the boredom he wrote to a contact (name not recorded) offering to play chess by correspondence. He outlined his first move. A note from the security service to the Tatura camp commandant says: 'Please furnish extracts of all further correspondence in each direction until chess game is over.'

Twice he escaped. Not with the intention of going 'home' to Austria, but because he wished to remain. Both escapes were on the eve of the serving of a deportation order. He was caught after a few days, having lived on canned food and berries. Prisoner V2127 Georg Gruber was deported to Austria in November 1947. He was taken straight from confinement to the ship. Herbert Strommer recalls: 'Some of us went to Port Melbourne to see him off. We could not approach him, but we saw him looking out of the porthole of the ship which was taking him away. We spoke across that short gap of water, while the boat was tied up. That was how we said goodbye.'

INTELLIGENCE FILES

Wartime Intelligence files in the Australian National Archives, now cleared for public inspection, give fascinating, and sometimes unexpected insights into the background of the Vienna Mozart Boys' Choir and the controversy which embroiled its choirmaster, Dr Georg Gruber.

Among the more interesting contents are the letters from Henrietta Marsh to the authorities 'dobbing in' Gruber. Her claims appear to have been accepted uncritically. Statements by the prosecuting officers, which are also on file, show a similarity in wording to her outpourings. There is an inference that she knew at least one of the investigators socially. Nowhere on file is there reference to her being the jilted mistress.

Also on file are the original handwritten pleas, in not-very-good English, from the choirboys to the authorities seeking Gruber's release. Though written well over half a century ago, there is a freshness and poignancy about them which is deeply moving. There is also a letter of support from Gruber's Jewish friend, Dr Schildberger.

Other correspondence suggests strongly that it was Gruber's moral shortcomings, not his Nazi links, which caused Archbishop Mannix to drop him like a hot potato. It should be stated that the files also contain letters, photos and documentation demonstrating that he was at least a nominal Nazi Party member.[2]

Other damaging material – sourced to expatriate (and strongly anti-Nazi) fellow countrymen – involves an allegation that Gruber, despite having resigned as a conductor with the Vienna Boys' Choir, had been secretly reinstated and promoted as the head of that world-famous organisation.

The claim was bolstered by reports that after the *Anschluß,* two SA stormtroopers and a civilian accompanied Gruber to the home of Rektor Joseph Schnitt, priest-director of the Vienna Boys' Choir, telling him that he was being compulsorily retired and that Gruber had been appointed 'Commissioner'.

Under interrogation Gruber partly confirmed this story, but said 'commissioner' merely meant someone who would examine the books prior to transfer of the choir, along with other hitherto privately run organisations, to State control. Gruber said he found the encounter with the priest, his former employer, 'not a pleasant situation'.

Yet another report – emanating from a former member of the Vienna Boys' Choir who had gone to live in New Zealand – said Gruber was sacked by Rektor Schnitt for having expressed satisfaction at the murder of the Austrian Chancellor, Engelbert Dollfuss. However, the priest was unable to find a suitable replacement, and restored Gruber to his post.

Gruber partly confirmed this story, which did not form part of the formal evidence against him, but told his Australian interrogators that he was not at all 'pleased' with the murder of Dollfuss – who was a personal friend – but disgusted. In fact, he had resigned from the Nazi party as a result. He said Schnitt told him to take a few months' leave at a lodge owned by the choir, and to return once the storm had blown over.

Otto Nechwatal, one of the few Mozart Boys' Choir choristers to have been a prior member of the Vienna Boys' Choir, told me there was a remarkable sequel to this story – namely that Rektor Schnitt, having been reinstated in his old position after peace returned, offered to re-employ Gruber.

This turn of events, if true, demonstrates remarkable Christian charity on the part of the Catholic priest, and seems to suggest that Gruber – despite having joined the Nazi Party in 1933 – was (as he maintained) an unwilling player in the coup that ousted Schnitt.[3]

People who write letters to government security organisations usually include a fair share of irrational people. A 'concerned citizen', whose letter is on file, said Gruber must be a Nazi because he 'keeps watching ships at Port Melbourne'. Another said he believed the printed programs of the choir's Sydney concerts contained Nazi code.

Albert Martin, the St Patrick's Cathedral organist,[4] declared that Henny Marsh, as well as Gruber, was a 'spy', and that he thought her hearing aid was an espionage device. Martin, who was appointed choirmaster after Gruber's arrest, also claimed the boys were billeted with anti-British elements, including an Irish family who had told neighbours they 'didn't care' if England lost the war. In a letter to the authorities he reiterated his own desire to be 'of service to the country'.

21
THE DISAPPEARANCE OF WILLY SIESZ

The visitor told him a hard luck story and asked for money. Otto instead bought him a meal. Willy disappeared into the night. Neither his friends nor relatives have seen or heard from him since.

Of the triumphs and tragedies experienced by the former Vienna Mozart Boys' Choir, possibly none surpasses the continuing human drama surrounding Willy Siesz, the second oldest of the choristers.

Siesz, 14 at the time of the group's arrival in Australia, looked up to only one person, and that was Georg Gruber. According to the others, he 'worshipped' Gruber, and was shattered by his arrest and incarceration in Tatura.

He got his own back on the authorities by making a nuisance of himself. By all accounts it was minor stuff, and included being cheeky to the desk sergeant at Brighton police station, where he was required (as an enemy alien) to make weekly visits. According to Otto Nechwatal: 'I believe on one occasion he went to a pub, though under age, and had a few beers. He then stood outside the station singing pro-German songs.'

Erich Troyna thinks Willy deserves understanding. 'It was just bloody mock heroism. His attitude was, "If you're interning Dr Gruber, you should intern me too." And of course they did, which was utter nonsense.'

Siesz, still only 15, was removed from foster care and sent to Loveday Internment Camp in South Australia, where he was imprisoned with Foreign Legionnaires, captured seamen and older enemy nationals of a rough and brutal disposition. The others believe that Siesz, who had 'fair wavy hair and striking good looks', was sexually abused, and made to suffer numerous indignities.[1]

He wrote to Gruber pleading to be transferred to Tatura. He began his letter: 'Dear Uncle Schorsch' (a pet name), which shocked the Tatura commandant. Gruber made a similar application: 'These boys are as dear to me as members of my own family ... If one of them is interned his proper place is with me.'

At the end of the war, Willy Siesz was released. For a while he was his old cheerful self, concocting all sorts of schemes to free Gruber, and taking the boys to night clubs and even a brothel.

One day Olav Schappacher and Willy Siesz decided to go to Canberra to personally plea for Gruber's release. Olav recalls: 'Willy and I were boarding at the same place. He told me, "We *must* go to Canberra; this is our last chance." We had to go by train and we didn't have any money. Willy said, "Look, there are some mad gamblers around. Let's play cards and take our chances."

'So we worked out some signals and played poker. We played right through the night, and we won. We got enough to go to Canberra. When we got there we went straight into Parliament House; just walked up the steps and asked to see the Minister.' The Minister for Labour and National Service, Edward Holloway, impressed by their boldness, saw them briefly, but was unrelenting. He told them flatly: 'Your choirmaster is a Nazi.'

As consolation, the boys were finally allowed to visit Gruber at Tatura, and found him resigned to his fate. He had heard them singing, in a radio program, which excited him. He seemed more concerned with their welfare than his own.

Sadly, as his moves to free 'Uncle Schorsch' failed, Siesz's mood and whole personality changed. He began to act strangely, then suffered an emotional collapse. According to Erich Troyna: 'It was all too much for him. His life had been ruined.'

Willy Siesz 'went bush', literally. He vacated his lodgings, avoided contact with his friends and, for all intents and purposes, disappeared.

In 1956, one of Willy's five brothers, a former Luftwaffe pilot, flew to Australia to look for him. The Melbourne *Herald* ran a front-page story about the quest, and Willy was located. Peter Siesz subsequently obtained permission to stay in Australia as a migrant.

For a while Willy moved in with Peter and Maria Siesz in a flat in Brisbane. According to Maria: 'It didn't work out. He was like a bird.' Tensions arose; Willy disappeared again. It was not quite the last sighting of Willy. About 25 years ago Otto Nechwatal, busy in the shop he ran near St Francis' Church, in Melbourne, saw a scruffy and hesitant figure watching him from the street. Otto looked again and recognised Willy Siesz.

The visitor told him a hard-luck story and asked for money. Otto instead bought him a meal. Willy disappeared into the night. Neither his friends nor relatives have seen or heard from him since.

On Tuesday, 31 July 1990, an evening of sacred music was held in St Patrick's Cathedral to mark (according to the printed program) '50 years of the Vienna Mozart Boys' Choir in Melbourne'. Half a century earlier, Otto Nechwatal had been a lad in short pants struggling with an unfamiliar language and in a new country. Tonight he was the conductor. Olav Schappacher and Franz Onger sang in the choir, and Leo Steger was usher.

According to the program notes a purpose of the concert was to commemorate 'Dr Georg Gruber, our highly respected director' and 'William Siesz and Alfred Homola,[2] whose whereabouts are unknown'.

The performance had received advance publicity, particularly among the Austrian community. Like the Jewish Passover custom of leaving a door ajar and an empty seat for Elijah, the main doors of the cathedral were left open. Even as he was conducting, Otto entertained 'the faint hope', as he confided to me later, that one or other of the missing men might quietly slip into a pew.

WHERE ARE THEY NOW?

When the war ended, all 20 members of the Vienna Mozart Boys' Choir elected initially to stay in Australia.

In 1952, Erich Troyna went back to Vienna, to be near his parents, later representing an English company in several European countries. Throughout it all, his bond with Australia and with the choristers remained strong. In 1993, having retired from business, he bit the bullet and returned permanently to this country. He says of that decision: 'It was just a natural thing. All those years had gone by, but it made absolutely no difference. I could resume a conversation [with the former choristers] as if we had never been apart.'

John Eder took a job in Africa and from there moved to Britain. The rest of the group lost contact with him in the 1960s.

Nine of the original 20 are known for certain to be alive (there is doubt about a further two) and living in Australia. They reside in Melbourne, Sydney, and on Queensland's Gold Coast.

Ernst Koller married an Italian girl who, as a young teenager, was interned in Camp 3 family camp at Tatura with her mother. Olav Schappacher brought his parents to Australia as migrants, as did Fred Mayerhofer, who was killed in a car accident in 1955. Another chorister, Kurt Gauwitz, died of multiple sclerosis about 25 years ago.

Kurt Schuster ('the Flea'), who had been the youngest of the choirboys, revisited his elderly parents for the first time, in 1982, some 43 years after their enforced separation. He introduced his wife and family at this emotional reunion.

Despite a disrupted and in some cases severely limited education, the former choristers pursued successful careers in arts, commerce, catering and the academic world. Possibly the best known was Stefan Haag, whose roles included producer with the National Opera Company in Victoria, director of Opera at Brisbane Conservatorium of Music, and executive director of the Elizabethan Theatre Trust. He was made an Officer of the Order of the Britich Empire (OBE) in 1968. He died in December 1986.

Otto Nechwatal, the oldest of the choristers, quickly adapted to the Australian way of life, and was the first in the group to get a job – initially as an errand boy, then in a china and glass importer's warehouse, where he received one pound a week. He was also the first, with fellow chorister, Stefan Haag, to own independent transport – a bicycle.

Unlike many of the others, he retained strong ecclesiastical connections. For many years he operated a shop in Melbourne, which sold vestments, prayer books, and what used to be called 'devotional objects'. Throughout his life he encouraged and trained church musicians in the ways that had been learnt in Vienna. According to Church historian, John Byrne, Otto Nechwatal, alone in Melbourne, 'kept alive the great tradition of European Catholic music'.

Otto Nechwatal died on 14 May 1995. Months before his death, it was known that he had terminal cancer. While he was still alive, his friends arranged a 'musical party' in the city's St Francis' Church, his spiritual home. He died before it could be held, and the 'party' became his funeral Mass. Nine of the 12 then surviving choristers were present.

Herbert Strommer died suddenly on 10 December 1995. He was found dead in his shop on the day of the group's annual reunion at Melbourne's Austrian Club. A cancelled hospital appointment possibly cost him his life. Franz Onger died in July 2001.

Olav Schappacher, who pursued a successful career in insurance, has retained a practical musical bent. He has sung in various choirs and still performs with 'fun' groups such as the Danube Musicians.

Not all the stories have had happy endings. Franz Hackl, golden-voiced star of the Vienna Mozart Boys' Choir, suffered a breakdown following a shattered romance. He became a recluse, and died, prematurely aged and alone, in 1982.

In November 1983, Fred Homola vanished mysteriously. His wallet, glasses and personal items were found in his car outside a public library. The sum of $8,000 went unclaimed in his bank account. In September 1995, after a police investigation called 'Operation Bolt', his son, Alfred Aldo Galli, was convicted of his murder.

Dr Georg Gruber, following his enforced return to Austria,[3] was reconciled with his wife and children. He appeared before a de-Nazification tribunal, which cleared him. He briefly promoted a scheme for an Olympic Games of choir music. In 1953, Gruber obtained the post of Professor of Music at Rhodes University, South Africa, where he is fondly remembered as a quiet man – elegant, distinguished, 'not a show off' on the platform, and 'everybody's kindly uncle'.

Students queried his excellent English, and noted that he declined to talk about his past. He founded the Rhodes University Chamber Choir, which has toured Britain, Germany and Austria.[4] He died in South Africa in 1979.

His son, George Gruber, a lecturer in physics at the same university, married an Australian, gaining the right – denied to his father – to settle in this country. He did not take up this option, but visited as a tourist. He died, while still in his forties, about 12 years ago.

Henrietta Marsh, the former lover who turned Gruber over to the authorities, died in Belgrave, Victoria, in 1981. Mother and daughter remained estranged, about which Ady feels uncomfortable. 'I heard about my mother's death from a stranger. It was too late to attend the funeral.'

Ady (Bobby) Gravenor, the teenager embroiled in an ill-fated love triangle, found refuge in anonymity. She went to England with a friend, Margaret Edmands, and together they ran a teashop in Surrey frequented by boys from Charterhouse School.[5] In 1965, the pair returned to Australia, and for the next 21 years they ran a motel, newsagency and general store in Cooktown, North Queensland.

Since 1987 they have been living quietly in an inner-Sydney suburb.[6] Ady was 17 at the time of her infatuation with the much older, married man, and refers to him, almost deferentially, as 'Dr Gruber'.

She maintains that, far from being a Nazi, he planned the US-Australian-New Zealand tour 'to get away from the Nazis'. She regrets being the trigger for his downfall. 'I loved him ... that was the problem.'

She is less forgiving of Archbishop Mannix, whom she calls 'a monster'. The choirboys disagree. Erich Troyna says: 'From her point of view it might have seemed so. I don't accept that at all. When you're an archbishop you have to take a moral stand, that a conductor was cohabiting with a strange woman, and that he was married with two children and so on.'

While they are grateful to the archbishop for offering them 'sanctuary', some feel he could have done more in the provision of practical needs. Troyna takes a middle view. 'I think Mannix was a far-sighted, kindly man; I came to realise this more later on. At the same time I think if he had taken more direct, personal responsibility, many things would have turned out for the better for us.'

Some of the choirboys claim their 'freedom' was less rosy than imagined, and state tongue-in-cheek that a year in Hay with the Dunera Boys might have been preferable to the rough and tumble of a Christian Brothers' education.[7]

Some years after the war's end a few of the former choristers, by now adults, asked the shipping company, somewhat cheekily, for a refund of the (unused) return half of their fare. They got it – but only as far as London, and at the juvenile rate. Small, though it was, the money received was enough to send one of their kin back to Austria to meet his parents. Additionally, he found a wife.

The (original) Vienna Boys' Choir, from which some of Georg Gruber's choristers were drawn, celebrated its 500th anniversary in 1998. It is facing lean times and has cut back on some of its activities.

The famed choir's archives make little or no reference to Gruber, whom many still consider was its finest conductor. In the words of former chorister, Erich Troyna: 'He's a non-person as far as they are concerned.'[8]

That this should be so is hardly surprising. The period of the *Anschluß* remains a taboo subject with many older Austrians, who are uncomfortable with the knowledge that some of their countrymen actually welcomed the union with Germany.

POSTSCRIPT

SURVIVORS

To a compulsive scribbler like myself, almost any form of writing gives pleasure. However, it is particularly satisfying to record the lives and experiences of those, who, in many cases, went through the ultimate in horrors, to survive triumphant.

Some have told their stories before – in personal biographies (many self-published), typewritten manuscripts or taped interviews, mainly through the Spielberg Foundation. Grandchildren and future generations are often the intended audience. For others it is a first time. As 'Horrie' Goldsmith said on first meeting the author: 'I've been waiting 64 years to tell my story...'

Many of those featured in this book were at one time refugees (the ubiquitous 'reffo'). Henry Lippmann, organiser of the Sydney Dunera reunions, says: 'One experience of being a refugee is that you are received with a kind of condescension and sometimes enmity. It applies, I think, to refugees everywhere. Some of our people have become more British than the Brits, or more Australian than Australians. I am myself a proud Australian, but I still have a strong feeling for Europe and European culture, which is my heritage.'

'Horrie' Goldsmith has also thought about the problem. 'I'm a citizen of the world, so to speak. I'm just a human being, who has moved around a bit. Now when I go to England or anywhere else I'm an Australian. I've got ties here and have lived here a long time, know about the politics of the place and so on. After a while you just identify with it.'

Holocaust survivors interviewed for this book are anxious that their experiences be known (and lessons learnt) among future generations. Some are angered that their offspring 'don't want to know'. Conversely, some first generation descendants are angry that their parents 'clam up' and will not speak about these matters.

Children who travelled on the *Kindertransports* have feelings of deep gratitude to the countries and foster parents who gave them shelter. At the 60th anniversary commemoration of the rescue operations in London, the Chief Rabbi, Dr Jonathan Sacks, had this to say:

'We now know the equally powerful truth that the countries that are truly strong are those that care for the weak and provide a place for those in danger. We know that open doors are mightier than closed walls and closed hearts. And how badly we still need those truths ...'

When survivors' groups and bodies such as the Dunera Boys meet for tea and cakes, there is discussion over 'then-and-now' attitudes to the intake and absorption of New Australians.

Nora Huppert, a *Kind* who married a Dunera Boy, wrote in her self-published memoir: 'At the beginning of the new millennium ... refugees, desperately fleeing horrific homeland situations, are neither welcomed nor easily accepted and are often pushed to outlying camps [in places] far away from legal help and access to their own communities. Sometimes I feel guilty for my good fortune to have arrived in this far-off land at a golden time in its history.'

Opinions hardened following a *Sydney Morning Herald* report (18 February 2003) that children in immigration detention centres were spending an average of 15 months behind the razor wire, and that one child had been detained for over five years. In December, 2002, it was officially stated that 120 children were in detention centres, and 79 of them were under the age of 12.

Critics of government policies feel these are the 'new child migrants' – meaning that they suffer the same disabilities and lack of care as the 'Leaving of Liverpool' kids in the 1950s.

This view is not universal. At a Dunera reunion, criticism of the handling of 'illegals' from a guest speaker produced audible 'tut tuts' from others present. Some made it clear that they endorsed mandatory detention and considered that children held for long periods in centres had been exploited as bargaining chips by their parents.

Likewise, among the Kindertransportees, there are the same divisions of opinion as in other sections of society. Many consider their own situation and that of the asylum seekers and 'queue jumpers' in no way comparable.

As reported in these pages, about 70 unaccompanied Jewish teenagers came to Australia from continental Europe under group-sponsorship schemes in the period immediately before World War II and between 300 and 500 afterwards (a figure often quoted is 316). It would be fitting if they could have a memorial, like those in Sydney's Darling Harbour honouring child migrants, 'Little Brothers' and the Dunera Boys.

For the record some 10000 children 'escaped' to Britain in the *Kindertransports*. Some 1.5 million Jewish children died in the Holocaust.

The plaque honouring the Dunera Boys was the first to go up and attracts attention from passers-by. The 'Boys', like other migrant groups, are getting old. The youngest (in 2004) was 80. About 150 of the 900 or so who decided to settle permanently in Australia were still alive, as this book went to press.

The 'Boys' paid for the memorial themselves, which seems unfair. However, as 'living treasures' they have much to be thankful for, including 'treasure' of an unexpected kind. As stated in Chapter 15, early in their enforced sojourn at Hay, the internees produced their own currency which (they quip) was 'legal tender for one week'.

The original paper money has now skyrocketed in value. In March 2003 five notes, originally 'worth' sixpence, one shilling and two shillings, were successfully auctioned in Sydney. They fetched prices from $4,200 to $8,300 each.

In Britain there is a plaque in the Palace of Westminster honouring the British people and Parliament for their role in the *Kinder-transports*. A more visible memorial was unveiled in the forecourt to London's Liverpool Street Station on 16 September 2003.

Designed and sculpted by Flor Kent, it shows a bronze figure of a little girl, life-size, standing in front of a laminated glass suitcase, nearly two metres high. Inside the case are numerous mementoes associated with the *Kinder*. These include children's clothes from 1938 and 1939, spare hangers, a teddy bear, documents, letters and diaries.

The overall appearance of this huge centrepiece echoes the look of the actual suitcases brought by the children. It may be opened and fresh items inserted. The stainless steel structure framing the glass walls is finished with a special coating to make it look like worn leather.

The plaque includes this line from the Talmud: 'Whosoever rescues a single soul is credited as though they had saved the whole world.'

Irene Schmied, of the organisation Kinder-Link, said she hoped the memorial, which has been titled *Für das Kind* (For the Child) would 're-enact the arrival of the *Kinder* before the hundreds of present and future Londoners who pass by every day.'

The space in which the memorial is located has been re-named Children's Square. According to Irene, London has a new meeting place. It is 'By the Suitcase'.

She believes that for the *Kinder* it will serve as an 'anchor of continuity between the past and present, between our lives in the vanished world of yesterday and our children's lives in the world of tomorrow, and a beacon of hope that our story will never be forgotten'.

AUTOGRAPH STORY

Reference has been made in this volume to the film director and actor Lord Attenborough (Richard Attenborough), who is unofficial patron of the British *Kinder*.

In the late 1940s I was a 12-year-old attending a preparatory boarding school in southern England. I was an avid autograph collector, and wrote to all manner of celebrities, seeking their signature. Among those to whom I addressed my epistles was Richard Attenborough, who – by coincidence – lived in the same town (Richmond, Surrey) as my parents.

I wrote from my school address asking for his autograph. I received a form letter in reply saying that if I sent two shillings to the Actors' Benevolent Fund I would receive not just an autograph but a signed photograph. I duly sent off my two bob, but was disappointed to receive, in return, a photo with a printed signature.

I dashed off a stiff protest – this time with my home address at the top – saying that I had been cheated. However, I failed to say anything about this to my mother, who answered the bell one day, surprised and a little embarrassed to find Richard Attenborough and his actress wife, Sheila Sim, on our doorstep.

He was holding an enormous brown envelope which he asked my mother to give to Alan Gill. Inside was a large studio portrait with the words – this time in real ink – 'To dear Alan with my very best wishes, Richard Attenborough'.

At the *Kindertransport* reunion I made a point of introducing myself to him, and reminding him of the incident, of which he had no memory.

Alan Gill
June 2004

APPENDIX

REGULATIONS
OF THE
LEEDS ORT TECHNICAL AND ENGINEERING SCHOOL

You are the <u>guests</u> of the British ORT-OSE Committee and your behaviour always, in and outside the Hostel, must be of the <u>highest order</u>.

Although you have all passed the Tribunal, you are, in the <u>eyes</u> of the Leeds Christian people, members of an enemy country at war with England. <u>DO NOTHING</u> at any time, to arouse the slightest hostility, and do not attract attention.

The <u>Jewish Community</u> of Leeds expects you to show a splendid example of respect and thankfulness to the people of the City of Leeds, for accepting you here in time of war.

1. Never speak German in the streets, so that you can be <u>heard</u>. Try not to speak German <u>at all</u> if you can help it, and in any case speak very <u>quietly</u>.

2. Do not go into the street at any time without a hat on, and keep your overcoat buttoned up, and your hands out of your pockets.

3. Keep your hair <u>always</u> cut short and neatly combed and brushed.

4. Do not walk in the streets in daylight in groups of <u>more than three</u>, and step into the road always to allow others to pass.

5. Do not have <u>any conversation</u> in trains, cars or buses.

6. Do not, at any time in the streets, <u>discuss the war situation</u>.

7. Obey always all orders given to you by the Police, the <u>Staff</u> of the Hostel and your <u>room leaders</u>.

8. Remember there are Christian neighbours on <u>all sides</u> of the Hostel; therefore be quiet at all times. Also, remember there are wounded soldiers <u>from the last war</u> living in the building opposite to the hostel.

9. We do not want to make your living here difficult, but you are now living in <u>exceptional circumstances</u>, which require <u>exceptional regulations</u>.

10. Be sure that no light is <u>ever visible</u> from any room during the <u>black-out</u> periods. The Leeds Police are sure to watch this hostel very carefully. The carelessness of one student may have <u>serious consequences</u> for all.

11. If you are ever <u>in doubt</u> about anything, ask your leader who will ask the Secretary, Miss Traube, or Dr Isaak.

12. Read the Notices on the notice-board in the Hall, <u>every day</u>.

13. Keep the Hostel, wash basins and lavatories <u>clean</u> at all times. Be tidy in your room, and do not leave things <u>lying about</u>. It is forbidden to take any reading matter into lavatories.

14. We are doing everything possible for your comfort, but remember we have only <u>very little money</u> and we must economise until you can earn money, or we get more funds.

15. Do not break rules by talking after lights are put out; if you are not sleepy, others are. <u>No smoking</u> is allowed in the <u>bedrooms</u> and no smoking on the <u>Sabbath</u> anywhere.

16. Eat <u>quietly</u> and cleanly at table, and do not upset grease on the tables. Any breakages will have <u>to be paid for</u>, so be careful.

17. Be <u>respectful</u> at all times to visitors.

18. Any complaints or special requests must be made in the first instance <u>to your leader</u>.

19. Whatever you are ordered to do such as cleaning of rooms, washing of dishes, etc. do <u>at once</u> and <u>do it cheerfully</u>. Everyone must help in their turn.

20. Slippers must be worn whenever possible in the Hostel. Go up and down stairs <u>quietly</u>.

21. If you are invited to the Leeds Jewish Young Men's Institute, remember you are there as an <u>Honorary guest member</u>.

22. Leave to remain out after 8 o'clock during the winter can only be granted as a <u>very special case</u> by the Hostel-Master, Dr Isaak.

23. Games, such as Chess etc. when finished with must be put away in the proper place.

24. We are trying to arrange as early as possible for English lessons to be given to you. You can however by <u>study</u> and <u>conversation</u> learn at once a good deal yourselves.

25. We are doing everything possible to get the <u>School opened</u> or find <u>paid work</u> for you in Leeds. Until then you must be patient and do other work such as gardening.

26. Read these instructions over <u>carefully</u> until you are sure you <u>understand</u> and remember them. They have been issued so that we may all be proud of our Hostel and School.

Signed: Lieut-Col. J.H. Levey, Acting Chairman and
                    Hon. Treasurer, British ORT-OSE.

Underlining of words and punctuation appears as they did in the original document.

NOTES

PREFACE

1. *Orphans of the Empire* (see Bibliography, page 292).

2. Pearl's book inspired a (1985) TV mini-series, *The Dunera Boys*. The Vienna choristers' story was told in Frank Heimans' (1983) Two-part SBS documentary, *Class of '39*.

3. The *Sydney Morning Herald* headline 'Hitler's Choirboys', though not intended to offend, caused anger and threats of lawsuits.

CHAPTER 1

1. Founder of the Melbourne-based Child Survivors of the Holocaust, and author of *Child Survivors: Adults Living With Childhood Trauma* (see Bibliography, page 296).

2. An organisation which brought out British youths.

3. A German Jew who came to Britain on a Kindertransport. Author of *Other People's Houses* (see Bibliography, page 295).

4. Leonard Montefiore, one of the aristocrats of British Jewry, publicly espoused this view at a London rally in October 1933. He later changed his mind, becoming a prime force in the Refugee Children's Movement, as it was called.

5. In the words of a later policy document: 'Jews as a class are not desirable immigrants for the reason that they do not assimilate; speaking generally, they preserve their identity as Jews.'

6. Author of *Edge of the Diaspora* (see Bibliography, page 295).

7. Now known as Jewish Care.

8. Author of *Reluctant Refuge* (see Bibliography, page 294). Her PhD thesis (University of Adelaide), on the 'need and pressures' to help refugee and migrant children in the years 1933–45, dealt specifically with this topic.

9. See Palmer, G., 'Seventeen Children: Australia's Response to German Jewish Refugee Children', *Australian Jewish Historical Society Journal* November 1995. Reprinted in an address to the 1995 Conference of the Australian Association for Jewish Studies.

10. Also some 1 000 adult Jews from Germany, Austria, Czechoslovakia, Hungary and Poland.

11. Later the New Zealand Government gave hospitality to over 700 Catholic Polish children. See Gill, A. 1998, 'Children of Pahiatua', in *Orphans of the Empire*, Random House Australia Pty Ltd, Sydney, pp. 519–29.

12. See Chapter 3, 'Gross-Breeseners'. There is disagreement about numbers.

13. A merger of two welfare organistions, OSE (*Oeuvres de Secours aux Enfants*) and ORT (Organisation and Rehabilitation through Training).

14. Anne Andgel, *Fifty Years of Caring*, Australian Jewish Historical Society in association with the Australian Jewish Historical Society, 1986.

15. See cartoon, 19 February 1947.

16. Some Jewish sources claim the number was much higher.

17. But not quite the first. Tom Keleman, a Welfare Guardian boy, arrived in Australia on 19 July 1947.

18. See Chapter 3, page 25.

CHAPTER 2

1. Suzanne Rutland, the writer and Jewish historian, has stated in lectures that she believes the Australian Government 'preferred Germans to Jews'.

2. See Chapter 1, page 6.

3. As previously pointed out, hostilities intervened, preventing all but a portion of the promised 15 000 from arriving.

4. Rowland James, MP for Hunter, believed German children from 'bombed-out ruins' of the industrial Ruhr should be brought to Australia and raised in schools 'of the Fairbridge model'.

5. One of the more extraordinary figures involved in immigration matters. He came to prominence as a journalist and 'immigrationist', author of *The Opportunity in Australia* (1914). After World War I Gullett was appointed first director of the Australian War Museum (1920). He served on the staff of the Prime Minister, William Hughes, at Versailles and shared the leader's view as to the fragility of peace. A pamphlet, 'Unguarded Australia' (1919) urged the consequent need for immigration. He briefly served as Superintendent of Immigration, but fell out with Hughes, whom he accused of talking big about immigration, yet doing little.

6. The 'Not a Prophet' speech, on 27 November 1946, was mainly concerned with defending the White Australia policy. In it Gullett stated: 'Whilst I am not a prophet, I believe it to be quite certain that within the next 10 years very heavy

pressure will be put on us to accept unlimited numbers of coloured migrants ... Australia is white today, and we support that policy ... simply because we have to support it.' He continued: 'The preservation of every standard that has been built up in this country is conditioned by the maintenance of a white Australia. Let us have a little less humbug and pious expressions about what white Australia means. It means no more nor less than our existence, and that is the way we must regard it.'

7. Non-Jewish (adult) German immigration was permitted officially from July 1952. I have met the man who was supposedly the first arrival. Some 50000 (Aryan) Germans arrived under government sponsorship during the remainder of the decade.

8. Then Professor of Social and Economic History at Deakin University, Geelong.

9. *Postwar Jewish 'Boat People', Parallels with the Tampa Incident*, presented to the Australian Association of Jewish Studies annual conference, February 2002, reprinted in the association's journal.

10. Drawn to readers' attention in the *Australian Jewish News*, 7 September 2001.

11. The original wording was 'of the Jewish race', which caused greater offence.

12. One of the officers was R.B. Armstrong, acting secretary of the department; the other is unnamed.

13. Volume 5, No. 2, 1991.

14. Dated 20 October 1949.

15. Cablegram, 'Policy with regard to DPs from various zones in German', 27 January 1948.

16. That is, the subjects of this book.

17. First post-war Jewish child migrant.

18. 7 July 1938.

19. There is a delightful story of how Porush, senior minister at the Great Synagogue, called on Gilroy at his private quarters, to be greeted by an Irish housekeeper who addressed him as 'Father'. 'Rabbi, actually,' said Porush. 'Yes, Father,' was the reply.

20. Or Jewish Christians.

21. Sometimes unkindly referred to as 'Christians of convenience'.

22. Adjunct Professor for Jewish Studies, and Roth Lecturer for Holocaust Studies,

University of Sydney.

CHAPTER 3

1. Wolfgang Matsdorf. See Chapter 3, 'Gross-Breeseners', page 30.

2. Many will consider this statement too modest in view of the achievements of both men.

3. Frances Barkman died in September 1946, after which the children's home was renamed in her honour.

4. Later re-named Employment Companies.

5. For good measure the production is what Germans call a *Männer-Oper,* in which women's roles are played by men.

6. Richard Dreyfus died on 21 June 1998.

7. The Dreyfus brothers were spared having their names changed, possibly through having a name well known to English speakers.

8. See also Palmer, G. 1997, *Reluctant Refuge,* Kangaroo Press, Sydney.

9. Author of *The Generation Between Fear and Hope: Jewish Youth in the Third Reich* (see Bibliography, page 290).

10. More grandiosely *Reichsvertretung der Juden in Deutschland* (Central Organisation of the Jews in Germany).

11. At least one Gross-Breesener, Alexander 'Wastl' Neumeyer, migrated to the Argentine colony, which folded in the 1970s. The survivors, including Neumeyer, subsequently migrated to Israel.

12. A book about the scheme, *An Unpromised Land,* by Leon Gettler (Fremantle Arts Centre Press) was published in 1993.

13. I had the privilege of meeting this unassuming man, who was intensely proud of his Australian citizenship, in Israel in 1986. Wolf Matsdorf died in Jerusalem on 13 September 1989.

14. Bert Cohn and others do not blame their companions for taking up this late option, since they had applied for US entry visas before the offer from Australia.

15. The average age was 18. One 'boy' was 25.

16. Officially known as Employment Companies.

17. Bert Cohn has collated three volumes of *Rundbriefe,* in German and English, under the title *The Gross-Breesen Letters. A Testament of the Survivors – A Memorial to the Dead.* The collection is housed in the Sydney Jewish Museum.

18. Theresienstadt has various claims to infamy, including its use for a propaganda film, supposedly showing well-treated inmates. See Bibliography, pages 299–300.

19. Useful information about the Gross-Breeseners is contained in Matsdorf, W. 1994, *No Time to Grow: The Story of the Gross-Breeseners in Australia*, Archive of Australian Judaica, University of Sydney.

CHAPTER 4

1. See Chapter 3.

2. Then head of the German *Sondereinsatzkommando* (Special Purpose Commando Unit). The man charged with implementing Hitler's 'Final Solution' – i.e. extermination – in regard to European Jews. Eichmann was later kidnapped and put on trial in modern Israel.

3. It has been claimed Eichmann was teased at school because of his 'Jewish' appearance.

4. Eichmann also featured in the life of a Kindertransportee, Walter Friedman. See Chapter 11, page 147.

5. Members of *Csenror*, a quasi-military force, formed officially as a supplementary force in non-metropolitan areas.

6. Two attempts were made, in July and August 1944, to deport the Jewish population of Budapest.

7. Through the diplomat, Raoul Wallenberg, declared a 'Righteous Gentile' by the State of Israel, and his assistant Per Anger, later appointed Swedish Ambassador to Australia.

8. The Hungarian Fascist Party in league with the Germans.

9. A Jewish-American welfare organisation that looked after displaced persons and Holocaust survivors.

10. As stated, Tom Keleman travelled independently (i.e. not as part of a group).

11. Founding president of the Australian Jewish Welfare Guardian Society, and for a time president of the AJWS Children's Committee.

12. See also account by Jack Schwartz who was in the same exodus.

13. In Hungarian, Karoly Keleman.

14. From 1952 to 1979, succeeding Saul Symonds in this role.

15. I was at that time a *Sydney Morning Herald* reporter.

CHAPTER 5

1. Also great-grandfather to the Halms' grandchildren, Syd and Billie 'momma' and 'poppa'.

2. See Chapter 7, page 92.

3. Pointing to a photograph of Mrs Peggy Lewinnek, wife of Braham's unofficial guardian, John Lewinnek.

4. The Isabella Lazarus Home was opened in 1939, and moved to Waverley in 1965. It closed in May 1968. A children's committee continued after this time.

5. An interesting contrast with the experiences of the English child migrants.

6. A Hebrew word meaning 'dedication'. It is also spelled *Chanuka, Hannukah* or *Hanukkah*. An eight-day Jewish festival, corresponding in time with Christmas, commemorating the re-dedication of the Temple of Jerusalem in 165 BC.

7. A popular Sydney dance venue.

CHAPTER 6

1. It remains a source of astonishment to Jack Schwartz and many others that the Germans, despite their own perilous situation, gave priority to the transport of Jews over more pressing military needs.

2. See also account by Tom Keleman, whose father was in the same transfer of prisoners.

3. See also account by Braham Stern.

4. See Chapter 6, page 80.

5. In 1983, assisted by his wife, Edi, Jack wrote his biography, *The Army-Cap Boy: The Story of a Teenage Boy's Survival in Hitler's Europe* (see Bibliography, page 295). A sequel, *Ex-Reffos,* was published in 1999.

6. Sponsored by the AJWS Children's Committee as opposed to the Welfare Guardian scheme.

7. See also description, Chapter 5, page 67.

8. Young migrants whom he had helped.

CHAPTER 7

1. Some sources claim the reverse – that more girls than boys survived the Holocaust, mainly because it was easier for girls to disguise their Jewish origins. Statistical evidence is not available.

2. In the same party as Braham Stern and Albert Halm.

3. Parents of Syd Einfeld.

4. Female Jewish child migrants, unlike boys, were accommodated from the beginning in private homes.

5. Founding president of the 'Welfare Guardians'.

6. The American Joint Distribution Committee.

7. According to former youth migrant Tom Keleman, who was later active in the pursuit of Nazi war criminals in Australia: 'My feeling is that a lot of these people who had leadership roles in the ghettos, perhaps head of the *Judenrat* (Jewish Council), and thus appeared to be collaborating with the Germans, were actually helping people. Certainly, they had to make shocking decisions about who to save and who not to save. I think it is wiser not to pass judgment.'

8. Mostly former concentration camp inmates.

9. She was 89 as this chapter was being written (late 2002).

10. Now deceased.

11. At that time still Mrs Freiberg.

12. The government of Paraguay, which was sympathetic to the Nazis, would not of itself have prevented German nationals from leaving. However, it is possible that the Americans, who were watching that country's air and sea lanes, would have intervened. It is claimed the 'deal' had the tacit support of the US, which was concerned about the fate of Jews in Europe.

13. David Gilbert died on 24 August 1998.

CHAPTER 8

1. Evidence suggests post-war Jewish child migrants were better treated than their pre-war equivalents.

2. In a foreword to the book *Child Survivors*, by Dr Paul Valent (see Bibliography, page 296).

3. Also known as *Schindler's List*.

4. Only Oriental Jews name children after people who are still living.

CHAPTER 9

1. Also in recognition of the *Kindertransports*, a statue of a child holding a suitcase was unveiled at London's Liverpool Street Station on 16 September 2003.

2. Children of political dissidents, intellectuals, certain categories of Christians.

3. It was to be a further three years before introduction of the 'Final Solution', i.e.

extermination, as a solution to the 'Jewish problem'.

4. Also immediate past-president, NSW Council of Christians and Jews.

5. Jews-free.

6. *No Longer A Stranger* (see Bibliography, page 295).

7. See Chapter 12.

8. See Ruth Rack, Chapter 12, page 151.

9. Grynszpan's own ultimate fate is shrouded in mystery.

10. Two weeks after *Kristallnacht*.

11. Only Sweden opened its doors in a similar manner. The US pointedly declined.

12. That first transport left Vienna on 10 December 1938. Two of the children on it, Kitty Finger and Anne Libter, now live in Sydney.

13. On 15 March 1939.

14. Many had much less.

15. Told in *Into the Arms of Strangers* (see Bibliography, page 293).

16. Buchenwald, Dachau, Kurzbach, Gross-Rosen and Bergen-Belsen.

17. Her son, at the age of six, weighed more.

18. Neé Eva Diamant.

19. Some *Kinder* preferred the hostel environment.

20. Government opinion in America was less forthcoming. A bill to allow refugee children into the US came to Congress in early 1939. It was resisted by the powerful anti-immigration lobby, one of the arguments being that it was 'against God's will' for children to travel without their parents. The bill died in committee.

21. To be precise 9354 German and Austrian children, of whom 7482 were Jewish.

22. Eichmann apparently considered her deranged. A fuller account of the activities of this extraordinary woman is contained in Inge Sadan's *No Longer A Stranger* (privately published, second reprint 2002) and in Gertruida Wijsmuller-Meijer's own privately published, but now out-of-print biography, *No Time For Tears* (see Bibliography, page 296).

23. A plaque, honouring the children, was installed many years ago in the Warner's holiday camp. It was moved to the town hall when the camp was demolished.

24. Erich Cahn did not have much time to find out. The food at Dovercourt was non-kosher, hence he and other Orthodox children were moved to a Jewish-run private hotel at Westgate-on-Sea.

25. This allowed many to disguise their 'enemy alien' origins. At school, competing

against English-born children, *Kinder* regularly topped their classes in English grammar and composition.

26. Pocket money they were allowed to take from Germany.
27. From an article in *AJR Journal*, magazine of the Association of Jewish Refugees.
28. Kurt Fuchel, past-president of the Kindertransport Association of America, made his observations in a letter to the reunion committee.
29. See Chapter 12, page 155.
30. His foster father.
31. Named after the Home Secretary in the Coalition Government, Herbert Morrison.

CHAPTER 10

1. From an article in *AJR Journal*, magazine of the Association of Jewish Refugees.
2. Old enough to travel alone at about the time of *Kristallnacht*, but young enough to be classified as a child.
3. Hence the appropriate title of her autobiography, *By the Moon And the Stars* (see Bibliography, page 293).
4. Lore is the author of *Other People's Houses* (see Bibliography, page 295).
5. Vera Gissing (Vera Diamant).
6. See *Pearls of Childhood* and *Nicholas Winton and the Rescued Generation* (see Bibliography, page 292).
7. See Nazi travel document photo on back cover.
8. To attend the *Kinder* 60th anniversary reunion.
9. Part of this report (by the author) originally appeared in the *Australian Jewish News*.
10. Indeed, they already have. Both Bertha and Bea star (with others) in the film *Into the Arms of Strangers*. Bertha is also the co-author of *I Came Alone: Stories of the Kindertransport* (see Bibliography, page 294).
11. David Jedwad died in February 2003.
12. *Life Is Beautiful*, directed by Roberto Benigni.
13. Dr Bernard Barnett, whose wife's experiences are quoted in this chapter, believes childhood regression is common among *Kinder*.
14. Notwithstanding her problem, Inge became (within six months of her arrival) top of her class in English.
15. See Bibliography, page 292.
16. See Bibliography, page 293.

17. See below.

18. Problems arose over an organisation known as The Barbican Mission, which took in several children. Though not realised at the time, one of its major aims was the conversion of Jews to Christianity.

19. The child, whose parents died in the Holocaust, eventually went to live with an aunt in America.

20. Though not strictly one of the *Kinder*, his experiences were similar.

21. Justin Jones subsequently became prominent in the Australian Jewish community. Posts he has held include that of vice-president of the NSW Jewish Board of Deputies.

22. See Chapter 14, page 184 and note 9, page 284.

23. Used on the cover of a book *And the Policeman Smiled*, by Barry Turner (Bloomsbury Publishing Ltd, 1990).

CHAPTER 11

1. 'Daddy' Robert Rainford. See Gissing, V. *Pearls of Childhood* (see Bibliography, page 292)

2. Aged 95, when this book went to press.

3. Martin Blake, a master at Westminster School. Winton had, on a number of occasions, helped Blake in supervising skiing parties of boys from the school.

4. The British Committee for Refugees from Czechoslovakia (BCRC).

5. A description of Chadwick's role is contained in Gottlieb, A. 1998, *Men of Vision*, Weidenfeld and Nicholson, London.

6. By this time a large number of endangered children from Germany, Austria and elsewhere were also present in the Czech capital.

7. *Nicholas Winton and the Rescued Generation* (see Bibliography, page 292).

8. *Pearls of Childhood* (see Bibliography, page 292).

9. By a twist of fate, because his mother and paternal grandparents were Jews, Winton (a baptised though purely nominal Christian) was unable to receive the Jewish honour of 'Righteous Gentile'.

10. See Postscript, page 265.

11. In her self-published book *From Holocaust to Haven* (see Bibliography, page 293).

12. Manufacturer of the chemicals used in Nazi gas chambers.

13. A good example of this genre is *All That Was*, by Lusia Przybyszewicz. The book

is more than the typical 'survivor's tale', giving an insider's view of the infamous Warsaw Ghetto, followed by a heart-stopping account of daily life, having adopted a disguised Aryan identity, in the heart of Hitler's Reich.

14. Though unable to talk about her own experiences, this lady willingly passed to me names of others who would.

15. The experiences of (and problems faced by) the children of Holocaust survivors are explored in an important book, *Children of the Shadows: Voices of the Second Generation*, edited by Kathy Grinblat (University of Western Australia Press). See Bibliography, page 292.

16. For an interesting commentary see Suzanne Rutland's keynote address *Our Children will be our Guarantors: Child Survivors in Australia,* to the 1993 Conference of the Australian Association for Jewish Studies.

17. Featured in the British BBC documentary, *Outwitting Hitler* (2002), screened in Australia as part of the ABC *True Stories* series.

18. See also 'Autograph Story' (see Postscript, page 266).

19. In fact, he never saw them again.

20. See also Chapter 14, page 184.

21. Adapted from *No Longer A Stranger* (see Bibliography, page 295).

CHAPTER 12

1. As told to the author and in her self-published memoir, *Book of Ruth* (see Bibliography, page 294).

2. Lory Cahn, another *Kindertransportee*, would respond to the Nazi greeting by calling '*Drei Liter*' (three litres).

3. According to Ruth: 'It is not unusual to doubt one's childhood memory, but I think I was there.'

4. Sachsenhausen, Buchenwald and Dachau were officially concentration camps (and as such also labour camps), as distinct from extermination camps such as Chelmo, Belzec, Treblinka, Sobibor, Majdanek and Auschwitz-Birkenau. Initially, Bergen-Belsen served as a special 'transit camp'.

5. Later, after her children were in England, it is thought Mrs Landesberg had a similar opportunity. She did not take it, believing in the faint possibility that her husband might be released from imprisonment, perhaps in a feeble state, and require her help.

6. 3 September 1939.

7. Her aunt had moved with her family to Llandudno, Wales, to avoid the bombing. Ruth, who had similarly been evacuated to Devon, found herself in a war zone.

8. Traditionally pronounced 'barrer' boy. Operator of a fruit or vegetable barrow.

9. Women's Royal Army Corps.

10. In the west country idiom, 'vurriners'.

11. Women's Royal Naval Service, the famous Wrens.

12. Over 3000 Jews were rounded up for extermination at Majdanek. A few hundred of the survivors – mostly women and children – were shot. After the war the Jewish community in Belzyce was not reconstituted.

CHAPTER 13

1. At that time, before the Nazis imposed their 'Final Solution', it was often possible to obtain release from internment if, for instance, the subject intended to emigrate.

2. Yiddish has no precise anglicised spelling. An academic source gave the quote as *'Ken Fish, ken Flaysh'*.

3. Armstrong, D., *The Voyage of Their Life* (see Bibliography, page 290).

4. Shooting of a German diplomat by Herschel Grynszpan. See Chapter 9, pages 112–13

5. The same voyage as Horrie Goldsmith. Unlike others on her 1947 voyage, she is tolerant about standards on the vessel.

6. Rita first told her story to an audience in the Great Synagogue, Sydney, to mark the 60th anniversary of *Kristallnacht*.

7. Of King George VI.

8. This story include extracts from the book *I Came Alone*, of which Bertha was co-author, and the film *Into the Arms of Strangers* (see Bibliography, page 299).

CHAPTER 14

1. The lowest category, until that time left entirely free.

2. There were also Catholics (including two priests), Protestants and Marxists.

3. There is some argument about numbers. The actual shipping lists show 1999 C-category internees (Dunera Boys), disembarked in Sydney; 354 German military and other prisoners (some with Jewish names) disembarked in Melbourne; and 199 Italian POWs, also disembarked in Melbourne. This makes a grand total of 2552.

4. Gill, Alan, *Orphans of the Empire* (see Bibliography, page 292).

5. The nationality question is delicate. Hitler's Third Reich, which had deprived them of citizenship, considered them stateless. The British considered them aliens. A handful had lived in England for 30 or more years.

6. As told in *No Longer A Stranger*, by Inge Sadan (see Bibliography, page 295).

7. The attack took place on Friday, 13 October 1939, causing the deaths of 833 crewmen.

8. An interesting work of fiction, *The Windsor Protocol*, by Peter MacAlan, canvasses the possibility that Prien thought the *Arandora Star* was a troopship.

9. Unlike the fury aroused by the sinking of the *City of Benares*, on 17 September 1940, taking British child evacuees to Canada. Of the 90 children on board, 77 died, as well as 179 adult passengers.

10. A reference to the Pocket Battleship class of the German Navy. The ditty was written and played on the piano by Ray Martin. (See Chapter 14, page 185).

11. Research by the late Cyril Pearl, author of *The Dunera Scandal*, confirmed that the German U-boat, U-56, did fire two torpedoes at the ship at a range of about 1500 metres.

12. Among the Dunera Boys, as elsewhere, stories improve with the telling. Some say the story about the shipboard Mass probably refers to another incident in which Professor Meyer (a Catholic) arranged a performance of the Oratorio, *Israel in Egypt*, with Jews and non-Jews forming a mass choir.

13. A fate which befell the first post-war child migrants.

14. A hallowed spot often revisited by Dunera Boys. It is now part of the Jones Bay Wharf commercial redevelopment. Items relating to the Dunera episode, including audiovisuals, a list of passengers and descriptions of life in Hay internment camp are displayed in a special 'heritage' area (ground floor, Doltone House Function Centre) open daily.

15. This highly entertaining mini-series, produced by Bob Weis and directed by Sam Lewin, was an interesting example of 'faction' – half fact, half fiction. As such, the Dunera Boys themselves are divided about its merits.

16. In an article in *Meanjin* in 1954, Walter Kaufmann described a conversation between a guard and 16-year-old Stefan Hermann. The guard, having heard some of the boy's experiences, disclaims: 'Never known a Pommy that was any good yet.'

17. The award was for 'conspicuous gallantry' in the battle for the Belgian town of Courtrai, on 14 October 1918. The citation read: 'When the advance of his

company [between the villages of Ledegem and Moorsele] was checked by two machine guns and an enemy field battery firing over open sights, at the head of 11 men he charged the battery, capturing four field guns, two machine guns, and 16 prisoners. Again, on the morning of 20 October 1918, Sgt O'Neill, with one man, rushed an enemy machine-gun position, routing about 100 enemy and causing many casualties.'

18. A sketch of this encounter, a prized *Dunera* relic, has been displayed in art galleries and museums.

19. 7 September 1940.

20. See below.

21. Quoted in full in Cyril Pearl's excellent book, *Dunera Scandal* (see Bibliography, page 294). Pearl died in 1987. His widow, Paddy Pearl, has maintained a connection with the Dunera Boys.

22. In 2004.

23. He is said to have written a memo to Scott, suggesting, with a hint of sarcasm, that if rings were to be removed, at least the prisoners' fingers should be greased first.

24. In an interview conducted in 1994.

CHAPTER 15

1. Later to achieve fame as a left-wing novelist.

2. Oswald Veit Von Wolkenstein.

3. As recorded in *Pomegranates: A Century of Jewish Australian Writing* (see Bibliography, page 292).

4. It is claimed one internee suggested the money be accepted and put in a fund to build a Spitfire.

5. The notes are now collectors' items (see Postscript, page 265).

6. The policy was, in fact, reversed whilst the *Dunera* was still on the high seas.

7. Apparently keeping their identities and Jewish origins a secret.

8. Julian Layton, having negotiated his charges' entry into soldiering, didn't quite disappear. By now Lieut.-Colonel, he continued to work on the sidelines and stayed several years, bringing his niece who married a Dunera Boy, Herbert Baer, first Jewish member of the Melbourne Stock Exchange.

9. *The Dunera Affair: A Documentary Resource Book* (see Bibliography, page 290).

10. Such was the general level of paranoia, there were warnings – made fun of in *Dad's*

Army and similar comedy sketches – of German parachutists disguised as nuns.

11. The figure most often quoted is 913.

12. At which point he and others anglicised their names.

13. From *No Longer A Stranger*, by Inge Sadan (see Bibliography, page 295).

CHAPTER 16

1. Told by his friend, Gordon Beale, at Oswald's wake in May 2003.

2. Mannix, as others have noted, showed compassion for the (mainly Jewish) internees, but offered practical help only to co-religionists.

3. A remarkable woman totally dedicated to the refugee cause.

4. Internees originally from the *Arandora Star* were separated, and were off-loaded in Melbourne (for transport to Tatura) whereas Dunera Boys disembarked in Sydney.

5. The period known as the 'phoney war'.

6. Hans states, in regard to his own encounters: 'I mean they have prefects who beat you with canes and they do all sorts of things, initiation rites. When you survive all that, the thing becomes just another experience.'

CHAPTER 17

1. Officially the Hay-Tatura Association. Its prime movers for many years have been Mike Sondheim, national president, and Horst Jacobs. Horst also edits the *Dunera News* with Mike.

2. The late Professor Henry Mayer, Emeritus Professor of Political Theory, Sydney University, and authority on media studies, was in this mould – even returning, unopened, copies of the *Dunera News*.

3. The initials stand for the grandiosely titled Organisation for the Distribution of Artisanal and Agricultural Skills among the Jews in Russia. ORT is now an international body whose work is much valued by the Jewish community. Its headquarters are in London.

4. Some sources claim 39.

5. At the time of writing, 17 ORT 'boys' were still living in Australia. A reunion is held annually in Melbourne.

6. He notes wrily that their names appear among two pages of Lippmann, all with the same spelling, followed by the one word '*verschollen*' (missing).

7. Perhaps influenced by hostile treatment from RSL branches in the immediate

post-war period.

8. See Chapter 6, page 83.

9. The film was *Quex*, directed by K. A. Schenzinger (1933), generally considered the first Nazi film of consequence. The story purported to show the sacrificial spirit of German youth.

10. Notably his friend Hans Marcus (see Chapter 16, page 212).

11. Mrs Margaret Thatcher, then British Prime Minister.

12. A senior United Kingdom source told the author at that time that an 'apology' by Britain was unreasonable and unlikely; the latter for fear that a demand for financial compensation – as had occurred among Japanese Americans – might result.

13. As a participant cheekily put it.

14. The event inspired a 60-minute documentary, *When Friends Were Enemies*, by Judy Menczel, for SBS Television (see Bibliography, page 300).

15. The Hon. Bill Hayden.

16. He still has the receipt.

CHAPTER 18

1. Men such as Hans Marcus, having attended English public schools, found unexpected use for the training received in their school Officer Training Corps.

2. There were other Employment Companies, comprising Australians as well as Greek and other non-naturalised persons. Like Britain's Pioneer Corps, units were not choosy about recruitment.

3. There is a story that a visiting drill instructor, apoplectic, said on parade: 'In *this* Army you don't ask, "Why should I?", every time an order is given.'

4. One former internee rose to Staff Sergeant.

5. Mike Sondheim was an exception: 'I was lucky. Colonel Courtenay of the Military Police liked foreigners. When he heard about this funny outfit, he asked Captain Broughton if he had anyone who could drive. I was told to report to HQ and become his personal driver. I was treated like a VIP in the Sergeants' quarters.'

6. Henry Lippmann recalls otherwise: 'We in the Employment Companies were foreigners, regarded with suspicion. I don't like to say it, but we were the scum of the earth. Yet we did a job second to none.'

7. The other was an Aboriginal, Lieutenant Reg Saunders.

8. Sgt Fischer.

9. See also Chapter 17, page 213 and Note 2, page 286. Professor Mayer died in May 1991.

10. Fashioned from photographs by Roche Lados.

11. There is disquiet that newspaper and magazine articles about the Dunera Boys tend to highlight only the 'famous'.

CHAPTER 19

1. There is disagreement about dates. For the record, auditions were held on 29 December 1936, and the first rehearsal on 6 January 1937.

2. Media references invariably confuse the Vienna Mozart Boys' Choir with the original Vienna Boys' Choir. It was left to Frank Heimans, producer of the 1983 SBS documentary program, 'Class of 39', to put things right.

3. Boys recall that, even after the Anschluß, Gruber avoided giving the Nazi salute and bowed, in the Austrian tradition, at the end of each performance.

4. In May 1939 the St Louis sailed from Hamburg with 937 Jews – some of whom had already been in concentration camps – who believed they had bought visas to enter Cuba. Before the ship was halfway across the Atlantic, a power struggle developed within the corrupt Cuban Government and the permits were withdrawn. This situation played into the hands of the Nazi leadership by suggesting that countries other than Hitler's Germany supported anti-Jewish measures. The ship began a return to Germany. What began as a journey to new pastures became what commentators have called 'the voyage of the damned'.

5. Literally 'School brothers', known in most of Europe as the Christian Brothers, but in Australia as the De la Salle Brothers.

CHAPTER 20

1. If he was, indeed, part-Jewish, the action by Gruber almost certainly saved his life.

2. Much of the evidence is trivial. For example, there are peacetime letters to Gruber, of a routine nature, from overseas diplomatic missions. He replied to one of these – the German consul in San Francisco – on the notepaper of Lennon's Hotel, Brisbane, ending with the greeting 'Heil Hitler'.

3. Monsignor Professor Joseph Schnitt (Rektor Schnitt) died on 26 September 1955. A service is held annually on the anniversary of that event.

4. Also known, after his conversion to Catholicism, as Patrick Joseph, or 'Paddy'

Martin. He was a partisan witness who had publicly and repeatedly stated his resentment at the power wielded by Gruber in the musical life of the cathedral.

CHAPTER 21

1. His dossier in the Australian Archives hints at such a situation.
2. Alfred Homola's fate was not known at that time.
3. In 1947.
4. The chamber choir, which is highly respected, celebrated its 500th anniversary in 2003.
5. Although I didn't realise it at the time, as a schoolboy I was among her customers.
6. Margaret Edmands died in November 2002.
7. By coincidence, Austrian-born Albert Karoly, a Dunera internee, was a member of the Vienna Boys' Choir from 1929 to 1931.
8. A privately produced book about the Vienna Boys' Choir, *Wir Sind Keine Lipizzaner Geworden*, by Alois Worlczek (Herold Druck, 1989), contains a chapter, largely based on hearsay, concerning the 'Affair Doktor Gruber'. *Lipizzaner* refers to the breed of horses used in Vienna's Spanish Riding School.

RESOURCES

BIBLIOGRAPHY

The following books have a bearing on issues raised in this volume:

Andgel, Anne 1988, *Fifty Years of Caring: The History of the Australian Jewish Welfare Society 1936–1986*, Jewish Care and Australian Jewish Historical Society.

Angress, Werner 1988, *The Generation Between Fear and Hope: Jewish Youth in the Third Reich*, Columbia University Press, New York.

Anon. 1999, *Kindertransport 60th Anniversary* (Reunion of Kindertransport), Association of Jewish Refugees, London.

Appignanesi, Lisa 2000, *Losing the Dead: A Family Memoir*, Vintage/Random House.

Armstrong, Diane 1998, *Mosaic: A Chronicle of Five Generations*, Random House, Sydney.

Armstrong, Diane 2001, *The Voyage Of Their Life*, HarperCollins. Flamingo paperback edition 2002.

Bartrop, Paul 1994, *Australia and the Holocaust 1933–45*, Australian Scholarly Publishing, Melbourne.

Bartrop, Paul, with Eisen 1990, *The Dunera Affair: A Documentary Resource Book*, Jewish Museum of Australia with Schwartz and Wilkinson.

Bauer, Yehuda 1994, *Jews for Sale: Nazi–Jewish Negotiations 1933–1945*, Yale University Press, New York.

Berk, Leon 1992, *Destined to Live*, Paragon Press, Melbourne.

Blakeney, Michael 2000, *Australia and the Jewish Refugees, 1933–1948*, Croom Helm Australia.

Brent, Bern 2000, *My Berlin Suitcase*, published privately.

Calwell, Arthur 1972, *Be Just and Fear Not*, Lloyd O'Neill, Melbourne.

Cesarani, David and Kushner, Tony 1993, *The Internment of Aliens in Twentieth Century Britain*, Frank Cass and Company Ltd, London.

Clayton, Tim and Craig, Phil 1999, *Finest Hour*, Hodder and Stoughton, UK.

Coldrey, Barry 1999, *Good British Stock: Child and Youth Migration to Australia,* National Archives of Australia Research Guide.

Collins, Alan 1989, *Jacob's Ladder*, Lodestar Books, E.P. Dutton, New York. First published in Australia under the title *The Boys from Bondi*.

Dacy, Marianne 1994, *Pathways to Understanding*, Archive of Australian Judaica, Sydney.

David, Janina 1992, *A Square of Sky, Memoirs of a Wartime Childhood*, Eland Publishers, London.

David, Ruth 2003, *A Child of Our Time: A Young Girl's Flight from the Holocaust*, I.B. Tauris, London.

Drucker, Olga Levy 1992, *Kindertransport*, Henry Holt, New York.

Dwork, Deborah 1991, *Children With A Star: Jewish Youth in Nazi Europe*, Yale University Press, New Haven and London.

Emanuel, Muriel and Gissing, Vera 2001, *Nicholas Winton and the Rescued Generation*, Vallentine Mitchell, London.

Epstein, Hedy 1998, *Erinnern ist Nicht Genug* (Remembering is Not Enough), published privately.

Epstein, Helen 1979, *Children of the Holocaust: Conversations with Sons and Daughters of Survivors*, Penguin Books, New York.

Flesch, Carl F. 2001, *Where Do You Come From? Hitler Refugees in Great Britain Then and Now*, Pen Press Publishers, London.

Foster, John 1999, *Community of Fate: Memoirs of German Jews in Melbourne*, Allen & Unwin.

Fox, Anne and Abraham-Podietz, Eva 1999, *Ten Thousand Children*, Behrman House, West Orange, New Jersey, USA.

Gershon, Karen 1990, *Postscript*, Victor Gollancz.

Gershon, Karen 1994, *A Lesser Child*, Peter Owen Ltd, London.

Gershon, Karen (Ed.) 1966, *We Came as Children*, Victor Gollancz.

Gettler, Leon 1993, *An Unpromised Land*, Fremantle Arts Centre Press.

Gilbert, Martin 1981, *Auschwitz and the Allies*, Michael Joseph, London.

Gill, Alan 1998, *Orphans of the Empire*, Random House, Sydney.

Gillman, Peter and Leni 1980, *Collar the Lot: How Britain Interned and Expelled its Wartime Refugees*, Quartet Books, London.

Gissing, Vera 1988, *Pearls of Childhood*, Robson Books/Chrysalis Books, UK.

Gissing, Vera and Emanuel, Muriel 2001, *Nicholas Winton and the Rescued Generation,* Vallentine Mitchell, London.

Gottlieb, Amy Zahl 1998, *Men of Vision: Anglo–Jewry Aid to Victims of the Nazi Regime 1933–45*, Weidenfeld & Nicolson, London.

Grenville, Anthony 2000, *German-speaking Exiles in Great Britain*, Research Centre for German and Austrian Exile Studies, London.

Grenville, Anthony 2002, *Continental Britons*, Association of Jewish Refugees.

Grinblat, Kathy (Ed.) 2002, *Children of the Shadows: Voices of the Second Generation*, University of Western Australia Press in association with Benchmark Publications.

Gutman, Yisrael and Krakowski, Shmuel 1986, *Unequal Victims: Poles and Jews in World War II,* Holocaust Library, New York.

Halm, Albert (Ed.) 1990, *The Gift of Life,* Published privately for Australian Association of Jewish Holocaust Survivors.

Hammer, Gael 1988, *Pomegranates: A Century of Jewish Australian Writing*, Millennium Books, Sydney.

Hammerton, A. James and Richards, Eric 2002, *Speaking to Immigrants: Oral Testimony and the History of Australian Migration*, Australian National University Press. One of a series of six books dealing with various aspects of migration.

Hammond, Joyce 1990, *Walls of Wire*: Tatura, Rushworth, Murchison, published privately.

Harris, Mark Jonathan and Oppenheimer, Deborah 2000, *Into the Arms of Strangers: Stories of the Kindertransport*, Bloomsbury/Allen & Unwin. The book of the documentary film of the same name.

Havell, Jane and Ryan, Marianne 2001, *Facing the Future: ORT 1880–2000*, World ORT, London.

Hayman, Eva 1992, *By the Moon and the Stars*, Random Century, New Zealand.

Holden, Robert 1999, *Orphans of History*, Text Publishing, Melbourne.

Horak, Olga 2000, *Auschwitz to Australia*, Kangaroo Press/Simon & Schuster, Sydney.

Humphreys, Margaret 1994, *Empty Cradles*, Doubleday, London.

Huppert, Nora 2002, *From Holocaust to Haven*, Published privately. Printed by Hippo Books, Sydney.

Josephs, Jeremy with Bechhofer, Susi 1998, *Rosa's Child*, I.B. Taurus, London.

Jupp, James 2002, *From White Australia to Woomera: The Story of Australian Immigration*, Cambridge University Press.

Kirby, James 1998, *My Mother's Diamonds: In Search of the Holocaust Assets,* Prentice Hall, Sydney.

Kociumbas, Jan 1997, *Australian Childhood: A History*, Allen & Unwin, Sydney.

Kostanski, Jan 2002, *A Gentile in the Warsaw Ghetto*, published privately, Puma Press, Vic.

Lack, John and Templeton 1995, *Bold Experiment: A Documentary History of Australian Immigration since 1945*, Oxford University Press, UK.

Lafitte, Francois 1988, *The Internment of Aliens*, Libris, UK.

Lehrer, Leon with Gill, Alan 2000, *From Horror to Haven*, Hippo Books, Sydney.

Leverton, Bertha and Lowensohn, Shmuel (Ed.) 1990, *I Came Alone: The Stories of the Kindertransports,* The Book Guild, Lewes, UK.

Levy, Herbert 1995, *Voices from the Past*, Temple House Books, The Book Guild, Sussex, UK.

Ligocka, Roma 2002, *The Girl in the Red Coat*, Hodder.

Lipstadt, Deborah 1984, *Denying the Holocaust*, Penguin Books, New York.

Matsdorf, Wolfgang 1994, *No Time to Grow: The Story of the Gross-Breeseners in Australia*, Archive of Australian Judaica, University of Sydney.

Mecham, Frank 1995, *The Church and Migrants*, St Joan of Arc Press, Sydney.

Modras, Ronald 1995, *The Catholic Church and Anti-Semitism in Poland*, Harwood Academic Publishers, Chur, Switzerland.

Moskovitz, Sarah 1983, *Love Despite Hate: Child Survivors of the Holocaust and Their Adult Lives*, Schocken Books, New York.

Murphy, Margaret (Ed.) 1999, *Wartime Memories.* Hurstville's Heritage, for Hurstville Civic Library.

Nagler, Eva 1995, *Massacre on the Baltic*, published privately, Fast Books.

Palmer, Glen 1997, *Reluctant Refuge: Unaccompanied Refugee and Evacuee Children in Australia, 1933–1945*, Kangaroo Press/ Simon & Schuster.

Patkin, Benzion 1979, *The Dunera Internees*, Cassell, Australia.

Pearl, Cyril 1983, *The Dunera Scandal*, Angus & Robertson.

Przybyszewicz, Luisia 2002, *All That Was*, Mini-Publishing, Sydney.

Rack, Ruth 2002, *Book of Ruth*, published privately, printed Southern Highland Publishers, NSW.

Reeson, Margaret 1993, *Whereabouts Unknown*, Albatross Books, Sydney.

Roe, Michael 1995, *Australia, Britain and Migration 1915–1940*, Cambridge University Press, UK.

Rosenberg, Elfie 2003, *Serry and Me: Kindertransport And Beyond*, published privately.

Rubinstein, William 1999, *The Jews in Australia (Vol. 2)*, William Heinemann Australia.

Rubinstein, William D. 1997, *The Myth of Rescue: Why the Democracies Could Not Have Saved More Jews from the Nazis*, Routledge, London.

Rutland, Suzanne 1997, *Edge of the Diaspora*, Collins, Brandt and Schlesinger.

Sadan, Inge 1999, *No Longer A Stranger*, published privately.

Saville, Annette 1999, *Little Grass-Orphan Annie.* A book for children, published privately, UK.

Schwartz, Zoltan and Adi 1983, *The Army-cap Boy*, Macmillan Australia.

Schwartz, Zoltan and Adi 1999, *Ex-Reffos,* Lina Publishing, Sydney.

Segal, Lore 1990, *Other People's Houses*, Victor Gollancz.

Selo, Laura 1992, *Three Lives in Transit*, Published privately, UK.

Sennott, Charles 2000, *Broken Covenant*, Simon & Schuster, Sydney.

Shadur, Joseph 1999, *A Drive to Survival*, Schoen Books, South Deerfield, Mass. USA.

Sherington, Geoffrey 1990, *Australia's Immigrants*, Allen & Unwin, Sydney.

Sherman, A.J. 1973, *Island Refuge: Britain and Refugees from the Third Reich 1933–1939*, Paul Elek, London.

Snowman, Daniel 2002, *The Hitler Emigrés*, Chatto and Windus, London.

Spindler, Arthur 1997, *Outwitting Hitler, Surviving Stalin*, University of NSW Press, Sydney.

Stone, Nina (Ed.) 1999, *Silent No More: Melbourne Child Survivors of the Holocaust*, Child Survivors of the Holocaust, Melbourne, Vic.

Tatz, Colin 1995, *Reflections on the Politics of Remembering and Forgetting,* Centre for Comparative Genocide Studies, Macquarie University.

Thomas, Gordon and Witts, Max Morgan 1974, *Voyage of the Damned,* Stein and Day, New York.

Turner, Barry 1990, *And the Policeman Smiled: 10,000 Children Escape from Nazi Europe,* Bloomsbury Publishing Ltd, London.

Valent, Paul 1994, *Child Survivors: Adults Living with Childhood Trauma,* Heinemann, Melbourne.

Verstandig, Mark 1997, *Rest My Case,* Melbourne University Press.

Wajnryb, Ruth 2001, *The Silence: How Tragedy Shapes Talk,* Allen & Unwin, Sydney.

Wasserstein, Bernard 1988, *Britain and the Jews of Europe,* Institute of Jewish Affairs and Oxford University Press, UK.

Whiteman, Dorit 1993, *The Uprooted: A Hitler Legacy,* Schocken Books/Plenum Press, New York; also paperback edition, 1993, Perseus Publishing, Cambridge, Mass. USA.

Whitworth, Wendy (Ed.) 2003, *Survival: Holocaust Survivors Tell Their Stories,* Quill Press in association with Aegis Institute, London.

Wijsmuller-Meijer, Gertruida 1961, *No Time for Tears,* published privately.

Winter, Barbara 1986, *Stalag Australia,* Angus and Robertson, Sydney.

Worlczek, Alois 1989, *Wir sind Keine Lipizzaner Geworden,* Herold Druck, Austria.

Information about the availability of privately published books featured in this bibliography may be obtained by writing to:
Alan Gill
c/- Simon & Schuster (Australia)
PO Box 507
East Roseville, NSW 2069.

Books on the Evacuation

The following books describe the situation and experiences of young people evacuated from Britain to Canada and Australia, also evacuation within Britain, in World War II.

Fethney, Michael 1990, *The Absurd and the Brave: The True Account of the British Government's World War II Evacuation of Children Overseas*, The Book Guild, Lewes, Sussex.

Holman, Bob 1995, *The Evacuation: A Very British Revolution*, Lion Publishing, UK.

Parsons, Martin and Starns, Penny 1999, *The Evacuation, The True Story*, DSM, Peterborough (originally for BBC Radio 4).

Stokes, Edward 1999, *Innocents Abroad: The Story of British Child Evacuees in Australia 1940–45*, Allen & Unwin, UK.

Wicks, Ben 1995, *No Time to Wave Goodbye*, Stoddart, Canada.

A five-part radio series, 'The Evacuation: The True Story', was produced by David Prest (Presenter, Charles Wheeler) for BBC Radio 4, in 1999. For information on availability contact Whistledown Productions, 66 Southwark Bridge Road, London SE1 OAS, England.

A similar series, 'The Child Migrants', went to air in Britain in July 2003. Information as above.

Theses and Special Articles

Coldrey, Barry. Author of a large number of essays, articles and contributions to specialist journals on migration issues (including child and youth migration). Contact c/- Tamaranaik Press, PO Box 12792, A Beckett Street PO, Melbourne, Vic 8006. Website: www.barrycoldrey.com

Cohn, Bert. Has collated three volumes of *Rundbriefe*, in German and English, under the title *The Gross-Breesen Letters: A Testament of the Survivors: A Memorial to the Dead*. The collection is housed in the Sydney Jewish Museum.

Mendes, Phillip 2002, 'Jews, Nazis and Communists Down Under: The Jewish Council's Controversial Campaign Against German Immigration', *Australian Historical Studies*, vol. 33, no. 119.

Palmer, Glen 1995, 'Seventeen Children: Australia's Response to German Jewish Refugee Children', *Australian Jewish Historical Society Journal*, November 1995. Reprinted in an address to the 1995 Conference of the Australian Association for Jewish Studies.

Rutland, Suzanne 1994, 'Our Children will be our Guarantors: Child Survivors in Australia', *The Australian Journal of Jewish Studies*, vol. 8, no. 1, 1994. Also 'Are You Jewish? Post-war Jewish Immigration to Australia 1945–54', vol. 5, no. 2, 1991, and 'Post-war Jewish boat people: Parallels with the Tampa incident', vol. 16, 2002.

USEFUL CONTACTS

The Association of Jewish Refugees

2nd Floor, Jubilee House, Merrion Avenue, Stanmore, Middx HA7 4RL, Great Britain.

Tel.: 020 8954 7272

Fax: 020 8954 0606

Australian Association of Jewish Holocaust Survivors and Descendants

Contact Dr George Foster or Marika Weinberger, c/- Sydney Jewish Museum, 148 Darlinghurst Road, Darlinghurst NSW 2010.

Tel.: 02 9361 3678

Child Survivors of the Holocaust

Sydney Group: Contact Eva Engel or Litzi Lemberg, c/- NSW Jewish Board of Deputies, 148 Darlinghurst Rd, Darlinghurst NSW 2010.

Tel.: 02 9360 1600

Melbourne Group: Floris Kalman c/- Jewish Holocaust Museum and Research Centre, 15 Selwyn Street, Elsternwick Vic. 3185. A Melbourne adult survivors' group also meets at this address.

Tel.: 03 9528 1985

Films and Videos

Class of '39, 1983 documentary mini-series by Frank Heimans for SBS TV about the Vienna Mozart Boys' Choir and its enforced stay in Australia. Available on VHS from Cinetel Productions, 15 Fifth Avenue, Cremorne, NSW 2090. Email: cinetel@bigpond.net.au

The Dunera Boys, 1985 TV mini-series and feature film starring Bob Hoskins, Warren Mitchell, director Ben Lewin. Video distribution Prism Entertainment (US). Available from US video retail outlets.

The Fifth Continent, 1999 documentary about migration to Australia of young Jewish Holocaust survivors. Made for ABC TV, directed by Steven Salgo. ABC Program Sales.

Into the Arms of Strangers, Oscar-winning feature-length documentary, directed by Mark Jonathon Harris (*The Long Way Home*) and produced by Deborah Oppenheimer (*The Drew Carey Show*). Made in co-operation with the United States Holocaust Memorial Museum, Washington DC. Available from Warner Video (VHS and DVD). Also from Association of Jewish Refugees (see address above). See Bibliography, page 293. See also websites: www.intothearmsofstrangers.com and www.ushmm.org.

Kindertransport: The Children Who Cheated the Nazis (1 hour), Directed by Sue Reed, narrated by Richard Attenborough. (Replaces earlier version called *Rescued: A 60-Year Journey.*) Golden Reed Productions, 72 Galveston Road, Putney, London SW15 2SA. See also: www.childrenwhocheatedthenazis.co.uk

My Knees Were Jumping: Remembering the Kindertransports, Directed by Melissa Hacker, narrated by Joanne Woodward (1 hour). Distributed by National Centre for Jewish Film, Brandeis University, Waltham, MA 02254, USA. Email: ncjf@brandeis.edu or mykneeswerejumping@yahoo.com

The Power of Good [about Nicholas Winton], director Matej Minac, Iofilm UK.

Prisoner of Paradise, Award-winning documentary about the life and times of Kurt Gerron, German-Jewish actor, entertainer and film director. Gerron was forced, as an inmate, to make a propaganda film for the Nazis about how good conditions were in Theresienstadt. Imagine Entertainment, Melbourne. Website: www.prisonerofparadise.com

A Taste of Freedom: The Kindertransports, BBC TV (30 min.)

Whatever Happened to Susi? Susi Bechhofer (Grace Stocken) (1 hour) BBC TV. See also, *Rosa's Child,* Bibliography, page 293.

When Friends Were Enemies, Judy Menczel, 1990, for SBS TV. Inquiries to Fortian Productions, 16 Courtenay Road, Rose Bay NSW 2029. Tel.: 02 9371 0706

Kindertransport: 60th Anniversary Reunion Video, Available for £7, including postage, from the Association of Jewish Refugees (see address above). Information about the Kindertransports is available from the Association of Jewish Refugees and from the Wiener Library, 4 Devonshire Street, London W1W 5BH. Tel.: 020 7636 7247. Website: www.wienerlibrary.co.uk

Kindertransport, Unveiling of *Kinder* statue and memorial at Liverpool Street Station, London, on 16 September 2003. Video available, price £5.50 plus postage, from KT Publications, 8 Canons Park Close, Donnefield Avenue, Edgware, Middlesex HA8 6RJ, Great Britain.

A number of films and videos have been produced about the ill-fated voyage of the St Louis. These include *The Double Crossing: The Voyage of the St Louis,* Holocaust Memorial Foundation of Illinois and Loyola University of Chicago (Ergo Media Teanek, New Jersey, 1992); *Sea Tales: The Doomed Voyage of the St Louis* (A and E Home Video, New York, 1996); *The Voyage of the St Louis* (Galafilms, Montreal, Canada, 1995); *Voyage of the Damned* (Avid Home Entertainment, Van Nuys, California, 1992).

INDEX